D1372790

Profiles in Humanity

Profiles in Humanity

*The Battle for Peace, Freedom,
Equality, and Human Rights*

Warren I. Cohen

ROWMAN & LITTLEFIELD PUBLISHERS, INC.
Lanham • Boulder • New York • Toronto • Plymouth, UK

Published by Rowman & Littlefield Publishers, Inc.
A wholly owned subsidary of The Rowman & Littlefield Publishing Group, Inc.
4501 Forbes Boulevard, Suite 200, Lanham, Maryland 20706
http://www.rowmanlittlefield.com

Estover Road, Plymouth PL6 7PY, United Kingdom

British Library Cataloguing in Publication Information Available

Library of Congress Cataloging-in-Publication Data
Cohen, Warren I.
  Profiles in humanity : the battle for peace, freedom, equality, and human rights /
Warren I. Cohen.
      p. cm.
  Includes bibliographical references and index.
  ISBN 978-0-7425-6701-6 (cloth : alk. paper)
  ISBN 978-0-7425-6703-0 (electronic)
  1. Political activists—Biography. 2. Civil rights workers—Biography. 3. Human rights
workers—Biography. 4. Pacifists—Biography. 5. Religious leaders—Biography.
6. History, Modern—20th century. I. Title.
  JZ5540.C64 2009
  323.092'2—dc22

                                                                    2009002249

Printed in the United States of America

∞ ™ The paper used in this publication meets the minimum requirements of
American National Standard for Information Sciences—Permanence of Paper
for Printed Library Materials, ANSI/NISO Z39.48-1992.

For Geoff and Anne
May they always do right
(at least from now on)

Contents

Part IV: Human Rights

Part V: Freedom from Want

Acknowledgments

For every book I've written over the last forty-odd years, I've accumulated debts, mostly of the intellectual sort. For this one, my initial debt is to Jonathan Glover, whose *Humanity: A Moral History of the Twentieth Century* led me to wonder who would best illustrate some of his ideas. I thought of such people as monuments to humanity, men and women whose moral vision shone through the horrors of the twentieth century. As I wrote the book, friends, editors, and agents, forever asking what I was writing, warned that only a celebrity could publish a volume of biographical sketches of people he or she admired. I thought I *was* a celebrity, but they quickly disabused me of that notion, not hesitating to remind me of the narrowness of my world.

So, I am especially grateful to Susan McEachern of Rowman & Littlefield, who was willing to read the manuscript, liked it, and guided it to publication. I must also thank Peter Coveney, who taught me at this late age how to draft a proposal to a publisher. I rearranged the entire structure of the book after reading a brilliant critique of the manuscript by an "anonymous reader," who was easily identifiable as Alan Karras of the University of California, Berkeley.

My colleague at the University of Maryland, Baltimore County, John Jeffries, liked David Kennedy's take on Margaret Sanger better than mine, but my work is *almost* always improved by his suggestions. The late Josephine Woll and Abe Brumberg were painfully gentle in their response to my essay on Holocaust rescuers—one of whom had saved Abe's life. Jim Mann and Caroline Dexter have nurtured me over the years, listened to my ideas, and shared theirs. And, of course, there's Nancy Bernkopf Tucker, my wife, who put up with the book's long gestation—encouraging me even though she knew its publication would put her yet another volume behind in the in-house competition. The alternative was for both of us to live on *her* royalties.

Introduction

God does not want to do everything.

—Machiavelli, *The Prince*

All of the men and women of whom I have written tried mightily to improve the human condition. Circumstances of birth—when and where they were born, gender, nationality, or color—and the historical context in which they lived shaped their efforts. They took risks that others, perhaps of like mind, were unwilling to accept. Some were ridiculed, some ostracized, and some murdered. Women everywhere had to fight for rights that men rarely conceded without a struggle—and in most parts of the world, have yet to concede. Men and women living under tyrannical regimes, whether homegrown or imposed by imperialist powers, had to fight for their freedoms, actively or passively. People of color, confronted by the apartheid regime of South Africa or the Jim Crow laws of the United States, had to battle for equal rights. Economic misery such as that caused by the Great Depression of the 1930s or the extreme poverty to be found in much of Africa and South Asia prompted men and women of good will to seek solutions, to lead people out of the Depression, out of poverty. And then there were other men and women who, when confronted by evils such as the Holocaust or racial discrimination, risked their own well-being and that of their families—and sometimes gave their lives—in the effort to end the evil or rescue some of its victims.

Most of their names will be familiar to the general reader: Mahatma Gandhi, Franklin and Eleanor Roosevelt, Martin Luther King Jr., Nelson

Mandela, Václav Havel, and Mikhail Gorbachev, for example. However, the contribution of Pope John XXIII, the great humanist, has been overshadowed by that of his recent, more charismatic successor, John Paul II. Although Aung San Suu Kyi, Andrei Sakharov, and Muhammad Yunus have all won Nobel Prizes for their efforts, few Americans know much—or anything—about their lives and work. How many young women anywhere are aware that Margaret Sanger was responsible for the single most important advance toward the liberation of the women of the world? What of the women who have fought at far greater personal risk for equal rights in Muslim communities? How many people are aware of the role Jack Greenberg played in the struggle against Jim Crow? Or the role of Bram Fischer, Donald Woods, and Helen Suzman in the fight against apartheid? Too few, even in China, remember Liu Binyan's efforts to win freedom of the press and end abuse of power by the Chinese Communist Party. And to find the names of some of the thousands of men and women of many nationalities, from many walks of life, who rescued Jews across Europe from Hitler's minions, one must turn to Yad Vashem in Israel—or its website. I have told only a handful of their stories.

I offer these biographical sketches in an effort to humanize, to put faces upon the principal movements for human rights in the twentieth century. I've arranged them into five sections: (1) nonviolent resistance, (2) women's rights, (3) racial equality, (4) human rights generally, and (5) freedom from want. I should note that this division, while useful, is arbitrary. Several of my subjects might fit readily into other categories. For example, I include Martin Luther King Jr. in the section on race, but I might easily have included him among the men and women who employed nonviolent resistance in their struggle against oppression. Similarly, I have left Eleanor Roosevelt with her husband, Franklin, in the section on freedom from want, although she spent her last years as a leader of the international movement for human rights.

The first section focuses on Gandhi, Havel, and Suu Kyi, three extraordinary leaders in the struggle against oppression. Gandhi, as a young barrister in South Africa, stumbled into the role of fighting for justice for that territory's substantial Indian population, both Hindu and Muslim. Despite his British legal education and London finery, he was not spared the harassment that white South Africans inflicted on South Asians as well as black Africans. After returning to his native India, he developed a successful program of nonviolent resistance to British imperialism, a program that would be emulated by men and women across the globe who confronted overwhelming power in their quest for freedom.

Havel perceived himself as a writer, a playwright, but found himself hemmed in at every turn by the totalitarian regime imposed on Czechoslovakia by the Communist Party. Violent revolution was not an option, especially after Soviet-bloc troops suppressed the Prague Spring of 1968, a valiant effort by enlightened party leaders to create "socialism with a human face." Gradually Havel, after several imprisonments for speaking out or writing critically of the regime, developed his concept of the "power of the powerless." He rallied other intellectuals, pressed ceaselessly for human rights, and as the communist world disintegrated in 1989, led his country's return to democracy, ultimately serving as its president.

Suu Kyi's story does not have a happy ending, although she lives and fights on in as nearly hopeless a situation as can be imagined. Her father was the great national hero who led Burma's fight for independence in the mid-1940s—and was then assassinated. She was educated in England, married a British scholar, and was leading a comfortable academic life at Oxford when her mother's illness brought her back to Burma. The country was under the control of a military dictatorship headed by a former colleague of her father. Angered by the political repression she witnessed, the corruption and incompetence that was wrecking the country's economy, she chose to stay in Burma and fight for democracy. A charismatic woman, aided by her father's name, she quickly emerged as leader of the opposition. Familiar with the writings of Gandhi and Havel, she insisted on a nonviolent approach. For her efforts she has lived under house arrest for most of the last twenty years, unable to see her children and denied the opportunity to have her dying husband see her one last time. Periodically, the military eases the conditions under which she lives, but each time it is frightened by her overwhelming popularity among the people of Burma. There seems little prospect of the brutal junta, indifferent to the suffering of its people, surrendering power in her lifetime. Only international pressure and her celebrity as a winner of the Nobel Peace Prize have prevented the military from taking her life as well as her freedom.

The second section centers on the actions of women who dedicated themselves to seeking equal rights for themselves and others of their gender. Sanger almost single-handedly fought to legalize the sale of contraceptives in the United States. She became the worldwide symbol of the battle to spare women from unwanted pregnancies that too frequently killed them or impoverished their families. She freed women to seek and hold jobs—and to have sex for the sheer enjoyment of it. It is unlikely that any young woman today, in the world of the Pill, with easy access to condoms and diaphragms, can imagine what women endured in the early years of the twentieth century in America—and still must endure in many parts of the world. Sexual freedom and the option to plan families, wherever they exist today, are largely the result of Sanger's crusade.

Sanger had to endure fines and brief imprisonment for her efforts to make contraception available. In much of the Muslim world, the struggle to enable women to achieve anything approximating gender equality can be far more dangerous. Inaction can also be dangerous in cultures where "honor killings"—the murder of daughters and sisters alleged to have sullied a family's reputation—are frequent, where women who are raped are stoned to death for committing adultery. Today the battle is led by women as disparate as Irshad Manji, a gay, Ugandan-born Canadian television personality, and Shirin Ebadi, the Nobel Prize–winning Iranian human rights lawyer. My focus is on two Egyptians, Huda Sha'rawi and Dora Shafik, notable for their efforts to end "harem culture," the seclusion of middle- and upper-class women in Egyptian society, and to achieve more equitable marriage and divorce practices. Nonetheless, Manji's challenge to the clerics is too provocative to ignore.

The men I discuss in the third section, the fight against racism, might also have been included in the following section, on human rights more broadly defined—or perhaps in the first section, on nonviolent resistance (admittedly a stretch for Nelson Mandela, leader of a group that fought a guerrilla war). Jack Greenberg, as a young associate of Thurgood Marshall, argued *Brown v. Board of Education* before the U.S. Supreme Court in 1954, the beginning of the end of segregation in the United States. When Marshall was appointed to a federal judgeship, Greenberg succeeded him as director of the NAACP Legal Defense Fund (NAACP-LDF), a post he held for twenty-three years. Martin Luther King Jr. chose him to oversee the court battles of the Southern Christian Leadership Conference (SCLC). Before he went to teach at Columbia Law School, Greenberg founded the Mexican-American Legal Defense Fund and Asia Watch.

King needs no introduction. He is almost certainly the best known of the men and women of whom I write—so well known that I hesitated to include him. But as the greatest American spokesman for human rights, I could not leave him out. I regret that he did not live to see the election of President Barack Obama, unimaginable without King's efforts.

Bram Fischer, Donald Woods, and Helen Suzman are surely unknown to most Americans, hardly known to anyone outside of South Africa. Fischer was a lawyer, scion of a very prominent Afrikaner family. He was perceived as betraying his class by becoming a communist and his race by defending Nelson Mandela and other ANC leaders. In 1952 he saved them from conviction in a treason trial, and in 1962 he saved them from the gallows when they were convicted of sabotage. Driven underground by government harassment, he was caught in 1965 and spent most of the rest of his life in prison, released just before he died of cancer. Woods was a journalist, a classic white liberal, who constantly challenged the apartheid regime, playing cat and mouse with the security forces. He befriended the charismatic young black leader Steve Biko, who was murdered by the police. Woods's efforts to expose the murder endangered his life and that of his children. He fled South Africa for England, disguised as a priest, and spent the rest of his life writing and lecturing in opposition to apartheid and in hope of gaining justice for Biko. Their story was told in the 1987 film *Cry Freedom*. Suzman was for many years the lone voice against apartheid in the South African parliament. Sharp of tongue and wit, she challenged and embarrassed government officials during her long years as a member of Parliament (MP). Concerned about the treatment of prisoners, she visited and befriended Nelson Mandela on Robben Island. Vilified at home, internationally she was South Africa's most admired politician. And Mandela had her at his side when he signed the constitution as his country's first black president.

Of course, Woods, Fischer, and Suzman were minor cogs in the machine that ultimately brought down the apartheid government of South Africa. The great symbol of that victory—and of graciousness in victory—is Nelson Mandela. Mandela, after years as an ANC leader planning guerrilla warfare, spent twenty years in prison, where by force of personality and intellect he won the respect of his jailers. When international pressure forced the regime to seek a way out of its pariah status, he was the obvious choice as an interlocutor to represent the majority black population of the nation. His subsequent election as president of the Republic of South Africa, like that of Havel in Czechoslovakia, was one of the great moral victories in world history.

The men and women upon whom I focus in the fourth section are a disparate lot, united only by a common sense of decency and their commitment to human rights. In the midst of World War II, thousands of people risked their careers, their lives, and the lives of their families to save Jews from murderous Nazis and their anti-Semitic collaborators all over Europe. A few, such as the Swedish diplomat Raoul Wallenberg and the German industrialist Oskar Schindler, received international recognition for their efforts. Most went unnoticed, except by those they saved—or the Gestapo that executed them or the neighbors who murdered them for daring to harbor the detested Jews.

Pope John XXIII was widely admired in his brief tenure atop the Catholic hierarchy, but some of his achievements and the main thrust of Vatican II, his legacy of Catholic humanism, have been blunted by his conservative successors. No other pope, no other religious leader of the twentieth century, could match John's efforts on behalf of world peace and social justice. Certainly no other pope tried as hard to reach out to non-Catholics, to end the tensions between Roman Catholics and other Christians, between Christians and those of other faiths. Indeed, he even found a place in his heart for communists, to the dismay of many American Cold Warriors.

Andrei Sakharov, a key figure in the Soviet development of the hydrogen bomb, sacrificed a life of privilege in the Soviet Union to fight for freedom of speech and freedom from fear for those of his countrymen who were critical of their government. He became an opponent of Soviet imperialism and a leader in the international movement to win respect for human rights. The government struck back by stripping him of his honors and his positions, exiling him to a remote town far from his native Moscow, and subjecting him to constant, sometimes life-threatening harassment. His suffering ended with the emergence of Mikhail Gorbachev as leader of the Soviet Union. Gorbachev's ultimate concern was to revitalize the Communist Party and the nation. He believed he could do this by opening Soviet society, by granting its citizens the rights for which Sakharov had long fought. Gorbachev had the power to carry out many of the reforms Sakharov demanded; although the two men had little affection for each other, together they created a country in which, for a brief time, the prospects for liberal democracy were great.

Liu Binyan thought of himself as a good communist and a Chinese patriot. His dream was to see communist China develop as a nation unsurpassed in social justice. As an intellectual, as a journalist, he worked assiduously to reveal flaws in the system, points at which the Communist Party failed to live up to its principles. Insisting on the freedom to expose corruption, to recommend policy changes, he was thrown out of the party twice, in 1957 and in 1987. After the first time he was forced to spend twenty-one years doing manual labor, including carrying human excrement from Beijing to the countryside and living among animals, separated from his family. When he was "rehabilitated" and allowed to resume work, he picked up where he left off—fighting corrupt party leaders, challenging their abuse of power. Once again, his efforts brought him grief—and ultimately exile in the United States, where he died, his efforts to see a just society in China all in vain.

The final section examines two very different approaches to the quest for freedom from want, the most essential of human rights. The Great Depression of the early 1930s facilitated the rise of totalitarian regimes in Europe and Asia, of Hitler, Stalin, and the Japanese militarists. Peoples across the globe were willing to sacrifice their freedom for economic security. Totalitarian movements arose in the United States and the critical question was whether democracy could survive so severe an economic crisis—the collapse of the banking system, massive unemployment, millions of Americans facing hunger. In 1932, the American people voted for change, risking their future on the amiable governor of New York, Franklin D. Roosevelt. He responded by restoring their hopes and putting many of them to work. The first and essential freedom he promised them was freedom from want. His New Deal did not end the Depression, but it mitigated the suffering greatly and provided a degree of social democracy hitherto unknown in the United States. There would be no totalitarianism there. And where his vision fell short, at his side stood an extraordinary first lady, Eleanor Roosevelt, to point him in the right direction and to nag him to do the right thing. After his death, she emerged as one of the world's leading advocates for human rights.

Muhammad Yunus, an American-trained Bengali economist, returned to teach in his native land of Bangladesh, newly independent from Pakistan. Confronting extremes of poverty beyond the comprehension of most Americans, he developed the concept of micro-lending, of providing his country's poorest peasants with tiny loans to enable them to become entrepreneurs on a very small scale. He lent them enough to buy a goat, to buy seeds, to buy something that would enable them to bring in a minuscule income that would allow them to climb out of wretched conditions. Most of his borrowers were women whose new income gave them enhanced status in the family and in the village. The success of his program led to micro-lending all over the world, including the United States. None of his "entrepreneurs" became rich, few reached the middle class, but almost all were able to provide more for their families and gained enormously in stature and dignity. No one has done more to fight the extremes of economic misery than Yunus.

Given the victims of Hitler, Stalin, and Mao, given the genocide in the Ottoman Empire, in Europe, and in Rwanda, the mass killings in Cambodia and Bosnia, and the many millions of victims of imperialists and homegrown dictators, the twentieth century was probably unsurpassed in the annals of human rights violations. But wherever men and women suffered, there were others who stepped forward, who had the moral vision to intervene, often at great personal cost, to alleviate human misery as best they could. This book tells the stories of a handful of them, heroes for our time.

PART I

NONVIOLENT RESISTANCE

Mahatma Gandhi, Library of Congress, Prints & Photographs Division, NYWT&S Collection, LC-USZ62-111091

CHAPTER 1

Mahatma Gandhi and Nonviolent Resistance

There are doubtless a few Hindu nationalists—of the sort who assassinated him—and more than a few Muslims on the subcontinent who think otherwise, but Mohandas Gandhi probably comes closest to a universal conception of saintliness of any of my current (or previous) subjects. His story and writings were an inspiration to Nelson Mandela, Martin Luther King Jr., Aung San Suu Kyi, and countless others who sought justice from opponents too powerful to confront with force. The image of this odd-looking little man, clad only in a loincloth, challenging the mighty British Empire and infuriating Winston Churchill, is known to educated men and women the world over. And millions more learned the outlines of his life in Richard Attenborough's 1982 film *Gandhi*.

Of course, Gandhi had his detractors, too. Numerous South African and British officials despised him for his successes in organizing against them. Many who knew his life were appalled at what they perceived as his mistreatment of his wife and children. He and Kasturbai were married at thirteen, and he claimed to have been an especially lustful teenager. Later in life he decided to become celibate without consulting her. Life's material pleasures were also denied her. When she was dying he refused to allow her doctor to administer the modern medicine that might have saved her life. He was arguably a lousy father as well, denying his children the education they sought, with tragic consequences for his eldest son. Saintliness, greatness on the world scene, are clearly no guarantee of good family life.

Mohandas Gandhi was born in October 1869 in a small town a few hundred miles northwest of Bombay, the youngest of three brothers. What we know of his childhood comes from his autobiography, written when he was in his fifties, already a prominent Indian nationalist leader, and intensely conscious of the image he was seeking to project. His father was a respected official in Rajasthan, now an Indian state bordering Pakistan. Gandhi describes his father as truthful, brave, and generous—as most of our fathers were—but also short-tempered and perhaps given to carnal lust. Why else would a man marry again and again after each of his first three wives died?

Mohandas appears to have been a bright child who thrived as his mother's favorite. He remembered himself as a shy, timid boy who found it difficult to speak publicly, even as he grew older. He insisted he was an earnest child, committed to truth and morality—which did not prevent him experimenting with smoking, eating meat, or making a brave but unsuccessful attempt at sex in a brothel. George Orwell imagined him as a boy with a strong ethical sense rather than being notably religious. Young Gandhi had an uncomfortable sense of being different from others his age and feared ridicule. He also recalled playing the role of peacemaker when his friends quarreled.

His father married him off at thirteen, apparently to save money by having a double wedding for two of his sons. The boy was delighted by the attention. The bride, Kasturbai, was an illiterate child of the same age. Instructed by his sister-in-law on the duties of his wedding night, he performed to his satisfaction, enjoyed the activity, and gave his young bride little rest in the next several years. What respite she found came when she was recalled (frequently) to the home of her parents.

By all accounts, including his own, the critical experience of his adolescence came with the death of his father when Mohandas was sixteen. When his father became ill, he eagerly accepted the role of principal nurse, preparing medicine and massaging the dying man to ease his discomfort. But at the moment that his father died, he was not at his patient's bedside. Lust had consumed him and he had slipped off to arouse his wife. He needed no psychotherapist to explain his feeling of guilt, although Erik Erikson, in his magnificent psychobiography, refers thoughtfully to Gandhi's lifelong "existential debt." There is an obvious relationship between this guilt and his view of children as evidence of a lack of self-control, and of course, his ultimate turn to celibacy. And like many other men, he was not above blaming women for his desires: the woman as temptress, from whom a man's vital juices had to be protected—an Indian variation on sublimation, Erikson suggested.

Although he insisted he was but a mediocre student, Gandhi won prizes and passed the necessary examinations to graduate from high school in 1887.

He dropped out after one term at a local college and gradually formed the idea of going to London to study law. With some difficulty, the necessary funds were raised, his mother's objections overcome, and off he went—leaving behind his nineteen-year-old wife with a baby, their first child.

He arrived in London shortly before his twentieth birthday and remained there for nearly three years. Having promised his mother he would have no sex, eat no meat, and drink no liquor, he was limited in his diversions. His principal interests seem to have been vegetarianism and theosophy, and he quickly became active in groups studying both. Not surprisingly, given his mother's religiosity, he thought and read a good deal about religious and ethical systems. Christian friends, noting his fascination with the New Testament, were hopeful of his ultimate conversion. Gandhi found Jesus an extraordinarily attractive figure and his teachings unquestionably influenced the young Hindu.

Gandhi enjoyed and was drawn to English culture. In particular, he was affected by the liberalism, humanism, and relative egalitarianism he found in London, elements he found more attractive than the culture in which he had been raised. Issues of British imperialism do not seem to have had any relevance for him in his years in England, and his Anglophilia lasted for many more years. Photographs of Gandhi in London portray a properly attired English gentleman.

Once he completed his legal training, he returned to India in 1891 to begin his career as a barrister in Bombay. He panicked in court in his first appearance, abandoned case and client—and never went back. He found speaking in public excruciatingly painful, a handicap he did not easily or quickly overcome. After six months, he gave up and joined his brother, "a petty pleader," in his hometown of Rajkot. There he was able to support himself and his family by drafting legal papers for minor cases. There, too, he had his first unpleasant experience with a British colonial officer. He called on the official, whom he had met in London, hoping to use the past acquaintance to reverse the man's poor opinion of his brother—and for his presumption was physically removed from the office. Outraged, he appealed for advice on how to take action against the official and was told by his seniors to get used to it, that better men than he had been treated thus by British officers.

Suddenly, an offer came to represent an Indian firm that had a major case in South Africa. They wanted an Indian barrister and they chose Gandhi for his British education and his command of English. The fee was good, the assignment seemed manageable, and he was ready to leave India. His homecoming had been less than glorious and the idea of starting over on a new stage was most attractive. In April 1893, he "set forth full of zest to try my luck in South Africa."

He arrived in Durban wearing a frock coat and a turban and quickly discovered that Indians were held in contempt by Europeans in South Africa and referred to as "coolies." He became known as a "coolie barrister." Approximately a week after his arrival in Durban, he won the confidence of his employer and set off for Pretoria to deal with the case for which he had been recruited. En route he had another defining experience. Despite his first-class ticket on the train, a white passenger who boarded farther down the line, in Maritzburg, objected to his presence in the first-class compartment. The conductor immediately ordered him out of the compartment and called the police when he refused to leave. Gandhi and his luggage were removed from the train and he sat through the night in the station waiting room, stewing and trying to decide whether to return to India immediately or swallow the insult and continue on to Pretoria. He chose to go on, encouraged by other Indians who related their own experiences. But he also resolved to do something about racial discrimination, a determination that intensified as he was treated roughly on subsequent legs of the trip and was spared difficulty finding lodging in Pretoria only by the good graces of an "American Negro" he chanced to meet at the train station.

The case that had brought him to South Africa involved financial intricacies that Gandhi succeeded in mastering. As a junior barrister, he prepared the plaintiff's case for the attorney who would try it and also translated much of the correspondence between plaintiff and defendant, mostly in Gujarati. In due course he concluded that his client would win, that the evidence supported his claims, but that with legal fees and court costs, both parties to the suit (who were in fact relatives) would be hurt. Somehow, he persuaded them to accept arbitration and when the arbitrator declared in favor of his client, he succeeded in working out an installment plan for payment that would not destroy the loser, who had to come up with £37,000 and costs. Gandhi was very pleased with himself: He had united the parties, both of whom gained esteem in the merchant community for the way in which they settled the case. He was beginning to see how he might enjoy legal practice—and he was becoming aware of his gift for persuading adversaries to compromise.

He stayed in Pretoria for a year, doing a little legal work, teaching English to Indian workers, dabbling in Christianity, and studying the condition of Indians in South Africa. Indians had been recruited as indentured labor after native Africans, freed from slavery, refused to work on the plantations of British settlers in Natal. Indian merchants had followed to market goods to the growing Indian community, but both the merchants and the laborers who remained after serving their five-year terms lived with restrictions that denied them equality with Europeans. Gandhi discovered that in the Afrikaner-controlled Orange Free State, Indians were by law denied virtually all rights. They could remain in the territory only as menials. In Transvaal, also Afrikaner-controlled, they could neither vote nor own property. They were charged a poll tax for entering. They were not allowed outdoors after 9 p.m. without a permit. Gandhi quickly concluded that South Africa "was no country for a self-respecting Indian." Gradually he was seized by a sense of mission, a sense that he should attempt to lead the Indian community toward acceptance as equals to whites, to put an end to the denial of their rights. His law practice became secondary to his public work—his efforts to organize Indians of all religions, from all parts of India, into a cohesive force to challenge discrimination against them.

The timid young barrister from India, the man who had fled the Bombay courtroom rather than address the judge, was transformed. He called a meeting of all Indians in Pretoria, recommended formation of an association to confront the authorities, and offered his own services. Those assembled responded favorably. Gandhi made representations to the British agent in the city and to the railroad without significant success. And then, his case settled, it was time to return to Durban for the trip back to India.

Of course, he did not go back; on the contrary, he remained in South Africa, except for brief trips to England and to India, for a total of twenty-one years—long enough to help the British against the Boers and the Zulus, as well as struggling against mistreatment of Indians. At his putative farewell party, he discovered that the legislature of British-controlled Natal was preparing a bill to deprive Indians of the right to elect members of the first independent Natal parliament. He urged his merchant patrons to fight against the bill, to prevent it from becoming law, and they agreed—if he would stay to direct the fight. That he did, emerging as the spokesman for Indian émigrés.

Gandhi and his colleagues quickly obtained a postponement on discussion of the bill and submitted a petition to oppose it. The petition won favorable comment in the press and in the parliament, but the bill passed nonetheless. Appeals to Natal's premier and governor and to the colonial secretary in London were also to no avail. Gandhi had better luck fighting a tax the legislators imposed on any Indian indentured worker who chose to stay in Natal after completing his five-year term. He was unable to have the tax eliminated entirely until many years later, but was able to have it reduced from £25 to £3.

It was evident that the fight against discrimination would not be an easy one and that victory, if it ever came, would be distant. A permanent organization to represent the interests of the Indian community was essential; Gandhi called it the Natal Indian Congress, an obvious allusion to the Indian National Congress that was leading the struggle against British rule in India. Sustained by retainers from leading merchants for his legal work, he spent most of his time organizing the community, making its wishes known to the white overlords of Natal, and developing an Indian consciousness among the émigrés and the African-born Indians. He had found his calling and had come to see himself as the man chosen to lead his people out of their benighted condition.

When he left India in 1893, he had left his family behind, although not before he had increased it with a second son. In 1896, he decided to return to India to fetch them and create a home for all in Africa. He remained in India for six months, where he assisted in fighting a bubonic plague epidemic that had swept in from China and established contact with nationalist leaders, eager to inform them of how their compatriots were being treated in Natal.

Gandhi returned to Durban with his family in December 1896 and barely survived the landing. His criticism of South Africa's treatment of Indians had been reported in the local press and a white mob at the dock, determined to prevent more Indians from coming ashore in Durban, recognized an opportunity to intimidate an antagonist and nearly lynched him. Kasturbai doubtless wished she'd stayed in India.

Gandhi's family could not have derived much pleasure from life in South Africa. He maintained his status as a leader in the Indian community, but was not satisfied with himself or his role. He wanted to be of greater service to humanity and purer, perhaps closer to God than he found himself. The penchant for nursing revealed when his father was dying provided one course of action. He began to volunteer at a hospital for indentured Indian laborers. He even took up midwifery and delivered or helped to deliver his two additional sons born in Africa. His sons suffered from his unwillingness to send them to either public or missionary schools and from his failure to give the time necessary for the homeschooling he preferred.

The arrival of the children troubled him, as did the demands of parenting the first two boys—at which he appears to have been an abysmal failure. He soon concluded that having children, caring for them, was inconsistent with public service. He could not allow the needs of his family to keep him from serving the larger community. He was stuck with four children he had already fathered, but determined to have no more. He knew something of contraception, having read about it during his stay in London, but concluded that sex for fun, to satisfy one's lust, was unworthy. Kasturbai, he acknowledged, was no temptress and probably appreciated the rest when Gandhi opted for separate beds. He had to master his lust, gain control over his will, save his vital juices for public service. In due course he decided that celibacy was the only answer. We have no indication of Kasturbai's response, although he notes in his autobiography that she did not hesitate to complain about other steps he was taking toward asceticism, such as refusing to accept gifts of jewelry some of his admirers sought to bestow on his family.

Perhaps even stranger for the man who played the principal role in winning India's independence from Great Britain was the persistence of his loyalty to the empire. When the Boer War broke out in 1899, most Indians sympathized with the Boers as covictims of British imperialism. Gandhi conceded that the British were in the wrong, but insisted that as British subjects, Indians owed allegiance to the empire. He persuaded the British to allow him to mobilize an Indian ambulance corps of over a thousand volunteers and ultimately won a medal for his service to the Crown.

Before the war ended, he decided to return to India, presumably to prepare himself for a leadership role in his country's fight for independence, a role he believed he had won by his activities in South Africa. The Indian National Congress met in Calcutta in 1901; Gandhi attended and presented a resolution calling for equality for Indians in South Africa and the abolition of the tax on Indian émigrés. He found Congress leaders apathetic, warning him not to expect such a resolution to have much impact, given that Indians were second-class citizens in their own country. When his resolution was put before the meeting, the delegates were obviously prepared to pass it without reading or understanding it. It passed unanimously—as did all resolutions endorsed by the chair. Gandhi was pleased that it passed but troubled by the indifference he perceived.

In general, Gandhi was underwhelmed by the meeting and by the Congress membership. He thought Congress leaders lived too well and that their followers lacked any commitment to service. He found the delegates lazy and the volunteers no more inspiring. He was troubled by the poor sanitary conditions that they tolerated and to which they contributed. They pissed off the verandas of their cottages and refused to clean the latrines. He found the stench unbearable and cleaned his own—and might have cleaned them all had he had the time, clean latrines the most understandable of his obsessions. The other delegates were appalled, insisting it was the task of scavengers, underlining the caste segregation that angered him.

The nationalist leader for whom Gandhi had the most respect was Gopal Krishna Gokhale, a moderate, apparently Anglophile intellectual who argued that India needed reforms, especially of the caste system, before it would be ready for independence—none of which kept him from being a trenchant critic of imperial rule. Gandhi stayed with him for a month after the Congress meeting and later described Gokhale as his political guru. Certainly there were similarities in their views of Indian customs and of the appropriate way to struggle for independence, but Gandhi was uneasy with Gokhale's upper-class ways—billiards at the club, travel by private carriage—and dissatisfied with Gokhale's explanations.

Gandhi was already beginning to exhibit some of the patterns that were soon to become central to his identity. In addition to latrine cleaning, he was convinced of the value of the exercise routine he had begun in London, of the necessity for daily walks. He became an advocate for animal rights, insisting that "the life of a lamb is no less precious than that of a human being," a view easily consistent with his vegetarianism. When his son nearly died from typhoid and pneumonia, Gandhi refused to give him the eggs and chicken soup the doctor recommended, substituting his own cure of wet sheets and hip baths. He insisted that diet and home remedies were preferable to modern medicine. He decided to give up life insurance so as not to deprive his wife and children of their self-reliance, and to devote the money saved on premiums to the good of the community. And he tried always to travel third class, with the masses—despite their habits, which he found dirty and inconsiderate.

Gokhale persuaded him to stay in India, to settle in Bombay, practice law, and help with public work—much as he had been doing in South Africa. Gandhi was dubious, but decided to give it a try, beginning in the provinces before he returned to Bombay with its memories of past failure. The legal work went a little better, but he was not engaged. He was not doing anything important, anything worthy of his growing sense that he had been put on earth for a special purpose. He needed a greater mission, something which he alone could do—and again, the call came from South Africa.

Britain's victory over the Boers had added the Transvaal and the Orange Free State to the empire, and the colonial secretary was headed for South Africa to examine the situation. Gandhi's patrons wanted him to return and present the case for the Indian community. He was delighted, and left as soon as the money for passage arrived, leaving behind his wife and family for an assignment he thought would take him about a year—another easy way to contain his lust.

Back in Africa, Gandhi drafted a statement of grievances and remedies for the Indian community to present to the colonial secretary who, alas, was uninterested. Gandhi followed him to Pretoria, but local authorities refused to let him attend the scheduled meeting. Gandhi recognized the fact that although Transvaal was now under British rule, discrimination against Indians continued unabated. Rather than go back to Natal, he decided to remain in Transvaal and carry on the fight from there. He chose Johannesburg as his headquarters, enrolled as a barrister before the Supreme Court, organized the Transvaal Indian Association, and resumed the kind of service in which he had reveled before his return to India.

Clearly this was the life for him. He led an Indian delegation to make representations to the British governor. He wrote reports about the situation that he sent to Indian Congress representatives in London as well as India—and these reports were widely circulated among British officials in England and India. To all who would listen or read his writings he insisted that Indians, as British subjects and desirable citizens, were entitled to equality with Europeans in South Africa. He started his own newspaper in which he criticized the British governor for attempting to recruit—and exploit— more and more indentured Indian workers, but being unwilling to allow them to stay when their terms expired. To British officials in South Africa in particular, but in London as well, Gandhi was becoming a great annoyance. In the Indian community in South Africa, he inspired the admiration he craved. He kept Gokhale informed of his activities, but he had not yet won the attention of other nationalist leaders in India.

Even his legal practice was enormously successful, and he had to hire several European assistants. He concluded that he would have to stay longer than he had anticipated, probably for several years. There was the small matter of his family, left behind in India. His solution was to propose that his wife and children remain in India for three or four years so as not to distract him. He reminded Kasturbai of how little time he had had for her in India and warned he would be even busier in Johannesburg. But he lost the argument: Her husband may not have been all she dreamed of in a mate, but living with him was far better than being stuck with her in-laws. Gandhi's quest for total control of his household failed, but his genius for defining himself in ways that tormented Kasturbai was far from exhausted.

Some years earlier, when Gandhi was studying various religions, especially Christianity, a friend sent him Tolstoy's *The Kingdom of God Is within You*, by which he was greatly moved. In 1904, another acquaintance gave him a copy of Ruskin's *Unto This Last*. Both books seemed to confirm and help him to articulate and act in accord with his evolving philosophy. Tolstoy argued that man's goal was to seek and tell the truth. One of those truths was that all men had the right to be free and equal. Gandhi had been fighting for that truth, against injustice, throughout his years in South Africa. Tolstoy promoted pacifism, rejecting anger, violence, passion—even sexual desire. Gandhi also saw a need to control all these emotions, to be in control of himself. Both Tolstoy and Ruskin had strong reservations about modernity, stressing the value of the simple life, a rustic life away from the noise and filth of the city. Tilling the soil and preserving traditional crafts were unmatched virtues—and Gandhi decided to buy a farm.

Shortly after reading Ruskin's book, he bought a hundred acres of land near Durban, to which he moved the operation of his newspaper, *Indian Opinion*. The paper's staff was to move to the farm, with their printing press. All who accepted the idea would work the farm, be paid equally, and turn out the paper in their spare time. He was able to persuade enough friends and relatives to join him, to surrender the quest for wealth that had brought them to South Africa, to bring his idea to fruition. Thus was born his Phoenix Settlement in 1904, the first of his experiments with ashrams.

Much as he would have liked to leave his practice, live at Phoenix, and earn his living by manual labor, Gandhi had to spend most of his time in Johannesburg, where Kasturbai and the children joined him. Still, he was determined to achieve simplicity even in the city. He refused to buy bread from a bakery and instead had his children grind flour ("a very beneficial exercise" for them) to make unleavened bread at home. He refused to have his servant clean the water closet, assigning his children the task of collecting the night soil— "good training for the children . . . and they naturally got a good grounding in general sanitation."

As Gandhi strove for control of his body and emotions and to reduce daily living to premodern forms, he continued to work for the betterment of the condition of his fellow Indians in South Africa. Black Africans were not a significant concern of his, but he was not unaware of their plight at the hands of the Afrikaners and British. As a loyal British subject, he once again organized an ambulance corps under British army control during the Zulu revolt of 1906. He insisted later that his sympathies had been with the Zulus and that he and his men tended only to Zulus—who would otherwise have been left to die of their wounds. But he was close to the end of his patience with British imperialism, gradually concluding that the British would never stop discriminating against Indians voluntarily. Demonstrating loyalty to the Crown was bringing no benefits for his people.

On a trip to London in 1906, Gandhi had an unpleasant encounter with the then colonial undersecretary Winston Churchill—the latter in his best imperial and racist form. Petitions to local authorities occasionally won respectful hearings, but the hopes of the Indian community were never fulfilled. Nonetheless, awareness of the Japanese victory over the Russian

Empire in 1905 allowed Gandhi to conceive of the day he might hope to rock the British Empire. Unfortunately, unlike the Japanese, he had neither army nor navy at his disposal. Of course, the use of military power was alien to his evolving philosophy. If petitions and legal action were ineffective and demonstrations of fealty to the Crown brought nothing, if military force was not an option, he would have to lead his people in other forms of resistance. Henry David Thoreau's essay on civil disobedience helped shape his thoughts.

The need to act became increasingly pressing. The 1906 Asiatic Law Amendment Ordinance passed by the Transvaal legislature required all Indians to register and be fingerprinted in the process. It deprived the Indian community of what few civil rights any of its members still enjoyed, and contained provisions that facilitated various forms of harassment. Labeled the "Black Act" by Gandhi, it was unquestionably designed to drive the Indians out of Transvaal.

Gandhi called together the Indians of Johannesburg in September and at a mass meeting outlined a plan for passive resistance. He called upon his audience to take a vow to oppose the government's action, to resist nonviolently in the face of abuse, imprisonment, even death. Stanley Wolpert, a prominent specialist in Indian history, finds Gandhi sublimating all of his power and sexual energy to fight against racial bigotry: "Fearing nothing, loving no one . . . , he had made himself invulnerable to physical coercion . . . and to human temptations." This was the beginning of an approach Gandhi called *satyagraha*, meaning, he explained, "truth and firmness"—a force born of truth, love, and nonviolence.

The resolutions passed by the Indian community and the resolve shown by Gandhi and his followers failed to move Transvaal or British officials. Once again Gandhi sailed for London in an effort to persuade the colonial secretary to overturn the Transvaal ordinance. This time, by intensive lobbying and with the support of John Morley, India's secretary of state, he won an apparent victory: The British government vetoed the ordinance. But the victory was ephemeral, as Great Britain proceeded to grant "responsible" government to the Transvaal, allowing that government to pass the same ordinance under the name "Asiatic Registration Act" in March 1907. Registration would be required as of July 1.

Gandhi was determined to resist and called upon the Indian community to refuse to register. His followers picketed the registration offices and only a few hundred of the thousands of Indians in the Transvaal chose to obey the ordinance. Supporters in London and in India worked frenetically to exert pressure on the British government to intervene and to awaken world opinion. Transvaal officials began to arrest unregistered Indians in November and in December ordered Gandhi and other community leaders to appear in court to explain why they should not be deported. Deportation orders were issued but Gandhi refused to obey.

In January 1908, Gandhi and several of his colleagues were imprisoned and other Indians flaunted their refusal to register, courting arrest. By the dozens they began to fill the jails of Johannesburg. General Jan Smuts, the widely respected Boer, acting as colonial secretary, contacted Gandhi and agreed to have the Black Act abolished if Indians would register voluntarily. Gandhi agreed and was released from prison—but Smuts failed to deliver on his end of the bargain.

Gandhi gave Smuts an August deadline to repeal the Black Act; when the deadline passed, he rallied his forces and over two thousand Indians publicly burned their registration cards. Smuts and his colleagues would not budge, but there were no immediate reprisals. Gandhi's followers then tested immigration laws designed to keep Indians out of Transvaal and were imprisoned, again filling the jails. Some were sent back to India, where their treatment enraged merchants as well as intellectuals and demanded the attention of the Indian National Congress. Gandhi was himself imprisoned once more in late 1908 and then again early in 1909.

Although his acts of civil disobedience brought little tangible benefit to the Indian community, the publicity Gandhi's acts and words began to attract throughout the British Empire won the admiration of Indians everywhere and was troubling to Smuts and to imperial authorities. He was the unquestioned leader of Indians in South Africa. His willingness to suffer on their behalf and to fight oppression without resort to violence, his faith that right would prevail and freedom and justice would be won, led them to see him as a saintly figure. Indeed, the role he had assumed could easily be equated with that of a medieval Christian martyr—or even that of Jesus of Nazareth.

Released from prison in May 1909, he departed again for London in June. Despite five months of effort there, success continued to elude him. He found countless sympathetic listeners, but none with the authority to meet the demands of the Indians of South Africa. His confidence in the British system of government and in the British commitment to fair play and decency, battered continuously by the realities of British policy, evaporated. On the ship back to Africa, he heatedly wrote *Hind Swaraj* (*Indian Home Rule*), a pamphlet that revealed his frustration and loss of faith in Western civilization. His argument in favor of simple village life over modern industrialism was a further evolution of thinking derived from Ruskin and Tolstoy. He also acknowledged the influence of Thoreau and Ralph Waldo Emerson on self-reliance.

As confidence in civil disobedience waned among his followers, he led the most faithful to Tolstoy Farm, on land provided by a supporter of German origin. He seemed to have a Jeffersonian fear of the corrupting influence of cities. As at Phoenix, Tolstoy Farm would be a place where his supporters could learn a new simple life as they persisted in their resistance to laws discriminating against Indians. They would learn useful trades such as carpentry and shoemaking. They would retain continuity with Indian culture. Books were not needed—Gandhi was not training intellectuals. He perceived all who lived there as a family, with himself as the father who would direct their purification. Men lived separately from women to facilitate celibacy. Diet was simple. Gandhi had concluded that flavorful food inflamed the passions; he would eat only what his body required to survive, and he imposed his views on the Tolstoy community.

As Gandhi trained his troops, Gokhale, representing the viceroy of India, traveled to South Africa to negotiate with Smuts. The negotiations appeared to have been successful and Gokhale left believing he had achieved repeal of all of the noxious legislation—but once again, Smuts backed away from the agreement.

In March 1913, South African authorities went a step too far in their harassment of Indians. The Cape Supreme Court ruled that non-Christian marriages were invalid: The marriages of Indians conducted according to Hindu or Muslim rites were nullified and the legitimacy of Indian children denied. Gandhi went to war. He ordered the enraged Indians to begin crossing the Natal-Transvaal border, those in Natal marching to Transvaal and vice versa. Cleverly, he sent women first, and when the Indian women were arrested and jailed, Indian miners were outraged and went on strike. As the authorities began to arrest them as well, the prisons filled rapidly. Leading the striking miners on a march from Newcastle to Pretoria, Gandhi was also sent to jail.

Word of the furor almost immediately reached India and England and prompted intervention by the viceroy and the British cabinet. A commission of inquiry was set up and Gandhi was released from prison. But Gandhi refused to cooperate with the commission because it had no Indian members. It was at this time that he first removed his Western clothes, donned those of an indentured laborer, shaved his head, and insisted on living the life of the poorest. The march would go on.

The denouement did not come until June 1914, after Gandhi offered to postpone resumption of the march at a moment when the government was confronted by a threatened work stoppage by European railway workers. Smuts and his colleagues accepted the peace offering and Smuts met once again with Gandhi. Agreement was reached in January 1914, and this time an Indian Relief Act was passed by the legislature. Gandhi had won the battle. It was time to return to India. He left South Africa on July 18, 1914, traveling first to London, where Gokhale was receiving medical treatment. He arrived only days after war had begun and once again raised an Indian ambulance corps to aid the British Empire, but a combination of poor health and British arrogance led to his resignation a few weeks after the corps was organized. As soon as he was able—perhaps a little sooner, fearing that he would die abroad—he left for India.

Gandhi's success in South Africa had been trumpeted throughout India. He returned in January 1915 as a hero to Indian nationalists and a source of concern to British officials on the subcontinent. He went home determined to lead his people, Hindu and Muslim alike, to independence. He was a man with a mission, and he was convinced that in satyagraha he had found the winning weapon and that he alone could lead India to its freedom.

Unfortunately, Gokhale died soon afterward, and other Indian leaders lacked Gokhale's sense that one day Gandhi would lead them. Gandhi found himself pushed aside, an upstart whose views were welcomed only when he addressed the plight of Indians overseas. Confident of his future role, Gandhi retreated to Ahmedabad, where in May 1915 he established Satyagraha Ashram, the base of his future operations and a training ground for his disciples.

At the ashram Gandhi pushed ahead with the experiments that he had begun at Phoenix and Tolstoy Farm. Those who joined him had to be committed to nonviolence, celibacy, simple food, and handmade clothing. He was reimmersing himself—and his followers—in an imagined Indian culture through which they would be freed of British influence and regain their identity. But he also demanded a vow against untouchability and admitted untouchables to the ashram—a decision that almost cost him his marriage to a distraught Kasturbai.

He had promised Gokhale that he would be silent for a year as he took the pulse of the country. In February 1916, he was free to speak out and he did at Benares Hindu University, where he gave a fiery speech belittling the be-jeweled maharaja and princes on the platform with him and announcing his willingness to die for the cause of Indian independence. When he declared that self-government would come only if Indians seized it, the program was ended abruptly. But his student audience was aroused, as were those who heard him speak as he traveled the country. Erikson suggests the Benares remarks were Gandhi's equivalent of Martin Luther nailing his theses to the Wittenberg church door.

In 1917, when peasants at Champaran appealed to Gandhi for help in their struggle against the indigo planters who brutalized them, he chose to fight with the tactics that had gained victory in South Africa. He prevailed against the planters with the first satyagraha in India. The colonial official to whom he first appealed ordered him out of the district and had him arrested when he ignored the order. Gandhi continued to refuse to leave, pled guilty to the charge against him, refused to pay the fine, and as in South Africa, chose jail. Wiser senior officials, familiar with Gandhi's reputation, arranged for his release and agreed to facilitate his investigation with a commission of which he would be a member. Despite intimidation by the planters, Gandhi won the abolition of the existing system of forced, uncompensated labor and stayed on to attempt to improve peasant life with schools and lessons on sanitation. His image as a man to whom the afflicted masses might turn continued to grow.

Gandhi's next mission took him back to Ahmedabad to take up the struggle of the local textile workers. Here was another opportunity for him to refine his techniques for achieving goals without resort to force, to demonstrate that his approach would work anywhere in India, under any circumstances. He advised workers to strike for the pay increase they wanted, and when they weakened, he chose to fast, to the death if necessary, to keep them at it and to increase the pressure on the mill owners, the most prominent of whom was his friend. He succeeded in keeping both strikers and owners from resorting to violence and won a decent wage raise for the workers. It was the first time he used the fast to achieve his goals, and his ambivalence about the tactic soon melted away. Over the years Gandhi's fasts became worldwide concerns as anxious sympathizers everywhere feared for his life—although certainly not Churchill, who was never a sympathizer.

Gandhi's international reputation came as a result of his leadership of the Indian nationalist movement for independence from Great Britain. In 1918, he attempted to win British gratitude by raising an Indian army to aid the Entente cause in its war against the Central Powers led by Germany. He rationalized his tactic by contending that military training would be useful for his people—however difficult it might have been to reconcile with his commitment to nonviolence.

The British were unmoved by Gandhi's support and, at the end of the war, passed the Rowlatt Acts, suspending civil liberties and threatening imprisonment for sedition, a category in which agitation for Indian independence fit comfortably. Gandhi and other nationalist leaders quickly resolved on a campaign of civil disobedience, demanding the repeal of the acts. The results were horrifying. In March 1919, police in New Delhi fired on unarmed protesters, killing several. There were also outbreaks of violence committed by Indians. The ultimate disaster came a month later at Amritsar when a deranged British officer, notorious Brigadier Reginald Dyer, ordered his troops to fire on thousands of Indian peasants at a festival, resulting in the deaths of four hundred and the wounding of more than a thousand others. Indians rioted in response, and Gandhi was forced to wonder whether nonviolence would work. He concluded that he had underestimated the intransigence of British officials and overestimated the readiness of the Indian people to carry out a campaign of civil disobedience. He would need more time to train the latter.

In 1920, he argued the case for satyagraha to the Indian National Congress. He contended that British rule depended not merely on force but on the cooperation of Indians. Were Indians to withhold that cooperation, the raj could not survive. Nonviolent civil disobedience was the answer. Among Congress leaders there was no lack of skeptics, but there was also no doubt that Gandhi had won the support of Indian peasants, to whom he had become "the Mahatma," or "Great Soul." He was the Congress's best hope of forging a mass movement. In 1921 the leadership grudgingly granted him the authority to reorganize the Congress, and he found himself where he had long wanted to be: the spiritual and political leader of the Indian people.

Gandhi's drive for Indian independence progressed but little in the 1920s. These were years when it also became apparent that he was as much a social reformer as he was a nationalist leader. He continued to fight against untouchability, arguing that Indians would never be free if they continued to treat "untouchables" as pariahs. Increasingly, he attacked the caste system, willingly alienating Hindu fundamentalists. And he struggled mightily to win Muslims to his side, insisting that an independent India would be a nation in which all religions would be respected. He met with Muslim leaders to persuade them that his tactics were consistent with Koranic teachings, that the Koran allowed for a nonviolent response to one's enemies. In 1924 he fasted for Hindu-Muslim solidarity. His principal supporters in South Africa had been Muslims and he imagined he could win them to his side in India as well—a dream he never surrendered.

In particular, Gandhi was concerned with rural poverty, some of which he attributed to the introduction of Western machine industry and Western imports. He insisted that a resurgence of cottage industries, of what a later age called "appropriate technology," was the answer. He demanded that his followers give up clothing manufactured by machines, that they wear nothing but *khadi*, a traditional, coarse Indian cloth produced on a manual spinning wheel. If a sufficient number of people followed suit, they would create a market for domestic products and income for poor peasants. To underscore his point, he cast away forever his Western clothing—his once-beloved English suits—shaved his head again, and dressed himself in a khadi cloak and loincloth. One scholar, Sunil Khilnani, suggests that Gandhi had transformed himself into an icon for his cause.

At approximately the same time he began to manifest an obsession with young women, especially attractive Western women, who were drawn to his side by his charismatic spirituality. Almost to the end of his life, he kept young women close to him, allowing some of them to bathe him, to massage him, to sleep in the same room with him. Given his commitment to celibacy and his conviction that sexual energy had to be sublimated, he was appalled by any intimation of impropriety. Even the most intense of these relationships, that with the Danish missionary Esther Faering, does not seem to have alerted him to any awareness of his sexuality. Sometimes he seems to have imagined he was testing himself, proving that his body was under control. At one time, troubled by a hint of sexual desire, he began sleeping naked with young women from his ashram with the intent of conquering the stimuli that aroused other men. Were he able to do that, he was convinced he could overcome Hindu-Muslim animosity. Perhaps his failure to unite Muslims and Hindus indicates a similar lack of success with his efforts to deny himself erections. None of this endeared him or his female following to Kasturbai.

But it is, of course, the nonviolent struggle against the raj that must remain central to any Gandhian narrative. His followers multiplied as he traveled around the country in 1919, 1920, 1921—and then disaster struck again in February 1922. A group of peasants with a limited grasp of his principles, apparently responding to a perceived provocation, set fire to a police station and butchered the policemen stationed in it. Gandhi had been on the verge of calling for massive civil disobedience, but horrified by the violence, he halted the campaign; this cost him support among the less patient of his followers. He was convinced that his people needed more training and greater discipline, and he fasted for five days as penance for his failure. A month later he was arrested and sent to prison, where he served two years of a six-year sentence; he was released early because of ill health and British fear that his death would be blamed on them and inflame the country.

Over the next few years he seemed preoccupied with his health and his various eccentric programs for coping with the failings of his body. He wrote an autobiography. But he also pushed on with his efforts to win Muslim support and to reform Hinduism. When urged to resume his political role, he indicated his belief that the country was not yet ready for the campaign he wanted to lead. Frustrations with British intransigence grew in the country, but a successful satyagraha led by one of his followers in 1928, a nonviolent campaign won by withholding taxes, seemed to reinvigorate him.

Searching for a target for a massive satyagraha, Gandhi chose the salt tax. The British authorities monopolized the sale of salt, selling it only in government shops and taxing it heavily. In March 1930 Gandhi led a band of followers to the coast, where they gathered salt illegally. Thousands of women joined in the activity, one of the earliest indications of Gandhi's success in finding a place for women in the nationalist movement. (His treatment of his wife may have been abominable, but he was unquestionably as much concerned with improving the lot of women as he was that of untouchables.) Soon millions of Indians defied the raj and trooped to the sea to collect salt. There was some violence, but this time Gandhi did not attempt to halt the satyagraha—he had learned from his experience in 1922.

The British, however, had not learned. In May 1930, they arrested Gandhi once more. Thousands of satyagrahis were jailed and thousands protested across India. The outcry against Gandhi's incarceration was worldwide—and the authorities blinked. The viceroy released Gandhi in 1931 and worked with him to reach an agreement to end civil disobedience in exchange for the release of all nonviolent political prisoners and Gandhi's participation in talks in London on the creation of a new Indian central government—which would remain under British domination. The talks failed, largely because of differences over the representation of religious and other minorities. In India, Gandhi's concessions to the viceroy angered many of his younger and less patient followers. Similarly, British policemen and civil servants were outraged by the viceroy's concessions to Gandhi. Terrorist acts and repression quickly resurfaced, and a new viceroy proved less accommodating.

When Gandhi returned to India late in December 1931, he found that many Congress leaders had been arrested. An effort to communicate with the new viceroy elicited no response. Gandhi had no recourse but to have his followers resume their acts of civil disobedience and to resume their boycott of foreign cloth. Almost immediately he was arrested, as were all leaders of the Indian National Congress. The British had decided to crush the independence movement, nonviolent or not.

In March 1932, Gandhi announced that he would begin a fast "unto death" in response to a British policy that seemed to reify untouchability. When London refused to back down, he began his fast in September. Soon thousands were fasting in sympathy. As the world watched and his weight dropped until it was down to about ninety-three pounds, the British beat a strategic retreat. Hindu leaders who had never been supportive of Gandhi's campaigns against the caste system and untouchability gave the British cover by accepting Gandhi's position. No one wanted to be perceived as responsible for his death.

In 1933, Gandhi began another fast, apparently to "purify" himself. The British quickly released him from prison: If he were going to kill himself, a prospect they might have welcomed by this time, they preferred that the end come under someone else's roof. But Gandhi intended only a three-week fast, during which he accepted water. When he met his goal, he resumed meeting with Congress leaders to plan future action.

Gandhi found the British authorities contemptuous of his efforts and convinced that his support was waning. Many of his Congress colleagues had lost confidence in civil disobedience. His efforts to reach out to Muslims were bearing little fruit. And his Hindu following had been weakened by defections provoked by his struggle on behalf of untouchables. When he announced a new satyagraha, he was immediately arrested and sent back to prison, where he found conditions more difficult than in the past. He decided to resume fasting and after eight days was granted an unconditional release.

This time, it appeared that his political career might well be over. He resolved to leave the Indian National Congress and devote himself to issues of social and rural reform. He was sixty-four years old and his eccentric eating habits and occasional fasts kept his weight below a hundred pounds. Hindu thugs, angered by his commitment to ending untouchablity, harassed him and Indian intellectuals wearied of his homilies about the joys of village life, but he gave no ground. Indian independence, he insisted, would be worthwhile only if India was purified by the end of untouchability and of Hindu-Muslim communal strife.

During this period, when Gandhi had withdrawn to his ashram, Margaret Sanger called on him. His young colleague and prospective leader of an independent India, Jawaharlal Nehru, had encouraged her to see Gandhi. Nehru and Gandhi stood together in an uneasy alliance, each admiring qualities in the other, each recognizing the other's appeal to an otherwise unreachable constituency, but each also skeptical of the other's core values. Nehru was impatient with Gandhi's glorification of rural life, certain that industrial modernization was essential for the Indian state, and suspected birth control would do more to ease poverty than wearing khadi. Gandhi listened to Sanger politely, agreed that Indians probably had too many children, but rejected her arguments in favor of contraceptives. To enjoy sex—as he had in his youth—was wrong: Sex could only be justified for purposes of procreation. Otherwise, abstinence, such as he had practiced for many years, was the only acceptable answer. The use of contraceptives denied men and women the discipline of self-restraint. Sanger moved on and Gandhi slept naked with young women to prove to himself that he no longer felt any sexual desire, to continue his pursuit of perfection.

When, in the late 1930s, Gandhi endorsed the appeasement of Hitler and suggested that Great Britain win him over by disarming, it seemed clear that Gandhi had outlived his usefulness, that his approach to the world was absurd. His subsequent suggestion that the Jews of Europe should have committed mass suicide to protest Hitler's persecution of them was decidedly unhelpful. The German blitzkrieg in the spring of 1940 did not undermine his faith in nonviolence. At a time when the convictions of pacifists the world over were shaken by the existence of such evil as personified by Hitler, Gandhi held firmly to his convictions. At the end of the war, he argued that Churchill and Roosevelt were no less war criminals than Hitler and Mussolini.

Twice before, when England went to war, Gandhi had rallied Indians to remain loyal to the empire. By 1939, Gandhi's respect for the British had evaporated, along with his expectation that they would grant India its independence voluntarily. This time, he had no qualms about taking advantage of Britain's desperation to press India's cause. In 1940 he accepted the Indian National Congress's call to lead a satyagraha against the British. One after another he sent his younger colleagues out to make seditious speeches urging the people not to support Britain's war effort. One after another they were imprisoned by the British authorities, although Gandhi remained free until August 1942, when he was arrested for launching his "Quit India" movement, his last great satyagraha. Imprisonment at the Aga Khan's palace followed—and the satyagraha turned violent. Nehru, for one, had no regrets: He was ready to fight for India's independence, as was Subhas Bose, who defected to the Japanese.

During Gandhi's wartime imprisonment, his wife became seriously ill. He refused to allow doctors to give her any modern drugs, despite the failure of the natural cures he prescribed, his chanting, or the efforts of a doctor who practiced traditional Indian medicine to help her. She died. No one can say that she would have lived had Gandhi been less rigid, less convinced of his own wisdom and righteousness, but it is hard not to imagine that in sickness as in life, Kasturbai had paid too high a price for her husband's saintliness.

And then one day the war was over and in England, the Labour Party led by Clement Attlee had prevailed over Churchill and the Tories. Churchill, who famously declared that he had not become the king's first minister to preside over the destruction of the British Empire, was pushed aside and India's leaders sensed that independence would soon be theirs.

Gandhi wanted to be the founding father of an independent *and* united India. Hindu-Muslim antagonism and the demand of the great Muslim leader M. A. Jinnah for partition, for a separate Muslim state, became the critical issue. Gandhi was convinced that partition would be disastrous, that communal violence would increase, and, of course events proved him correct. He spent the last years of his life in a desperate and successful struggle to tamp down violence between Hindus and Muslims. He marched, he fasted, he used every technique for which he had become known. And then, on January 30, 1948, he was murdered by a Hindu nationalist, a man affiliated with the same organization that controlled the Indian government when I decided to write about him fifty-four years later.

Many people have written about Gandhi over the years, and I cannot claim to have read everything published. Of the few works I have read, I found a short essay by George Orwell, "Reflections on Gandhi," most congenial. Like Orwell, I am repelled by Gandhi the man. His treatment of his wife and children was appalling. His bizarre sexual behavior and ideas about human sexuality have been explored gently by Erik Erikson, but strike me as pathological. His ideas about diet, medicine, and health were sheer quackery—tolerable as he practiced them, but not as he imposed them on his wife. His program for relieving poverty in India was absurd and, much as I must respect his commitment to nonviolence, his prescription for coping with Hitler was inane.

And yet everything he fought for in his life was admirable. Without resort to force, he gained a modicum of decent treatment for Indians in South Africa. He achieved his principal goal, the peaceful surrender of the raj, the independence of India. He won tremendous gains for India's "untouchables." He could not prevent the partition of India into Muslim and Hindu states, but his efforts to prevent communal violence met with considerable success while he lived.

Orwell felt "a sort of aesthetic distaste" for Gandhi and was not much taken with claims of his saintliness, but ranked him nonetheless among the century's great leaders. Despite the fact that Gandhi reveled in his fame and the worship of the masses, there was never a hint of corruption, of abuse of power. He was a great and decent man—just not one with whom you'd want to live.

Václav Havel at the United Nations, courtesy of Karel Cudlin

CHAPTER 2

Václav Havel and the
Power of the Powerless

October 27, 1989: Once again, the police came for Václav Havel, playwright and reluctant dissident. But this time his incarceration by the moribund communist regime of Gustáv Husák proved mercifully brief. On December 29, 1989, a mere two months later, Havel was elected president of the post-communist government of Czechoslovakia. It was one of history's great triumphs for moral man, a victory of good over evil. There was no lack of moral clarity in the "Velvet Revolution," which allowed the proponents of democracy to prevail over totalitarianism in Prague.

Havel was born in 1936 into a wealthy and well-educated family. His father was a prominent architect and his maternal grandfather had served as ambassador to Austria. The Havels do not appear to have suffered greatly under the German occupation, but fared less well under the communists who seized power in 1948. By the early 1960s, most of their property had been confiscated. Potentially more damaging to the life of Václav and his brother was the decision by the communist regime to deny the boys, scions of a bourgeois family, the educational opportunities that led to advancement in Czech society. But they nonetheless enjoyed a culturally privileged home life, and Václav enjoyed a brief stay at an elite boarding school before the class struggle began. He managed to get a high school education by attending night school. He did not require a college degree to become an intellectual.

Young Havel perceived himself as a writer, but from the outset there was a Jeremiah-like quality to his thoughts and writing. Eda Kriseova, a Havel biographer, points to the influence of the philosopher Josef Šafařík, whose work on moral responsibility profoundly impressed him. Havel's first publication, at the age of twenty, was a letter to a magazine for fledgling writers in which he pointed to the contradiction between the editors' efforts to encourage poets to write about life in Czechoslovakia while accepting only such work as proved consistent with official ideology. As a result of publication of the letter, he was invited to an officially sponsored conference for young authors, at which he rose to make a similar point. The conference came amidst the Soviet suppression of the Hungarian revolution of 1956, and Havel called his hosts hypocrites for claiming to be reformers seeking truth while they tolerated the suppression of literature that did not follow the Communist Party line.

From 1957 to 1959, Havel served in the Czech army. It seems to have been a painless experience, perhaps even beneficial. He later suggested that his ability to understand all sorts of people, specifically nonintellectuals, derived in part from his military companions. It was during his army days that he wrote his first play, in collaboration with a friend. When his tour was over, his father was able to get him a job as a stagehand—which he much preferred to his initial assignment as a carpenter's apprentice and the work as a lab assistant that preceded induction.

The 1960s were exciting years in Prague, as they were in much of the Western world. Small theaters were springing up across the city, and Havel was drawn to them. He had time to write and he reveled in the relative spontaneity of the times. Several of his plays were performed and awareness of his work spread across Europe to critics in the United States. Looking back, he concluded that the theater was a "seismograph" of the era. It was a celebration of uncensored life, of pure fun and contempt for ideology. Czech society was straining at the bonds with which the communist regime had bound it, and this was apparent in the theater and encouraged by the theater. And the Communist Party was itself caught up in the process that ultimately manifested itself in what came to be known as "the Prague Spring."

In 1965, Havel joined the editorial board of *Tvar*, a magazine founded in 1963 and designed for young readers. In frequent conflict with the authorities, it was shut down permanently in 1969. Havel's immediate task was to defend *Tvar* at a meeting of the Writers Union. At the meeting and in a subsequent essay, he demanded freedom of expression. He condemned censorship, executions, rehabilitations, and self-criticisms—the control mechanisms of the totalitarian state. He assailed the Writers Union for serving as an instrument of the state, for presuming to tell writers how or what to write.

At the meeting, he set off an explosive debate, but it was indicative of the political climate in Czechoslovakia that he appears to have emerged the victor: He was not bundled off to prison.

A few years later, in April 1968, Havel pushed even harder, writing an essay demanding that the Communist Party, with its newfound pretensions to reform, permit the organization of an opposition party. He argued for rewarding personal responsibility over party loyalty and insisted that the Communist Party could be reformed only if there were sufficient outside pressure—a need to compete with an opposition party for popular support. A two-party system, with both parties committed to democratic socialism, was, he insisted, essential. Again, Havel was not threatened with arrest and was allowed to travel abroad, even to New York, where his *Increased Difficulty of Concentration* won an award for best off-Broadway play.

In January 1968, Moscow-trained Alexander Dubček had become first secretary of the Czechoslovakian Communist Party. He and several of his comrades on the central committee believed in the socialist vision and were deeply troubled by the gap between that vision and the reality of the Stalinist state. They were determined to change things, to put an end to the totalitarian system that oppressed their people, to create "socialism with a human face." Dubček was prepared to go a considerable way along the path to which Havel had pointed.

Very much aware of the Soviet response to the Hungarian revolution, Dubček and his allies were determined to avoid antagonizing the men in the Kremlin. As they reined in the secret police and the censors, released political prisoners, and allowed Czech society to enjoy freedom of expression, even freedom to criticize the government and organize opposition to it, they assured Moscow that Czechoslovakia would remain a loyal member of the Warsaw Pact alliance and that the Communist Party would retain the leading role in Czech politics.

In the Kremlin, however, Soviet leaders were not reassured. They were fearful that the opening of Czech society would embolden dissenters elsewhere in the Communist bloc, perhaps even in the Soviet Union itself. Their anxiety mounted with every democratic reform Prague attempted. In August 1968, Soviet first secretary Leonid Brezhnev decided he had seen enough. On August 21, Warsaw Pact forces invaded Czechoslovakia. Dubček was seized, flown immediately to Moscow, and forced to renounce his policies. The world was informed subsequently of the Brezhnev Doctrine, in which the Soviet Union claimed the right to intervene in the affairs of any communist country that strayed from the fold.

The Soviet invasion changed Havel's life. Prior to Brezhnev's actions to crush the Prague Spring, Havel perceived himself as an aspiring playwright, albeit with a powerful concern for intellectual freedom and a growing recognition of the need for political change. Afterward, the playwright became a political activist, whose ultimate goal was an end to totalitarianism and the creation of a democratic state in Czechoslovakia. Given the public positions he had taken ever since 1956, it was not a difficult transition. His plays, influenced by the absurdist writings of Eugène Ionesco, would not likely have brought him comparable fame.

Years later he argued that Soviet intervention could have been avoided if the party leadership had worked harder to win the full support of the Czech people, citing the examples of Tito in Yugoslavia and Ceauşescu in Romania. In 1969 he published a letter to Dubček, calling upon the deposed party secretary to speak out in defense of his 1968 efforts to reform the party and open Czech society. He urged Dubček to denounce the Soviet invasion and the Stalinist practices of the regime that succeeded his. Dubček was a good and decent man, who doubtless would have liked to have responded as Havel wished, but he was not suicidal. Havel, perhaps whistling in the dark, concluded that the Soviet seizure of Dubček had the important positive effect of stimulating nonviolent resistance among the people of Czechoslovakia.

By the end of 1969, Havel's writings were banned from publication and his plays could not be performed. But his essays continued to circulate and to bring hope to all who dreamed of democracy. In the early 1970s, Havel was declared an enemy of the state and removed from every position he held, but he was no less determined to be heard. He continued to meet with friends of like mind and with former communists who had resigned or been thrown out of the party. He found work in a brewery.

Havel was appalled by détente, by Western efforts to improve relations with the Soviet Union and other Soviet-bloc states by seeking rapprochement with their governments and avoiding contact with dissidents. He called détente a "naïve, thickheaded and suicidal way of 'easing tensions.'" His own approach was a frontal attack on the Prague government, laid out in an open letter to Husák in April 1975. Havel refused to live a lie and spelled out the many ways in which the regime had diminished life in Czechoslovakia. All the government asked of its citizens was that they avoid politics and pretend loyalty, and in return they would be granted an acceptable material existence and social order—the calm of the morgue or the grave, according to Havel. The people were being spiritually, politically, and morally violated. The social contract was based on hypocrisy.

Havel noted that the whole society lived under constant threat from a state police whose power to intervene in the individual's life was unchecked. He expressed disgust with the bureaucratic control of culture, which led to "mental sterility, petrified dogmas, rigid and unchangeable creeds leading inevitably to creedless despotism." Truth had been driven underground. What, he demanded to know, had the regime done to enhance the human dimensions of life, for the moral and spiritual revival of society? And, of course, he contrasted Husák's rule unfavorably with that of Dubček.

The letter to Husák was part of Havel's struggle to escape the passivity forced upon intellectuals by the authorities. It may have made him feel a little better. It may have encouraged others of like mind, but it had no discernible impact on the men and women who governed Czechoslovakia. Further evidence of the absurdity of official efforts to control culture came a year later in the celebrated trial of the rock group Plastic People of the Universe. Their "crime" had nothing to do with politics; they were not dissidents in the usual sense. Influenced by the Beatles and Frank Zappa, they played raucous music of the sort that appealed to young people everywhere and offended cultural conservatives everywhere. But in the totalitarian state, the cultural commissars had the power to arrest those whose music they did not like, just as they could imprison writers who displeased them.

Friends of the musicians turned to Havel—who was himself a Frank Zappa fan—for help. He saw the case as a marvelous opportunity to fight for intellectual freedom. These were young people with no political past. In their music he professed to sense "an experience of metaphysical sorrow and a longing for salvation." The attack on them was an attack on life itself, on human freedom and integrity. If Czech society did not oppose the arrests, the regime would have a precedent for imprisoning anyone who dared to think independently. He organized a human rights group and a petition drive, wrote to the German novelist Heinrich Böll, sent protests to all the embassies in Prague, and won international media attention to the trial. Nonetheless, all members of the Plastic People were sent to prison. On January 1, 1977, Havel and his associates in support of the musicians formed Charter 77 to fight for human rights in Czechoslovakia.

The government had had enough of Havel. Two weeks later, he was imprisoned and vilified as a counterrevolutionary and a Zionist agent. All who had signed the Charter petition were interrogated, lost their jobs, their passports, their driving licenses, and their telephones. They were lucky: In the 1950s they would have been executed.

Havel's initial experience with extended imprisonment was upsetting. He was profoundly depressed and easily manipulated by his jailers. Told that the other signatories had repudiated Charter 77, he signed a statement declaring that he would no longer serve as the group's spokesman—and won his release after four miserable months.

Once he learned that he had been tricked, Havel was humiliated and went on the offensive. He resumed his efforts on behalf of human rights, insisting he had not resigned as spokesman for Charter 77, merely declared his intention to do so. Again and again, he challenged the authorities. He traveled to the Polish-Czech border to meet with Polish dissidents and was arrested and convicted of injuring the interests of the republic abroad, although on this occasion he received a suspended sentence. Fully aware that prison awaited him, he pressed relentlessly for fulfillment of the Helsinki Accords on human rights. It was better, he insisted, "not to live at all, than to live without honor." In January 1978, he began a six-week prison sentence.

Havel was convinced that the Charter and the counterculture—of which the Plastic People were but a small part—were having an impact on Czech society. He and his friends formed the Committee to Defend the Unjustly Persecuted. They monitored trials such as that of the Plastic People, but also those involving the state's abuse of the criminal code. They wrote reports, complaining to the authorities and informing the outside world of the conditions in which Czechs were forced to live. Havel was becoming the moral and political authority for thousands of his countrymen. He hoped he was laying the foundation for civil society.

In October 1978, he wrote "The Power of the Powerless," probably the most important and most widely read of his essays. In it, the maturation of his thought is evident. The core question he posed was whether dissidents—the powerless—could influence the social system. Some of his thinking had changed since 1968. He no longer saw creation of an opposition political party, of a Western democratic system, as sufficient. The change he sought required individuals to stop living a lie, to stop conforming, stop mouthing slogans in which they did not believe. Acceptance of the modern dictatorship's ideology forced people to live in conflict with reality; the system worked only while people were willing to play along, complicit in an arrangement that stripped them of moral integrity and dignity, denied them the fulfillment of their own freedom. They could fight it by "living in truth," by refusing to put up slogans to humor the authorities, by refusing to vote in meaningless elections, by speaking out at political meetings. Denying the lies would threaten the entire system. He called for letter-writing campaigns by intellectuals, strikes by workers, rock concerts, student demonstrations, hunger strikes, public speeches—a revolt against manipulation and a rediscovery of freedom.

Havel argued that the central question was whether, in a society such as existed in Czechoslovakia, it was possible to live like a human being, with dignity. Did the system serve the people rather than forcing them to serve it? He defined as dissidents any individuals who did what they felt they must and found themselves in conflict with the regime—no matter whether scientists, workers, or poets. Certainly the government perceived anyone who avoided manipulation, who denied the principle that the system had an absolute claim on the individual, as a member of the opposition.

The driving force behind dissident movements such as Havel's came from nonpolitical people. Charter 77 was founded on the notion that human rights and freedoms are indivisible. It was a defensive movement, committed to nonviolence, determined to defend people and the genuine aims of life as opposed to the aims of the system. Its goal was to awaken the society and renew the feeling of responsibility among an apathetic people. The alternative could only be an Orwellian nightmare. Havel offered no timetable for success. It would be a creeping process, as in 1968. Change would come when the people refused to sacrifice human identity to politics, when they recognized that to live within the truth was a moral act.

Dissidents in Eastern Europe, especially Poland, were heartened by Havel's words—as were their supporters in the West. He had made a forceful case for victory over tyranny without military power, without political power, in countries where the regime had a monopoly of both. One by one the people could be won over to reject the lies of the state. Those determined to live in truth would spread like an ink blot until they prevailed. But however hopeful his words, memories of Soviet action in Hungary in 1956 and in Czechoslovakia in 1968 shadowed his vision. Change might well have to come first in Moscow.

It was quickly apparent that Prague was not ready for change. Havel was placed under continuous police surveillance and harassed persistently. The government was trying to drive him into exile, but he had no intention of relaxing his efforts. He understood that prison was inevitable, but he had come to terms with that prospect. He had found his role in life and was very much at peace with himself, pitying rather than hating those who tormented him. The arrest came in May 1979.

Again, he was offered the opportunity to leave the country, to take up a position offered in the United States, but he refused. He realized how quickly exiles were forgotten, how little they could contribute to their cause from abroad. His place was in Czechoslovakia, where even as a prisoner he could be a symbol of resistance, if necessary a martyr to the cause of freedom. His calculation proved to be correct. He was brought to trial in October 1979, and the regime's heavy-handedness was almost laughable. It was crude in terms of whom it allowed to attend the trial and in the absurdity of the evidence in the case it made against him. His conviction brought him more international attention. Kriseova suggests that he was more dangerous to the regime in prison than when free.

This time imprisonment lasted nearly four years, ending early only because he contracted pneumonia and the state presumably feared he would die in custody. He was allowed to write only to his wife, once a week, on four sheets of paper, to be cleared by the prison censor. If one sentence, one phrase, perhaps even one word, offended the censor, the letters were destroyed. Even under those conditions, he managed to write letters of sufficient interest and importance that they were published later. He was able to receive letters from his brother as well as from his wife, and they found ways to keep him informed about the world outside. His brother's letters in particular seem to have buoyed his spirits and enabled him to transcend the humiliations of prison life. His wife, Olga, was allowed four visits a year, and the guards did not prevent them from discussing matters other than the prescribed family affairs.

Four years in prison allows much time for reflection, and Havel does not appear to have wasted it. Not surprisingly under those conditions, some of his thoughts bordered on the religious, although he defined himself as a nonpracticing Catholic. He told his "official" biographer that he had always felt there was some great mystery above that was the "focus of all meaning and the highest moral authority." He complained that modern science had killed God and taken his place. In the age of science, man was playing God, and sacrificing tens of thousands of lives in search of utopian solutions such as collectivization. He was critical of the "arrogant anthropocentrism of modern man," who thinks he can know and control everything. Many of his thoughts, as evidenced in his *Letters to Olga* and in a volume on Havel as political thinker by James Pontuso, were clearly the product of a dialogue in which he was engaged with the writings of the German philosopher Martin Heidegger. Good Pope John XXIII doubtless would have agreed with Havel's argument that the trouble started when man began considering himself the source of the highest meaning in the world—and with his demand for spiritual renewal.

Havel perceived an awakening of religious feeling in the country, the inevitable consequence of herd life in a socialist consumer society, with its "intellectual and spiritual vacuity, its moral sterility." At no time, however, did he suggest prayer or the church as the solution to the oppressiveness of the Czech state. For Havel, it remained the individual, drawing strength from within, taking a moral stand, living in truth, who would ultimately prevail over the system.

His own role, the role of the intellectual, was to be a Cassandra, always issuing warnings, always predicting horrors. He had to disturb the complacent, bear witness to the misery of the suffering, and provoke the government— serve as a constant irritant. No doubt the Husák regime would have conceded that Havel played his part well.

His goal expanded from a demand for social democracy in a multiparty state to include the need for a market economy. He was persuaded on the basis of what he had witnessed in Czechoslovakia that it was impossible for an economy to thrive without competition, without multiple economic initiatives, without the marketplace and its institutional guarantees. Human individuality required man to be able to participate in economic affairs with relative autonomy. Havel wanted genuine trade union rights, with workers having a voice in industry. He concluded that economic centralization was a less obvious and thus more dangerous method of manipulating life, much like the political and intellectual standardization that had a nihilizing impact on the populace.

Perhaps his most interesting position in the mid-1980s was his opposition to the Western peace movement. Havel argued that movement activists valued peace over freedom, peace over human rights. His critique was similar to his argument against détente. Peace advocates, especially those whose slogan was "better Red than dead," were surrendering their humanity. They were suggesting there was nothing worth dying for. Havel called for heroes who knew what they were dying for. Peace and tranquility were what totalitarian governments promised their people in exchange for surrendering their dignity, their humanity. Men were deceived if they believed that they could prevent war if only they could forestall the deployment of weapons—presumably a reference to well-meaning Europeans who opposed the introduction of new American missiles into their countries.

The saintly Havel seemed to sneer with contempt at the failure of the Western peace movement—in all its congresses and demonstrations—to protest the Soviet invasion of Afghanistan. But it was his insistence on the transcendent importance of human rights that was central to his argument.

Most tellingly, he argued that a state that did not respect the rights of its citizens could not be trusted to respect the rights of other peoples. A state that exercised unchecked power at home was not likely to submit to international supervision. And a state that denied its citizens their basic rights became a danger to its neighbors: "Internal arbitrary rule will be reflected in arbitrary external rule." True peace required respect for human rights.

Although Havel had few illusions about life in the United States—certainly he had reservations about capitalism—or the goals of American foreign policy, he had no doubt as to which side in the Cold War represented the best interests of humanity. He was horrified by the efforts of peace advocates to suggest a moral equivalence between the two superpowers. For him the difference was obvious and overwhelming: The degree of freedom enjoyed by the American people had no parallel in the Soviet bloc. The United States thus enjoyed a degree of international political credibility the Soviet Union could never equal. Ronald Reagan's America may have fallen far short of Havel's vision of the good state, but, he insisted, to equate it with the Soviet Union was a monstrous oversimplification.

In the mid-1980s, Havel seemed both optimistic and defensive about Charter 77. In March 1986, he wrote again about its purpose, reminding his audience that the signatories had banded together, despite ideological and political differences among them, to demand respect for the law and for human rights. The Charter stood for no political program: It was concerned only with the truth. His need to defend the Charter appeared to stem from the contempt Milan Kundera exhibited in *The Unbearable Lightness of Being* for petitions in support of political prisoners. Havel, whose prison experiences gave considerable weight to his argument, contended that prisoners were helped by knowing they had people outside supporting them publicly, alerting the world, exposing the arbitrariness, the oppressiveness of the government. Charter 77 existed now to monitor the state's exercise of power constantly. The regime could no longer assume that it could act as it pleased without criticism. Hundreds of people were daring to act in ways that would have been inconceivable in the early 1970s. He saw an explosion of samizdat books and an unstoppable development of an independent culture. And Husák and his comrades could not stop them: The Charter had become an integral part of Czech social life.

Musing about the nature of communism, Havel concluded that there had never been a nontotalitarian communist state. The ideology that had promised to oversee the withering away of the state gave rise to the most powerful state ever known, the totalitarian state. He was struck by the irony that workers liberated from their chains by communism now envied the rights of workers in capitalist countries.

By 1988, he sensed that important changes were occurring in Moscow. A Soviet journal published a relatively friendly account of conversations with Havel. He suspected that Mikhail Gorbachev's Kremlin was prepared to reassess the Prague Spring, that Gorbachev might be headed along the same route Dubček took in 1968. But he knew that Husák's apparatus would resist change. Charter 77 intensified its efforts, putting out a manifesto, "Democracy for All," in October. Demonstrations were planned for Prague, but the police rounded up those who had signed the manifesto and held them for several days. They roughed up the hardy folk who rallied in Prague's Old Town Square.

Undeterred, Havel and his collaborators organized an international symposium to celebrate the twentieth anniversary of the Prague Spring, to be held in November. The regime responded by gathering up the hosts, including Havel, and detaining most of them. But the tide had shifted. Several weeks later, after Havel had been released, French president François Mitterrand visited Prague and was allowed to have breakfast with Havel and other dissidents. A few days later, the authorities, for the first time since the Soviet invasion, authorized a demonstration sponsored by Charter 77.

Husák had not surrendered, however. Havel was arrested again in January 1989 while attending a demonstration in Wenceslas Square. He was sentenced to nine months in prison. The arrest did not have the deterrent effect for which the regime hoped. On the contrary, it appeared to galvanize the opposition, uniting the dissidents and reformers within the Communist Party. A petition drive for Havel's release succeeded in freeing him in four months. It was not, of course, the last time Havel was arrested—nor the last time the Czech government fought back, its survival at stake.

Over the next several weeks, Havel's attention was drawn to events in China, to the exciting prospect of a democracy movement taking root there as thousands of students demonstrated in Beijing's Tiananmen Square. And then came the tragic denouement on June 4, 1989, as the troops of the People's Liberation Army opened fire on the people, crushing the regime's critics. Havel contrasted events in China with the flood of reforms in the Soviet Union. Gorbachev was trying to save socialism by allowing free speech and moving toward a market economy, "while Li Peng protects socialism by massacring students." He was aware that Gorbachev, under fire from party conservatives, had to tack occasionally in their direction, but Havel admired his courage. He doubtless also understood that throughout the Soviet bloc,

Gorbachev and Li Peng were perceived as offering competing models for managing dissent. Which would Husák choose?

Initially the regime tried the middle road, merely arresting Havel once more in late October. Quickly, the party leadership relented and he was released. On November 9, the Berlin Wall came down. Ten days later, Havel and friends met in a small theater and proclaimed the existence of Civic Forum, membership in which was open to anyone who cared to join. They began to organize demonstrations in Prague and sent a delegation to meet with the prime minister, who made conciliatory gestures—although he barred Havel from the meeting. Husák and his comrades still imagined they could hold on by compromising: They promised not to impose martial law, to bring noncommunists into the government, and to begin a dialogue on reforms.

On November 22, Havel spoke to crowds of Prague demonstrators for the first time, and they all knew the end of communism in Czechoslovakia was imminent. On November 24, Dubček addressed a crowd of 300,000 roaring for freedom. That same day, Husák and the entire Politburo resigned. Before the week was over, Havel had met with the prime minister and the government had given Civic Forum a building on Wenceslas Square. On December 7, the prime minister resigned and on the December 29, the Velvet Revolution was completed: Václav Havel was sworn in as president of Czechoslovakia.

On January 1, 1990, in his first major address, President Havel expressed the hope that his country would become the "humane republic" that he had long imagined as an alternative to the totalitarian state it had replaced. His would be a government that would serve the people and earn the consent of the individual to serve it in return.

Several weeks later, in February, Havel spoke in Washington to a joint session of Congress. Reporters revealed some embarrassment at the degree to which his address surpassed that of the American president in both style and substance. He was, after all, a philosophical playwright rather than a professional politician. Commentators who frequently deplored the irresponsibility of American political leaders and the public to which they catered were delighted by Havel's emphasis on moral responsibility. He apologized for the passivity of his own people which, he contended, had allowed totalitarianism to flourish, and he stressed the need to put morality ahead of politics, economics, and science. If human actions were to be moral, they had to be based on responsibility "to something higher than my family, my country, my company my success—responsibility to the order of being where all our actions are indelibly recorded and . . . judged."

His audience may not have comprehended that part of his message when they applauded it, but his opposition to militarism and to the continued degradation of the environment brought him to subjects more familiar to congressmen and congresswomen. He spoke contemptuously of the "absurd mountains" of nuclear weapons that both the United States and the Soviet Union had stockpiled and spoke of his intention to reduce the bloated Czech military establishment. He would defend his country with moral strength—although he clearly perceived no imminent threat. And he warned that we were still destroying the planet "that was entrusted to us."

The most fascinating part of his speech came when he responded to the question of what Americans could do to help Czechoslovakia. Rather than hold out the anticipated tin cup and beg for aid, Havel astonished his audience by declaring that the United States could help best by aiding the Soviet Union. The peaceful movement of the Soviet Union toward democracy, toward political pluralism, toward a market economy, he contended, was what Czechs, Slovaks, and the entire world needed most. He was hoping the Soviet Union would move in the same direction he hoped to move his country—and that would be the best guarantee of his success and that of the rest of Eastern Europe. Not least, he noted, Soviet democracy would allow for the reduction of the burden of defense spending borne by the American people.

Havel traveled a great deal as president of Czechoslovakia and was consistently an eloquent advocate for human rights, moral responsibility, and democracy. He spoke for the aspirations of the oppressed everywhere and served as an inspiration to the powerless who dreamed of freedom and decent government. As he once put it, the victory of the Velvet Revolution was viewed as bringing hope of a better world in which poets might be as powerful as bankers. His nomination of Aung San Suu Kyi for the Nobel Peace Prize helped to win her that honor and to remind the world that the end of the Cold War would not bring an end to human misery, certainly not in Burma. Few world leaders were ever as widely admired as he was.

At home, the luster faded. The end of totalitarian rule did not bring instant prosperity to all of the people of Czechoslovakia. Havel never imagined it would, but many of his constituents had expected him to work miracles. His own finance minister and ultimately chief rival, Václav Klaus, was dissatisfied with the pace of economic reforms, more inclined to try the "shock treatment" being attempted in Poland and Russia, perceiving Havel as an obstacle. Slovaks, less well off on the whole than Czechs, concluded that they would fare better if they split the country—and they seceded in 1992. Some people in Czechoslovakia and elsewhere blamed Havel for the breakup of the country. They contended that he should have prevented it, presumably by a show of force if necessary. Obviously, the use of violence to hold the country together, to fight a civil war to hold in a people who wanted out, was utterly alien to Havel, morally and politically.

Perhaps nothing he did undermined his people's affection for him as did his remarriage less than a year after Olga's death. Saint Havel's affairs during Olga's life appear to have been without cost, but many Czechs were discomfited when he married a much younger actress who had once appeared bare-breasted in a film. Olga had satisfied the nation's image of a presidential wife: Dagmar Havlová did not. Havel's personal popularity ratings dropped sharply. For a man who did as much moralizing as he did, his choice of brides proved unacceptable. Surely a degree of jealousy was involved.

More damaging to his effectiveness was his inability to prevent the writing of a constitution that marginalized the president, reserving power for the parliament. Klaus, an unstinting admirer of Margaret Thatcher, quickly fashioned a right-wing party based on her principles and sustained by considerable corruption. The opposition Social Democrats, in theory determined to end the corruption and ameliorate the impact of Klaus's reforms on the poor, in practice seemed more interested in getting a piece of the action. Seeking to be above politics, lacking a base of power in Parliament, Havel could do little to bring about the necessary reforms. Politically and economically, the Czech Republic did not live up to the expectations aroused by the Velvet Revolution.

But Havel was reelected and ultimately served thirteen years as president, despite serious health problems and declining approval ratings. He remained enormously valuable to his country as its international symbol. Few people around the world realized what a mess the Czech Republic had become: Everywhere people knew it was Václav Havel's country. And he won for it admission to NATO and the European Union long before it was deserved and pushed and pulled his people into accepting that international role. And Havel's persistent demand for action to save the Bosnian Muslims and the Kosovars helped point the way for Bill Clinton to do the right thing.

In the end, he was tired and his people were tired of him. He felt less sure of himself after thirteen years as president than he had at the outset of his political career. He had doubts about the value of his work and of those he helped bring to power. He was not satisfied with what he had ac-complished—the world, "in the hands of poets," had not become a poem. There was still evil to be confronted and his call for moral responsibility in managing the world's problems was still heeded by too few. He knew the battle for human rights would be unending, but he would fight it hereafter as playwright and poet. In 2003 Havel stepped down as president.

Aung San Suu Kyi, used by permission of AP Photos/Richard Vogel

CHAPTER 3

Aung San Suu Kyi:
Martyr for Democracy

When I began this essay in February 2005, Nobel Peace Prize winner Aung San Suu Kyi was living under house arrest in Rangoon, the prisoner of a ruthless military regime which, largely impervious to international pressure, ruled Burma brutally. There have been moments of hope subsequently, as with the Buddhist monks' demonstrations late in 2007, but nothing has changed. The time may yet come when the generals, leaders of the Tatmadaw—the Burmese army—decide that it is expedient to kill her, given the threat she poses to their power and their inability to force her into voluntary exile. More likely, she will die alone in the decaying house to which the junta has confined her, her cause forgotten by the rest of the world, her people abandoned to despair.

In 1988, young intellectual Aung San Suu Kyi, daughter of the late Aung San, who was probably the most beloved figure in modern Burmese history, was enjoying life in England as the wife of British scholar Michael Aris and the mother of two children. She had warned Aris when he proposed that some day the call to serve her country might come, that she might need to pick up the fallen mantle of her father. She was not unaware that her heritage offered entrée into Burmese politics. On March 31, the phone rang and she learned that her mother, once a prominent diplomat, had suffered a stroke. Suu Kyi flew to Rangoon to care for her.

At the outset of World War II, the Burmese had endured the yoke of the British Empire, their economy dominated by Indian and Chinese merchants whose presence had been encouraged by the British to facilitate their rule over the restless native population. As in much of the region in the 1920s and 1930s, a small nationalist movement had arisen in Burma. In 1941, a group of young Burmese patriots, led by Suu Kyi's father, twenty-six-year-old Aung San, turned to the Japanese for help liberating their people from British domination. Known as the Thirty Comrades, they were sent to Hainan Island for military training, and then, as leaders of the Burmese Independence Army, returned to fight alongside the Japanese. After several years in the field, Aung San came to two conclusions: First, the Japanese were worse than the British; and second, the Japanese were not going to win the war. Astutely, he and his army changed sides and in the last months of the war, assisted the British in driving out the Japanese.

At the conclusion of the war, Aung San chose a career in politics, leaving the army he had founded and led. Obviously capitalizing on his stature as a military hero, he nonetheless insisted that the army be professional and nonpolitical. General Aung San became citizen Aung San, and in January 1946 he was elected president of his party, the Anti-Fascist People's Freedom League (AFPFL). His goal remained independence, and he proved to be as able a politician as he had been a military leader. In September 1946, the AFPFL organized a general strike that forced the war-weakened British to give it a role in the governing of the country. A few months later, in January 1947, a Burmese delegation in London negotiated the Aung San–Attlee Agreement, which, to the horror of Winston Churchill, set the stage for Burmese independence, achieved at last on January 4, 1948.

Aung San, however, was not there to lead the country he had labored so hard to free. In July 1947, he was assassinated by political rivals. His daughter, Aung San Suu Kyi, was two years old when he died.

Burma resumed its independent existence as a democracy, governed by popularly elected civilians. But the country's myriad ethnic minorities were restless and, like much of Southeast Asia, it was plagued by a communist insurgency, albeit small relative to the one that roiled nearby Malaysia. In the last days of the Chinese civil war, Guomindang troops fled into Burma where, assisted by the U.S. Central Intelligence Agency, they established bases, harassed the People's Republic of China, and gained a share of the narcotics trade. The government in Rangoon struggled ineffectually against these challenges and depended increasingly on the army to maintain stability.

As power accrued to the military, its leaders increasingly perceived the civilian regime as a hindrance. In 1958, General Ne Win, defense minister and one of the Thirty Comrades, stepped in as prime minister at the head of a caretaker government. In 1962, contrary to its founder's insistence that it stay out of politics, the army launched a coup and seized complete control of the government. Quickly, Aung San's erstwhile colleague established a military dictatorship. For the next quarter of a century, Burma practiced Ne Win's version of socialism and isolated itself from the rest of the world. The results for most Burmese were disastrous. A potentially prosperous country with an abundance of resources was crippled economically and its people oppressed by army leaders. The government, staffed largely by the military, its power unchecked, became increasingly corrupt. Only military families benefited from Ne Win's rule—and they were content to sustain it as conditions for most of the rest of the people deteriorated.

As the Cold War festered, Burma remained outside the contending blocs. Ne Win's suppression of human rights in his country surely did not trouble Soviet or Chinese Communist leaders, and the leaders of the "Free World" did not find it expedient to complain and risk provoking Rangoon's enmity.

Aung San Suu Kyi, her brothers, and her mother did not suffer under the imposition of military rule. The aura of Aung San, the George Washington or Ho Chi Minh of his country, protected them. They lived, as part of the elite, in a lovely house at the edge of a lake. In 1960, her mother, trained as a nurse, was named Burma's ambassador to India, and Suu Kyi attended high school in New Delhi. She majored in political science and philosophy at Delhi University before transferring to Oxford in 1964. In India, she discovered Gandhi, studied his writings, and was attracted to his conception of nonviolent political action.

At Oxford, she added the study of economics to her program and marveled at the boisterous and promiscuous behavior of her schoolmates. By all accounts she neither drank nor indulged in any of the licentious acts for which the 1960s were notorious. She did, however, acquire a suitor, Michael Aris, a young British intellectual and student of Tibet, to whom she was ultimately married in a Buddhist ceremony in 1972. But first, she obtained her bachelor's degree in 1967 and left England, intending to begin graduate work at New York University while Aris continued his in London. Once in New York, Suu Kyi was enticed into working at the United Nations. NYU would have to wait.

She remained in New York for three years before succumbing to Aris's proposal and returning with him to England. He completed his studies and received an appointment at Oxford. They had two children, and they lived the stimulating life of young faculty at great universities. She found time to read and to write, primarily about Burmese history and culture. She was troubled by conditions in her homeland, wondering whether there was a role she could play in the restoration of democracy and of her father's vision for the country. And then came the call informing her of her mother's stroke.

Suu Kyi returned to Burma the next day to care for her mother. Rangoon was already in turmoil as student radicals demonstrated against the Ne Win dictatorship. Some of those who visited her mother were political activists who asked her advice. Remembering her study of Gandhi and aware of Martin Luther King Jr.'s efforts in the United States, she spoke optimistically about the efficacy of peaceful protests and urged them on, stressing the importance of human rights. "People power" had ended the dictatorship of Ferdinand Marcos in the Philippines. Perhaps the people could prevail in Burma.

August 8, 1988—8/8/88—was perceived as an auspicious day, and the country was electrified by Ne Win's announcement that he would resign on that day. Demonstrators, generally peaceful, took to the streets in cities across the nation. In Rangoon, they knelt before the soldiers and sang freedom songs. To the astonishment of the demonstrators and the horror of the world, the troops were ordered to open fire. They killed more than three thousand people, wounded and dragged away hundreds more. Democracy would not be restored in Burma. The power of the people vanished before an army that did not hesitate to kill.

Suu Kyi, as the daughter of Aung San, perceived a responsibility to step forward. She wrote to Ne Win's ruling Burma Socialist Program Party, calling for an end to violence and the release of political prisoners. She urged the government to begin the process of creating a multiparty democracy. She may have been surprised to receive no response. There was no alternative, she concluded, to becoming more active. On August 26, unimpeded by the military, she addressed a crowd of more than half a million people at Shwedagon Pagoda, a mural portraying her father hanging behind her. She proved to be a charismatic speaker and became the de facto leader of the opposition. Her lineage was certainly not a liability.

In September, the government collapsed and there appeared to be what scholars call "an open historical situation," in which the future of Burma was uncertain. Suu Kyi continued to advocate nonviolence, but after the August 8 massacre enraged Burmese demonstrators were not always responsive and conditions verged on chaos. Once again, army leaders stepped in, announced the creation of the State Law and Order Restoration Council (SLORC), a military junta, and crushed the demonstrators. At the same time, however, they allowed new political parties to be formed and they promised elections to determine the next, presumably civilian government.

Suu Kyi and family friends and associates quickly formed the National League for Democracy (NLD). As the generals probably anticipated, scores of other parties representing various ethnic groups and political philosophies were also formed. The likelihood of any one party becoming powerful enough to challenge the military seemed slim. Elections were announced for May 1990. A fragmented parliament would be easy to manipulate. Suu Kyi recognized the problem and worked assiduously to unite the opposition.

In December 1988, her mother died and the SLORC worked with Suu Kyi to ensure her mother the funeral she deserved as the wife of Aung San. It was the last time they cooperated. As Suu Kyi resumed campaigning across the country, assuring minorities that an NLD government would be inclusive and protect their rights, the SLORC perceived a threat. Her assurances that she was leading a nonviolent movement for human rights were to no avail. The military began to harass her and to arrest people who came to her rallies.

As the SLORC maneuvered to hem in Suu Kyi and the NLD, she ignored the rules intended to hamper her campaign. Like Gandhi, like Martin Luther King, she practiced civil disobedience. At the same time, she wrote again and again to the SLORC, criticizing its tactics and appealing for a dialogue. The junta was unresponsive. The standoff ended in June 1989, a few weeks after the Tiananmen massacres in China. The SLORC placed her under house arrest and jailed other NLD leaders.

Suu Kyi's campaign, especially her emphasis on nonviolent action, had already won her international attention and Aris was not shy about spreading the word of her arrest—although the human rights community was focused on the appalling events in China. She demanded to be imprisoned with her colleagues and supporters, hoping that her presence might shield them from some of the more vicious practices in Burmese prisons. The junta refused, assuming that its relatively benign treatment of her could drive a wedge between her and her brutalized followers—as well as limiting whatever foreign concern for her well-being might be aroused.

Suu Kyi, in the best Gandhian fashion, began a hunger strike. The SLORC allowed Aris to enter the country before her life was in danger and he succeeded in negotiating a compromise. His wife ended her hunger strike in return for assurances that none of her imprisoned allies would be tortured and that they would receive due process—whatever that meant in a military dictatorship. Receiving further assurances from the authorities that he and his wife would be allowed to exchange letters and packages, Aris returned to Oxford.

The SLORC seemed uncertain what to do with Suu Kyi. Killing her would provoke anger in much of the world and quite likely sanctions, conceivably even foreign intervention. The greatest danger was that her death might prompt a massive uprising within the country. House arrest was a useful tactic for keeping her off the campaign trail, and they could make it more or less unpleasant, fine-tuning conditions in accordance with the junta's needs of the moment. Most desirable might be her voluntary exile. Should she return to England of her own accord, she would be perceived within Burma as having abandoned her followers—and once abroad, exiles historically have had a short shelf life.

To encourage her departure, the SLORC cancelled the Burmese passports of her children. They would not be allowed back into the country; Suu Kyi would have to leave to see them. However painful the decision, she chose to stay. Perhaps she imagined the SLORC would relent after the elections, which were less than a year away. They did allow her husband to visit over Christmas—but then cancelled his visa.

In the closing months of 1989, the Cold War ground to a halt. The Berlin Wall came down and the Velvet Revolution brought democracy to Czechoslovakia. Across Eastern Europe totalitarian dictatorships collapsed. Even the Soviet Union appeared to be evolving peacefully toward a more open, perhaps a democratic society. It was evident that the Chinese model, turning the people's army against the people, was not the only alternative. Suu Kyi and other friends of democracy in Burma and around the world could dream of peaceful change in Rangoon.

Awaiting the elections, she puttered around the garden, played the piano, read, listened to the radio, and meditated. She had no contact with her supporters or her family. Although the junta was confident that the result would be a parliament so divided that the military could control it easily, it took the precaution of removing Suu Kyi's name from the ballot. Otherwise, the elections appear to have been free and fair. The results, however, were shocking. The NLD and its allies won 392 out of 485 seats in the National Assembly. They even won in constituencies that were heavily military. Eighty-one percent of members were to be opponents of military rule.

The SLORC had only one option: It refused to recognize the results of the election. No amount of international outrage moved the generals. The Chinese supported them. They were not about to surrender power and the perquisites that went with it—or risk punishment for their misdeeds over the previous three decades. They closed the universities, arrested and imprisoned student activists, and issued a special decree extending Suu Kyi's house arrest for five years.

Confined to her home, Suu Kyi had ample time for reflection, ample time to develop her thoughts. She apparently had some access to world news and to books. In her initial foray into the political arena, she had indicated little of her program. Human rights were important to her. She wanted to restore civilian rule and democracy—and she wanted to pursue nonviolent means to achieve those goals. Now she immersed herself in the writings of Havel and tried to understand the lessons of the work of Martin Luther King and Andrei Sakharov. Eventually the approach of Nelson Mandela found a place in her rhetoric. All of these men had resisted the power of the state and ultimately prevailed against enormous odds. They were the beacons of hope.

Havel seems to have been most influential, especially his essay on the power of the powerless. SLORC had left her very much aware that she and her supporters were powerless in their confrontation with the military. She understood that she would have to find some way to work *with* the military, some way to assure the generals that it was not her intention to destroy the army, to punish its leaders. She had to speak of reconciliation rather than retribution, should she have the opportunity Havel and Mandela had won. Again and again, she called for dialogue to seek a peaceful and just resolution. Again and again, the junta ignored her.

On rare occasions, the plight of Suu Kyi and her country captured the world's attention. In general, the end of the Cold War had diminished interest in Burma. The Japanese were eager to exploit economic opportunities there, and the Chinese supported SLORC's repression of the movement for democracy, consistent with their policies at home. Burma's neighbors, no avatars of democracy themselves, hoped to integrate the country into regional organizations, specifically the Association of Southeast Asian Nations (ASEAN). They were not interested in confrontation. The government of the United States criticized SLORC occasionally, as did the European Union and the United Nations. Economic sanctions, urged by human rights activists, were attempted, to no avail.

In 1990, it became evident that Suu Kyi was becoming the new icon of the men and women for whom the fight for human rights was paramount. Sakharov was dead, Havel was ensconced in Hradny Castle, and Mandela had just been released from prison, his moment of glory yet to come. In July, Suu Kyi was awarded the 1990 Sakharov Prize for Freedom of Thought by the European Parliament. A few months later, following a campaign by Havel, she won the Nobel Prize for Peace. Havel portrayed her as the personification of what it meant to live in truth, as one who demonstrated the power of the powerless. He was himself a candidate for the award, but he clearly believed the values for which he had struggled now would be served best if she won.

Of course, SLORC would not allow her to travel to Oslo to deliver her acceptance speech to the Nobel Committee. Nor would the junta allow the Polish ambassador to deliver a letter informing her of the prize, insisting she was undeserving. Aris claimed to be uncertain as to whether she was still alive. But the award reminded the world of the tyrannical regime in Rangoon, further depreciated SLORC's currency on the international stage, and decreased its maneuverability in handling her. The price to be paid for mistreating her had gone up, as Havel and the Nobel Committee intended. One of her sons accepted the prize for her, quoting his mother: "To live a full life . . . one must have the courage to bear the responsibility of the needs of others . . . , one must want to bear this responsibility."

In a collection of essays Aris edited and published in 1991, Suu Kyi wrote about her father and her country and its culture—much as she had before she returned to Burma in 1988. But when she wrote "In Quest of Democracy," the evolution of her thinking in captivity was evident. Again, Havel's influence was often apparent. She pointed to her father and to Gandhi as models, men who were fearless and spoke the truth. She contended that Ne Win's totalitarian regime had survived so long because the people of Burma, much like those of Czechoslovakia after 1968, had lived a lie. They had been passive while Ne Win and his minions arrogated power to themselves. The citizens of Burma had failed to carry out the duties of citizenship.

She was scornful of those such as Singapore's Lee Kuan Yew and other authoritarian rulers, who argued that liberal democratic principles were a foreign import, inconsistent with traditional Asian values. She stressed the desire of the people of Burma to live an existence free from want or fear. She insisted that Buddhism, at the core of Burmese belief systems, provided the foundation for human rights. And she noted that Burma had voted for the Universal Declaration of Human Rights in 1948—without any suggestion that its tenets were alien.

SLORC's claim to be essential to law and order in Burma did not escape her contempt. Law and order without justice were of no value. And justice, like liberty, like democracy, had to be earned through courage, resolution, and sacrifice.

In another essay, "Towards a True Refuge," Suu Kyi was dismissive of the idea that improvement in material conditions would lead eventually to improvement in other social conditions. It was evident that she was not one to believe that economic development would lead inexorably to a rising middle class that would insist upon and attain democracy. For Suu Kyi, as for Havel, it was essential to promote social, ethical, and political reforms first. A democratic government protective of human rights was manifestly her priority.

In May 1992, a change occurred in the leadership of the SLORC and there was a notable easing of its grip on Burmese society. The universities were reopened and some political prisoners were released. Suu Kyi, however, remained under house arrest, although Aris and their children were allowed to visit her. In 1994, she was permitted to receive nonfamily visitors, including a reporter for the *New York Times* and the American politician/statesman Bill Richardson. It was a moment of hope, but there was no indication that the generals were any more interested in democracy. They were not yet certain they could maintain control if Suu Kyi were free to rally her supporters around the country.

Suddenly, unexpectedly, in July 1995, after nearly six years, the SLORC released her from house arrest. Quite likely pressure from Tokyo, an essential source of loans and investment capital, triggered the decision. Equally likely, the junta was convinced that the risk it was taking was minor. The NLD had been weakened in the six years of her imprisonment, and the generals had no intention of giving her free rein to invigorate the democracy movement. Once again, they miscalculated. The people of Burma had not forgotten her and the transgressions of the government had made her ever more attractive as an alternative. To her people, she had become "the Lady," a legendary figure they were eager to see and prepared to follow.

Suu Kyi emerged speaking of the need for reconciliation, insisting she harbored no bitterness toward her captors. As before, she called for dialogue, insisting she was not hostile to the military that her father had created. She pointed to the experience of South Africa, where the once-oppressed and their erstwhile oppressors found a peaceful means to work together. She clearly meant to wrap herself in the mantles of Nelson Mandela and Archbishop Desmond Tutu—who wrote the introduction to the 1995 revised edition of the essays Aris had collected in 1991. She contended that the democratic forces in Burma and the government had fewer gaps to bridge than did blacks and whites in South Africa.

For several months, Suu Kyi devoted herself to reviving and reorganizing the National League for Democracy, resuming her post as secretary-general of the party despite a SLORC ruling designed to prevent changes in the party hierarchy. She irritated SLORC further by labeling its proposed constitutional convention a farce, by calling for economic sanctions against Burma, and by urging tourists to boycott the regime's "Visit Myanmar 1996" campaign. Writing for the *Mainichi Shimbun*, she criticized Japanese companies that invested in Burma.

Despite these provocations, in October SLORC allowed her to travel out of Rangoon for the first time and to meet with the UN special representative on Burma—a critic of the government's human rights record. She was allowed to deliver public addresses to crowds—often more than a thousand people—that massed outside the gate of her home every weekend afternoon. She told her audiences that the NLD would not participate in the constitutional convention because the military had refused to talk to her, that there had been no dialogue since her release from house arrest. She denied charges that she was being confrontational, but it was evident that she was frustrated by the tactics SLORC was employing.

The regime's desire for legitimacy to facilitate the flow of foreign capital and tourists into the country was obvious. The generals were also uneasy after the United Nations approved American use of force to restore the democratically elected president of Haiti in 1994. Might it do the same in Burma? Releasing Suu Kyi from house arrest, allowing her considerable freedom to travel and to speak, were ploys to give the appearance of movement toward democracy or at least an improved performance on human rights issues. But the promise of multiparty democracy was derided by most observers, and few saw genuine progress on human rights. Foreign governments were aware that there had been no dialogue with Suu Kyi, and the junta's intent was readily apparent in the proposed constitution. One provision guaranteed the leading role of the military and another banned anyone married to a foreigner from serving as president. By December 1995, the *Christian Science Monitor* was reporting that hope was fading, that Suu Kyi was being marginalized, and the UN General Assembly condemned Burma for continued human rights violations.

Some analysts suspected divisions among the generals on the issue of how to handle Suu Kyi and the democratic movement generally. None of them was willing to surrender power to a popularly elected civilian regime, but it seemed likely that there were some who thought a more benign façade would be useful and were willing to risk giving her and the NLD some room to maneuver. Others presumably saw no need to disguise the iron fist of military power and perceived their best interests to be served by intimidating the opposition and cowing the people.

If the analysts were correct, it was apparent by the spring of 1996 that the hard-liners were growing restive. Suu Kyi was addressing crowds in excess of two thousand every weekend, speaking to them of the blessings of democracy, of the importance of free speech and freedom of the press and of assembly. The military began harassing her supporters, arresting some of them. She in turn became more critical of the junta. The NLD planned a meeting at her house in late May, but party members were arrested. In June SLORC banned her weekend meetings, which had drawn as many as ten thousand in recent weeks. Her godfather, the honorary Danish consul, was arrested and died in prison. Suu Kyi's freedom of movement ended, as did the access of foreign reporters and diplomats to her home.

In July, a videotape of Suu Kyi calling for international sanctions to force regime change was smuggled out of Burma. She insisted that political reform had to accompany economic development. Much as Havel had perceived earlier in Czechoslovakia, she understood that the junta hoped to buy the people off with improvement in material conditions—and she feared they might succeed. In the video she argued that sanctions would not hurt ordinary Burmese, that only the military and its sycophants were benefiting from the existing economic expansion.

Outraged, SLORC accused her of collaborating with subversives. The blockade of her house was tightened and SLORC defended the military dictatorship, pointing to the success the communist dictatorship in China had had with its economic programs. Beijing was delighted by the admiration expressed by the Burmese rulers and continued to provide economic and military support. The Chinese had no interest in seeing democracy bloom in Burma and perceived Suu Kyi as too pro-American. An NLD government in Rangoon would contribute to the encirclement of China by hostile forces.

But it was increasingly apparent that members of SLORC were ambivalent in their handling of Suu Kyi. The United States was threatening major sanctions and there were signs of unease among Burma's ASEAN neighbors. Her street was reopened in November, and she immediately drove out to address supporters. Along the way, her car was attacked by government agents and she was forced to return. The blockade around her house was reinstituted and the generals indicated it would remain indefinitely. And yet, on January 4, 1997, Burma's Independence Day, she was allowed to hold a rally at her home attended by twenty-five hundred people. The vacillation in SLORC's treatment of Suu Kyi did indeed suggest an unresolved policy division within the junta.

One major SLORC goal was admission to ASEAN. It is likely that what little freedom Suu Kyi and the NLD were allowed was designed to ease the consciences of the leaders of ASEAN nations—or at least, to make it easier for them to stand up to criticism from the West. In July 1997, Burma was admitted to the organization. It was also evident that, despite Suu Kyi's pleas, France, Singapore, and Thailand, as well as Japan, were seizing investment opportunities in Burma.

The junta continued to make cosmetic changes in its approach to support its claim to be moving toward democracy. In October, Suu Kyi was allowed to address an assembly of three hundred people on the outskirts of Rangoon—technically she had been given permission to leave Rangoon. In

November, SLORC, presumably at the instigation of public relations con-
sultants seeking to soften the junta's image, renamed itself the State Peace
and Development Council (SPDC). It also authorized Suu Kyi to hold a National Day celebration, attended by 360 people, at her house. Contacts with
the NLD were resumed, although they appear to have been aimed at driving
a wedge between Suu Kyi and other NLD leaders. Suu Kyi was allowed to
have weekly lunches with friendly diplomats, but in fact she was not allowed
to leave Rangoon and no known reporters were permitted to see her. Even
ambassadors seeking to visit her at her house were turned away.

Years passed without Aris being permitted to enter Burma. In the spring of
1998, the regime cut off Suu Kyi's telephone access to the outside world. The
house was crumbling around her and she had sold most of the furnishings to
buy food. She had some income from her articles for the *Mainichi Shimbun*, and
the police allowed supporters to bring her food. Her life was grim, but she continued her daily routine and dreamed of ways to bring about peaceful change.

In July and August, she attempted several times to run the blockade
to meet with supporters in the provinces. On each occasion the way was
blocked by soldiers, but she refused to turn back. She sat in her van for days
and nights—once for six days before the troops forcibly returned her, sick,
to her home. The SPDC rejected a request by seven Western nations that
American and Japanese diplomats be allowed to see her. The efforts by the
regime to prettify its brutality failed. Single-handedly, Suu Kyi prevented the
world from ignoring the horrors of life in Burma.

But for her, there was even greater misery ahead. Aris was dying of cancer.
Hoping to force her to leave, the junta refused to grant him a visa to visit
her. They brushed aside pleas from Western governments and human rights
organizations. She remained steadfast—the cause of her people ahead of
her husband. In March 1999, he died. They had not seen each other since
Christmas of 1995.

ASEAN's commitment to engagement with Burma accomplished nothing. Suu Kyi, appealing to the UN Human Rights Commission in April 1999,
called 1998 the worst year the people of Burma had suffered. Indeed, the
military was intensifying its efforts to crush the democracy movement, arresting and torturing NLD members. Over three thousand were imprisoned,
including women and children and 150 of the party leaders. An estimated
forty thousand were forced to resign. Rangoon's relations with the rest of the
world—other than China—deteriorated in the aftermath of Aris's death.
But what really hurt the regime was the Asian financial crisis of 1998–1999,
which caused a sharp drop in foreign investment in Burma.

Over the next several years, the cyclical pattern of hope and repression continued. Until the summer of 2000, Suu Kyi had limited freedom of movement within Rangoon. In May she met the British writer and human rights activist Timothy Garton Ash, friend of Havel and other East European advocates of democracy, at the home of a diplomat posted to the city. Not surprisingly they talked at length of the transitions to democracy in Eastern Europe and South Africa and of the South African "truth and reconciliation commission." But Ash was deeply pessimistic about the possibility for peaceful change in Burma. He thought the 1990 election had been the best opportunity for a "Silken Revolution" analogous to Havel's Velvet Revolution. The moment had passed and he anticipated a violent peasant revolt—which the government would suppress.

In late August, Suu Kyi provoked another long standoff with the military, in a vain attempt to travel outside the city. Once again she was forced home, held incommunicado, and placed under house arrest. In December there were indications the junta might release her. Talks between the SPDC and Suu Kyi were reported. While the world waited, the American president, Bill Clinton, awarded her the Presidential Medal of Freedom, but it had no more impact on the generals than had her Sakharov or Nobel prizes. They released some political prisoners in February 2001, and there were hopes in Washington that sanctions might be working, but Suu Kyi remained under arrest. By May, all hope disappeared. Talks had broken down. Perhaps hardliners in the SPDC had prevailed over more pragmatic colleagues, but no one outside the junta really knew. The UN envoy was not allowed to return to Burma. There were indications that Japanese corporations were undermining the sanctions and ample evidence that the Chinese were actively aiding the SPDC in countering them. A December appeal for Suu Kyi's release signed by twenty winners of the Nobel Peace Prize went unheeded.

Finally, in May 2002, after nineteen months under house arrest, Suu Kyi was freed again—and that hope that "springs eternal" sprang once more. She went to NLD headquarters where she was met and cheered by thousands of well-wishers. She was allegedly at liberty to travel outside Rangoon and to resume organizing her supporters. No one was quite sure what had happened: Perhaps the sanctions had worked; surely the UN role had been critical—or was it Malaysia? There were rumors of a deal, that Suu Kyi had negotiated a compromise with the junta. Certainly she seemed less defiant.

In July she drove to Mandalay, where she spoke to large crowds. Local officials treated her with respect. But the SPDC's promise to release political prisoners was not honored, and talks between the generals and Suu Kyi were not resumed. In August, one of the leading generals declared categorically that democracy would not come quickly; arrests of her student supporters resumed. She was openly critical of the failure to release political prisoners and of the new acts of intimidation. In the autumn of 2002, it became increasingly clear that the junta had lost interest in political compromise, and relations between the military and the NLD deteriorated once more.

By the end of May 2003, Suu Kyi was unquestionably disheartened. There had been no political dialogue for over a year. The SPDC was no longer allowing her the promised freedom of movement. She and her supporters were being harassed and intimidated. There were hostile and violent disruptions of her meetings. NLD offices were being closed again. She openly questioned the sincerity of the generals and returned to her demand for implementation of the 1990 elections results.

A shakeup within the SPDC apparently signaled the end of any hope for reconciliation. The most powerful general within the junta had no interest in working with Suu Kyi. She was manifestly too popular with the people. The crowds she was attracting were too large. On May 30, a caravan of cars in which she was traveling, her plans filed with the government, was attacked by government-organized thugs. Suu Kyi was injured and her bodyguards and several supporters were killed. It was an extraordinary act of contempt for international opinion. Even the Japanese—but not the Chinese—halted aid to Burma.

For months she was held incommunicado at a military base without access to her doctor. Her condition was unknown and the junta, backed by Beijing, resisted pressure to release her or to allow visitors. Finally, late in September, after undergoing surgery for an unknown condition, reportedly gynecological, she was returned to her home—under arrest. Throughout Burma, repression of the already brutalized Burmese people intensified.

Democracy and human rights activists all over the world demanded Suu Kyi's release. The SPDC freed a handful of NLD leaders in April 2004 and resumed plans to hold a constitutional convention, ostensibly to create the foundation for constitutional government. NLD participation in the convention was essential for it to have any legitimacy, and the party agreed to send delegates *if* Suu Kyi and her deputy were released. Nothing happened. A power struggle within the SPDC appeared to immobilize the regime. Months passed—and then, in October, the general who had ordered the 2003 attack on Suu Kyi was named prime minister; in November, her house arrest was extended for an additional year. Moreover, the number of guards—young supporters—she was allowed was cut in half and her doctor's visits were obstructed. Protests from the United Nations and the U.S. government once again proved to no avail—and the sanctions regime was undermined by Japan and France, as well as China.

And so, the democracy movement in Burma seemed moribund in early 2005. Suu Kyi survived under increasingly difficult conditions. Having battled for seventeen years, her health was not what it was when she began and she was no longer a young woman. The circumstances that allowed for the emergence of democracy in Eastern Europe and South Africa do not exist in Burma. There is no Gorbachev-like figure sitting in Beijing, carrying out political reforms at home and urging similar changes on his client states. Perhaps the South African situation comes a little closer: The majority of Burmese would doubtless prefer not to live at the mercy of the army, and most of the world treats the generals as pariahs. Suu Kyi has often put forward offers of reconciliation that might well have come from Mandela or Bishop Tutu. But Garton Ash was probably right: None of the generals seem likely to reach out to her in my lifetime—or hers.

There was another brief moment of hope in the fall of 2007, when tens of thousands of Buddhist monks demonstrated against the government. But the junta chose the Tiananmen option and crushed the demonstration violently. International pressure led the generals to send a representative to meet with Suu Kyi, but the arrests and beatings continued. For the first time in three years, she was allowed to meet with members of her party. She was conciliatory as always, to no avail. As the weeks passed, the world's media turned elsewhere, and there was no indication that the military had any intention of loosening its grip.

Right does not always prevail. Of all the good people of whom I write, Suu Kyi is most likely to be martyred in a losing cause. The 1950s movies with which I grew up—in which the good guys always won in the end—appear to have been inadequate preparation for life in the real world.

PART II

WOMEN'S RIGHTS

Margaret Sanger, Library of Congress, Prints & Photographs Division, LC-USZ62-29808

CHAPTER 4

Margaret Sanger and the Liberation of Women

I read a review a few years ago of *The Death of the West*, a regrettably popular book by Pat Buchanan. Buchanan, as is his wont, fears that non-Christian, nonwhite people will inundate Western Europe and the United States, to the detriment of his beloved—and imagined—white Christian culture. An important part of his explanation for the coming disaster is the reputed failure of white Christian women to accept their natural, God-given role as breeding stock.

Margaret Sanger had rather a different view of the role of women. She devoted her life, almost single-mindedly, to obtaining access to birth control information and devices for women all over the world. She understood that women, half of humanity, could not be free unless they could choose whether and when to have children. She understood that the progress, the wealth, and prosperity of nations would be retarded if women were not free, if women did not have equal opportunity to contribute to the advancement of the societies in which they lived. And she thought it would be wonderful if women could make love for the sheer joy of it rather than to maintain or increase population levels.

Sanger was born Margaret Louise Higgins in 1879, the sixth of eleven children in a Catholic family residing in Corning, New York. As a teenager, she trained to be a nurse. In her own writings and those of scholars who have studied her life, both parents appear to have been important influences on the woman she became and the cause for which she fought. Her father, a stonemason with radical political views, seems to have been at war with local

59

industrialists and the Catholic Church for failing to support the labor movement. She was attracted to his anti-establishment politics. Her mother's death, given variably at forty-eight or fifty, Sanger attributed to exhaustion from excessive child-bearing—an example of what had to be stopped.

Perhaps more influential was the period during which she lived in Greenwich Village, New York City, the center of radical bohemian life in the United States for much of the first half of the twentieth century. She had married William Sanger, an architect, in 1902, and gave birth to three children over the next several years. After residing in suburban Westchester, the Sangers decided to move into the city in 1910, to be where the action was—and where William Sanger could try his luck as a painter. Margaret returned to nursing to keep food on the table. Between 1910 and 1914, the Sangers associated with a prominent group of anarchists and socialists. Margaret joined the New York Socialist Party and participated in strike actions taken by the International Workers of the World (the "Wobblies").

Of all the radical intellectuals she encountered in the Village, who included "Big Bill" Haywood, John Reed, Max Eastman, and Elizabeth Gurley Flynn, Emma Goldman and her ideas seemed to resonate most strongly with Sanger. Goldman frequently argued that unwanted pregnancies were the bane of the working class and spoke eloquently of the power that would be liberated when women gained control of their bodies. Insisting on voluntary motherhood, she was articulating what Sanger had perceived in her own mother's life and had witnessed as a nurse working with poor immigrant women desperate to terminate pregnancies. Sanger had already begun speaking to socialist women's groups about both sexual issues and the plight of immigrant women. Ellen Chesler, a Sanger biographer, suggests that Sanger was indebted to Goldman for both her feminist ideology and her rhetoric.

Sanger began publishing her views on sex in 1912 in a column for *The Call*, a socialist daily published in New York. By 1913, she was in trouble, running afoul of the Comstock laws that banned obscenity, for writing about venereal disease. That column was suppressed and the censors kept her in their sights. She welcomed the challenge and demonstrated her determination to keep educating women about contraception and what a later generation would call "safe sex." She lectured on family planning and women's sexuality at the radical Ferrer Center in New York. During a brief trip to Paris, she met with French radicals who encouraged her focus on birth control. The historian David Kennedy suggests that she came to see control of contraception as "a weapon in the class struggle."

Early in 1914, she published a magazine, *The Woman Rebel*, intended to be a radical feminist monthly, questioning traditional notions of women as wives and mothers and stressing the importance of birth control. Several issues of the magazine were banned and, for sending information about contraception through the mails, a criminal offense at the time, Sanger was eventually charged with violating the Comstock laws. Undaunted, she wrote a pamphlet, *Family Limitation*, in which she offered details on various methods of preventing conception. When her case went to trial in 1914, she fled to Europe. Her husband, who distributed *Family Limitation*, was arrested, convicted, and jailed for his efforts in 1915.

In Europe, her meetings with Havelock Ellis, the British sexologist, and Johannes Rutgers, a Dutch medical researcher who was fitting women with flexible diaphragms, appear to have been definitive in her efforts over the next decade. Ellis's theories on female sexuality appealed to Sanger. His argument that women had a psychological need to enjoy sex added legitimacy to her own inclinations. He spent considerable time guiding her research in the British Museum and perhaps as much time sleeping with her. He was only one of several European intellectuals, including H. G. Wells, with whom she had an affair as well as intellectual exchanges.

There is no indication in any of her writings or those of her several biographers that she slept with Dr. Rutgers, but he changed her mind about the best approach to contraception. Until she visited his clinic, she had focused on means that women could manage by themselves, such as contraceptive foams. But Rutgers's work—and success rate—persuaded her that the diaphragm, fitted by medically trained personnel, made more sense. Sanger began to lean toward the conclusion that she would need the cooperation of the medical profession.

While in Europe she filed for divorce from Sanger and did not bother to visit him in jail when she returned to New York to stand trial in October 1915. Her intent was to use the trial as a media event, to attract attention to herself and her ideas, and to arouse the public to challenge the Comstock laws. Suddenly in November, her only daughter, Peggy, five years old, died. One does not need a degree in psychiatry to imagine a mother's sense of guilt. In pursuit of her ideas and her pleasures, she had left her husband and neglected her children. Now one of them was gone. At this point she appears to have committed herself to a crusade for birth control, conceivably as a means of relieving her guilt. The cause had to become important enough to justify neglect of her parental responsibilities—and she had to perceive herself as the only one capable of leading the crusade to victory. The cause and Margaret Sanger became one. Years later she wrote of having been part of something of unquestioned value, "something so fundamentally right."

The government was not eager to prosecute its case against Sanger, and after stories of her daughter's death circulated in the press, making her a sympathetic figure, charges were dropped. But Sanger was not to be denied. In the weeks that followed she toured the country in fulfillment of her mission. At each speaking engagement she did what she could to provoke local bluenoses and on several occasions was arrested for violation of laws banning obscenity. The resulting publicity was everything she hoped for, rallying more and more Americans behind her banner.

Upon her return to New York, she was ready for the next step, the opening of the country's first birth control clinic, in a section of Brooklyn populated largely by poor Jewish immigrants. She was probably not surprised when the clinic was raided by the police and she and her staff arrested. This time she stood trial, was convicted, and spent thirty days in jail. Her appeal, based on the argument that denying women access to contraception was unconstitutional because it denied a woman's right to enjoy intercourse without inviting pregnancy, thus obstructing a woman's pursuit of happiness, was rejected, but she reveled in the publicity. Her sister, arrested with her and jailed before her, went on a hunger strike, and reports of forced feeding won more sympathy and more support for Sanger's cause.

By 1917, Sanger's rhetoric had softened to the extent that she no longer gave primacy to arguments that had been popular in radical circles. Talk of class struggle faded, as did attacks on marriage. She spoke and wrote more often about the danger of abortion and the value of contraception in sparing women from its horrors. She emphasized the emancipation of women from their role as brood mares. Women's health and opportunities for development, a chance to enjoy life, were notes she sounded constantly. And she found, probably to her surprise, that her mission was more attractive to middle-class than to working-class women.

Of course, a world war was raging in Europe at this time, and most of her radical friends in America had focused their efforts on keeping the United States out of it. Sanger's ultimate concern never changed, but the war added one more arrow to her quiver: She argued that population pressure had sent the Germans marching. Obviously, if excess population caused war, birth control could preserve peace.

On the eve of American intervention in the war, Sanger organized a mass meeting at Carnegie Hall at which she distributed the first issue of the *Birth Control Review*, a broadsheet for disseminating her views. By all accounts she was extraordinarily successful in winning media attention. She was an attractive woman with a charismatic personality and exceptional organizing skills, pressing a controversial issue, and she fascinated the press. But her activities were overshadowed briefly when American boys marched off to make the world safe for democracy. She did make a modest contribution to the war effort when the venereal disease section of her *What Every Girl Should Know* was distributed to the troops.

In 1918, her appeal of her conviction for operating the Brooklyn clinic was rejected, but the New York State appellate court nonetheless advanced her cause. The court ruled that doctors could legally provide contraceptive advice to women whose health might be endangered by pregnancy. In other words, although Sanger's clinic run by two nurses had violated the law, the same clinic run by a doctor would be legal. A few years later, she opened just such a clinic, the Birth Control Clinical Research Bureau, staffed by female doctors. She warded off police harassment and the hostility of the Roman Catholic Church to keep the doors open and provide a model for clinics across the country.

The Catholic Church became Sanger's principal nemesis, and she and Church leaders waged open warfare, each demonizing the other. In cities where the Church was powerful, her lectures were occasionally cancelled or raided by the police. In 1919 American bishops distributed a pastoral letter forbidding artificial means of contraception: Sex was for procreation, not for fun. When she staged the First American Birth Control Conference in New York in 1921, the last session was blocked by the police; the evidence indicated that the action had been requested by the city's Catholic archbishop. Taking on the Church came easily to Sanger, whose father had quarreled with its leaders in the town in which she was born. Ellen Chesler suggests that Sanger had long held a grudge against the Church for its treatment of her father, but there can be no doubt that Church actions against her and her cause were reason enough for her animosity.

Sanger's activities in the 1920s gave her an international reputation as the world's single most important advocate of birth control. She lectured across the United States and in Europe and Asia as well. She wrote books that sold phenomenally well: 567,000 copies of her *Woman and the New Race* and *The Pivot of Civilization* were sold between 1920 and 1926. In 1925, she was the subject of a very favorable *New Yorker* profile. And she organized major international conferences. In addition to the First American Birth Control Conference, at which she announced the creation of the American Birth Control League, she sponsored the Sixth International Neo-Malthusian and Birth Control Conference, also in New York, in 1925, and joined a British feminist in organizing the Geneva Population Conference of 1927.

One reason for Sanger's incredible success in building support for her ideas was her willingness to join forces with and accept support from groups and individuals whose goals overlapped with hers, but whose rationales were different—and sometimes problematic. Sanger's ultimate concern was to free women by sparing them from unwanted pregnancies and allowing them to enjoy sex. Just as she had once justified her cause as part of the class struggle and then as a step toward world peace, she used neo-Malthusian arguments linking population pressure to poverty, and took money from John D. Rockefeller Jr. and other members of the New York elite eager to reduce the birthrate of the lower classes. The *New Yorker* profile noted that she was willing to argue—and always believed—that birth control would "cure the ills of home, of war, of most of the tangles and tragedies of all human relationships." Worst of all, she made common cause with eugenicists, some of whom were eager to prevent pregnancies among people of color and any other category of humanity they deemed unfit. Building coalitions is an obviously practical way to accomplish one's ends, but sometimes one's allies can be embarrassing and provide ammunition for the opposition.

Another reason for Sanger's extraordinary activity in the 1920s was her marriage in 1922 to Noah Slee. Slee was a wealthy businessman who had made a fortune manufacturing Three-in-One Oil; he was obviously enamored of her and enormously supportive in every sense of the word. It was his money that funded many of her activities and provided the financial security she had long craved but never known. And Slee was also generous in accepting her long absences and extramarital affairs. Marriage to an attractive, vivacious, world celebrity seemed to meet his needs. It appears to have been a wonderfully satisfying relationship for both of them—although she noted with amusement that he objected to her coming home alone in a taxi at night.

Sanger's travel to Asia in 1922 appears to have come as a result of an article of hers being translated into Japanese and the contacts of her friend and sometime associate, Agnes Smedley, a journalist later famed for her writing about Chinese Communist guerrillas during World War II. Smedley arranged for Sanger to be invited to speak in a lecture series along with Albert Einstein, Bertrand Russell, and H. G. Wells. Curiously, Sanger found Japanese men more responsive to her arguments for birth control than were Japanese women—perhaps failing to appreciate how difficult it was for Japanese women to express opinions publicly. In 1938, presumably aware of Japanese aggression on the Asian continent, she wrote that she had reached Japan too late—that Japanese perceptions of population pressure would lead to an explosion.

She went on to Korea, where she noted Japanese contempt for and mistreatment of Koreans, and to China, which she described as a Malthusian nightmare of overpopulation and incredible poverty. In Beijing she spoke at National Peking University, had dinner with its president, Cai Yuanpei, and lunched with Hu Shi, China's best-known Westernizing intellectual. Shanghai clearly shocked Sanger, and she was appalled by the contrast between the luxuriousness of the International Settlement and the conditions in which the average Chinese lived. Worst of all, the only birth control poor Chinese seemed to practice was female infanticide. Fifteen years later, with funding from Rockefeller and the apparent assistance of Pearl Buck, she was able to get a clinic started in Shanghai, but then came the Japanese invasion.

At home Sanger recognized the plight of African Americans, especially those in the South, and tried to reach them with ideas about birth control. She understood that solutions that worked for middle-class women might be beyond the means of poor blacks, and she sought a cheap, simple contraceptive for them. Long afterward, some blacks, aware of her flirtation with eugenics, suspected Sanger of a racist effort to reduce the African American population, but at the time, W. E. B. Du Bois endorsed the clinic she opened in Harlem and Mary McLeod Bethune supported her efforts in the rural South. Her clinics do not appear to have had much appeal to African Americans before World War II.

By the end of the 1920s, Sanger concluded that she needed federal legislation to overcome opposition to birth control. Her goal was to get doctors to provide information and devices. She would have to persuade the medical profession of the need and federal and state governments to decriminalize the process. In 1929 she published *Motherhood in Bondage*, a volume of five hundred letters out of what she claimed were more than a million addressed to her by women pleading for help in avoiding or terminating pregnancies. Shortly afterward, with anonymous funding from the Rockefellers, she established the National Committee on Federal Legislation for Birth Control and opened an office in Washington to commence lobbying. She sent speakers not only to the Hill but also all across the country.

Sanger failed in her ostensible goal of obtaining legislation. She won many supporters in Congress, but her efforts provoked the Catholic Church, which launched a major counterattack. The National Catholic Welfare Conference denounced birth control, and her opponents portrayed her plans as part of a Soviet plot to undermine American morality. Nonetheless, Sanger claimed to be pleased by her success in educating both Congress and the public, and it was evident that she was gaining supporters around the world. In 1930 the Lambeth Conference of Anglican bishops surprised clerical circles by approving the use of artificial means of preventing contraception. Liberal Protestants and Reformed Jews had the cover they wanted and followed quickly.

Even the Catholic Church gave some ground when a papal encyclical, *Casta Conubii*, allowed for recreational sex—the pope referred specifically to post-menopausal women—provided no artificial means were used. The rhythm method practiced by many of the faithful later was given the sobriquet "Vatican roulette," in a delightful song by social critic Tom Lehrer.

Equally important was the gradual acceptance of birth control by the medical profession. In 1931 the New York Academy of Medicine reported favorably on the operation of Sanger's New York City clinic, supporting her argument in favor of contraception for the prevention of disease. Doctors, unable to get needed training in medical schools, flocked to her clinics to gain the technical knowledge they needed. And eventually, in 1937, the American Medical Association finally agreed that contraception might be warranted even when disease was not involved.

In 1935, Sanger met Jawaharlal Nehru in London and found the prominent young Indian nationalist highly supportive of her views on the value of family limitation for his country. He encouraged her to establish birth control clinics in India—and to meet with Gandhi in the faint hope of winning him over to the cause. She eventually spent nearly three months in India, speaking across the country, and succeeding in opening several clinics there. Her meeting with Gandhi was enormously valuable in gaining her international publicity, but she failed to win him over. She recognized his appeal but was not favorably impressed by his economic program, an early version of insisting on appropriate technology, which she thought reactionary—and she was utterly appalled by his views on sex. She concluded that he had not the slightest understanding of women. His view that all sex acts were debasing and should be limited to procreation sounded like something out of the Vatican. But he did agree that families should be limited to no more than three or four children, imagining that intercourse three or four times in a marriage might be enough. Obviously, Sanger could expect no support from the Mahatma. But at an All-India Women's Conference at which she had been invited to speak, she found a much warmer reception. The middle-class Indian women who were her hosts had already recognized the need to make birth control part of their nation's public health program.

But Sanger's greatest victory came in the courts in 1936. Her lobbying efforts had failed to obtain the legislation she sought—primarily because she was outgunned by the Catholic Church, but she and her legal adviser, Morris Ernst, believed she had succeeded in educating the judges. They decided to try another tack, through the courts. In 1933, Sanger ordered a package of pessaries (diaphragms) from Japan. When the pessaries arrived, U.S. Customs officials were tipped off and confiscated the package pursuant to Section 305 of the Tariff Act of 1930, which incorporated the intent of the 1873 Comstock law prohibiting the import or mailing of contraceptives. Sanger sued to obtain her shipment, and in January 1936 a U.S. District Court judge in New York, obviously sympathetic to Sanger's cause, ruled that Customs had no authority to prevent the import of devices intended for legitimate medical use. The government appealed the decision. Before the year was out, one of the nation's leading jurists, Augustus Hand, speaking for the U.S. Court of Appeals in the case of *U.S. v. One Package of Japanese Pessaries*, upheld the lower court decision. He declared that the government could not question the judgment of physicians presumed to be acting for the good of their patients. The use of such devices had to be left to the discretion of the medical profession. And he went further, declaring that if Congress had understood the danger posed by pregnancy and had seen clinical data available in 1936 (thanks to Margaret Sanger), it would never have classified birth control as obscene. The likelihood of a Hand decision being overturned by the Supreme Court was minuscule and the government chose not to challenge his decision. Sanger's cause had triumphed—and Henry Luce ran a four-page spread on her in *Life* magazine. Gratified by her success, Sanger closed her Washington office and turned to other fronts.

Another measure of Sanger's success can be found in the "scientific" public opinion polls that began to appear in the 1930s. Although crude by current standards and less meaningful in the absence of earlier figures for comparison, the numbers suggest Sanger had overwhelmed her opposition. Chesler cites polls indicating that 70 percent of Americans, including a majority in every state, favored the legalization of birth control. A poll taken of its readers for the *Ladies' Home Journal* suggested that nearly 80 percent supported legalized contraception. And even 51 percent of Catholic women readers reported their willingness to defy the Church on this issue.

Given widespread public support for her cause and the court decisions in her favor, Sanger had visions of gaining President Franklin Roosevelt's endorsement of a plan for federal funding of contraception. She pulled a couple of new arrows out of her quiver: Birth control would alleviate the misery of the Depression and conceivably help the country out of it. Contraception was less expensive than the treatment of syphilis. And she knew she had the president's wife on her side. Eleanor Roosevelt had served on the board of Sanger's American Birth Control League in the 1920s, resigning when her husband was elected governor of New York in 1928. In 1931 she had spoken at a testimonial dinner in Sanger's honor. But the president would not touch the issue, and Sanger was convinced that he feared antagonizing the urban Catholic political machines so important to the Democratic Party. It was not until after he was elected president for a third term that Eleanor Roosevelt was able to throw off her husband's restraints and invite Sanger to the White House for a meeting on federal support for contraception. At that meeting in December 1941 and in the months that followed, White House pressure, orchestrated by Mrs. Roosevelt, forced the Children's Bureau to include birth control in its program. David Kennedy suggests that the president acquiesced because war industries could not afford to have Rosie the Riveter put out of action by an unwanted pregnancy.

Although Sanger was unquestionably the best-known figure in the birth control movement at home and abroad, and as such indispensable to the movement, her ideas and approach were not always admired by others who shared her goal. Many of her colleagues considered her to be too radical and too combative, and were dismayed by her confrontations with the Catholic Church. In the late 1920s tensions within the American Birth Control League, the organization she had created, led her to resign as president. She was losing control of the agenda and she found that intolerable. When she left she took her clinic with her. In 1939, however, she agreed to merge her Birth Control Research Clinic with the League, quite possibly as the result of pressure from major donors, such as the Rockefellers. The new organization was called the Birth Control Federation of America. Although its leadership never repudiated Sanger, she was increasingly marginalized. In 1942 her objections to changing the movement's focus from family limitation to child spacing were overridden, and the organization was renamed Planned Parenthood Federation of America.

Also in 1942, Sanger, then sixty-three, moved to Arizona, a climate better suited to fighting the tuberculosis that had plagued her since her youth. There she was able to comfort her ailing husband, who died in 1943. There were probably many birth control activists, as well as the Catholic hierarchy, that allowed themselves the luxury of believing that her retirement meant they were rid of her. They would, of course, be mistaken.

For the most part, Sanger was quiescent during the war. When it ended, she was ready to save what remained of the world. The neo-Malthusians were terribly fearful of the consequences of population growth, foreseeing famine in much of what came to be called the Third World. Birth control advocates everywhere looked to Sanger for leadership. Efforts to incorporate birth control into UN programs were blocked by the Roman Catholic Church, with support, amusingly enough, from the Soviet Union. Stalin apparently had concluded that birth control was a capitalist plot to weaken communism. In 1948, one great capitalist, John D. Rockefeller Jr., may have confirmed

Stalin's fears by funding an international conference organized by Sanger and convened in England.

By 1952, it was evident that neither the United Nations nor any of its member states would meet the widely anticipated problem of overpopulation. A nongovernmental organization, the International Planned Parenthood Federation, was founded, with none other than Margaret Sanger as president. She remained in that post until 1959, when she was eighty years old.

By the 1950s Sanger was no longer functioning at full capacity. Age and illness slowed her and she was reputedly addicted to painkillers. She remained, however, the world's best-known advocate of birth control, and her name and occasional presence were valuable for fund-raising. She was not ready to fade away. The women of the world still needed her. And, indirectly, she had two more enormously important contributions to make to the cause.

Sanger had never surrendered her quest for inexpensive and simple contraception. Condoms were important for preventing the spread of venereal disease, but they left too much to the whims of men. Diaphragms were better, in that women controlled them, but they required professional fitting and a degree of manual dexterity not all women had. Various spermicides she had investigated never matched her hopes for them. At one time she had been interested in the Gräfenberg ring, a device that could be inserted in the uterus and left there. Eventually, the IUD evolved, a great boon to poor women around the world.

Sanger also seemed obsessed with the idea of finding an oral contraceptive that could be taken like an aspirin. In 1959, a researcher working with funds she had helped him to obtain, came up with "the Pill" and pointed to Sanger as the driving force behind his discovery. Upon learning of the successful testing of the Pill, the conservative Catholic congresswoman Clare Boothe Luce declared that modern women were at last as free as men to dispose of their bodies, earn their living, and improve their minds.

As her physical condition worsened and her heart began to fail, Sanger, now in her eighties, was confined for the most part to her home in Arizona and largely retired from the fray. Nonetheless, the nomination of John F. Kennedy as Democratic candidate for president roused her. She was deeply troubled by his Catholicism, fearful that her archenemies, the hierarchy of the Roman Catholic Church, would use Kennedy to turn back the clock, to take back from women the protection and freedom she had won for them. Kennedy, eager to avoid confrontation with Sanger, was quick to defuse the issue, distancing himself from the Church and endorsing family planning.

Sanger lived long enough to revel in the 1965 Supreme Court decision in *Griswold v. Connecticut* overturning a state law banning the use of contraceptives and stating categorically that the use of contraception was a constitutional right. With the help of friends—and a straw—she greeted the news with champagne. Death found her in a nursing home in 1966.

She was probably not aware but would have been gratified had she known of the turmoil in the higher echelons of the Catholic Church over the issue of birth control and the use of artificial contraceptives. Throughout her life the Church had demonized her as an exemplar of moral relativism and sexual promiscuity. When she died, a *New York Times* writer claimed that powerful sections of the Catholic press despised her more than they did Hitler. But at the Vatican Council called by Pope John XXIII in 1962, highly placed ecclesiastics recommended reconsideration of the Church position on birth control. Pope John's successor, Pope Paul VI, later spoke of an agonizing reappraisal of Church teaching on the subject. Sanger would not have been surprised that conservatives prevailed and the Church remained opposed to artificial contraception, a tenet of Catholicism that the majority of the faithful apparently ignore.

Margaret Sanger was not a saint. She doubtless loved her children, but she neglected them all too often. She may have loved her husbands, but she was not faithful to them. Her involvement with eugenics can only appall a later generation. In the pursuit of her goals, she was arguably ruthless and unprincipled. She was not blameless in her struggle with the Catholic Church. Nonetheless, her efforts constituted an enormous contribution toward the freeing of half of humanity.

No other figure advanced the cause of women as much as Sanger did. Birth control is not the panacea for women or the world that she claimed it to be—and probably believed it to be. But the success of the movement was at least as important as the success of the suffragettes who preceded her or the demand for equal rights for women before us today. No one was a stronger or more successful advocate for the idea that women should control their bodies, that women should be able to determine when and if they have children—and no woman is free or equal without that power.

The historian David Kennedy, less sympathetic to Sanger than others who have written about her, insists that birth control information was more readily available in American society than Sanger alleged and that many Americans had begun limiting the size of their families before she took up the issue. But even Kennedy is forced to concede that it was Sanger who brought the issue into the open and gained access to the necessary information for working-class Americans—and perhaps he would have been less quick to discount her import had he not chosen to put aside her international role.

For much of the world, Sanger was the voice and the face of the birth control movement. Her dedication to the cause was extraordinary and it consumed her. She never deviated from her goal despite her intellectual growth and the striking changes in the sources of her support and in the status and ideology of her supporters. Without her campaign, who can say with certainty that the ever-conservative American medical profession would have come to its senses and agreed to provide women with the information and devices they required? Surely it would not have happened in the 1930s.

There will always be men who perceive of women as breeding stock and who are horrified by the thought that women might enjoy sex. Pat Buchanan is not alone in America, and men like him are probably in the majority outside of North America and Western Europe. Those women who are free, who control their bodies and have the right to choose when to conceive, who can make love for the sheer pleasure of that intimacy, owe a debt to Margaret Sanger. And those men—husbands, lovers, and fathers—who delight in strong, free women are no less indebted to her.

Doria Shafik, Egyptian feminist leader, courtesy of the Rare Books and Special Collections Library, from the Van-Leo and Angelo Boyadjian Photograph Collection, The American University in Cairo

CHAPTER 5

Muslim Feminists

There was a time, not very long ago, when I would have thought of "Muslim feminist" as an oxymoron. In the days of my enlightenment, I came to realize they exist wherever there are Muslims, in Muslim countries as well as in predominantly Christian countries or Hindu India. In response to my queries, every specialist in Islamic studies I asked could name several women, rarely the same ones. Bangladesh has had two female prime ministers, and both Indonesia and Pakistan have had female presidents. Muslim women were fighting vigorously for equality years before I was born—openly in Egypt and Iran, quietly in more repressive societies such as Saudi Arabia. Undoubtedly there are thousands, perhaps millions of women who qualify as Muslim feminists. I can write about only a few, focusing largely on those about whom there already exists a scholarly literature in English or who have themselves written.

The most outrageous of them is doubtless Irshad Manji, a Canadian of South Asian extraction, born in Uganda. Her prosperous family fled Uganda to escape the horrors of Idi Amin when she was four years old. Her father was a monster who brutalized his wife and children. In her early twenties, she declared herself a lesbian and in 1998 started hosting *Queer Television*, a program focused on gay and lesbian culture. She insists that it is possible to be both queer and a devout Muslim. Her book *The Trouble with Islam Today*, published initially in 2003, became a best seller and was reprinted in a paperback edition.

Manji's ultimate concern is to open debate among Muslims over interpretations of the Koran and especially to challenge those interpretations that subordinate women. Much of what she objects to derives not from the Prophet Muhammad, but from later commentators. She argues that fear of disunity, perhaps a thousand years ago, led to the rejection of debate within Islam and an end to independent thought—an end to the exciting role of Islamic intellectuals in the intellectual and cultural history of the world. She writes of the need for *ijtihad*—the freedom to think for oneself, to challenge traditional practices.

Her father, who made a pretense of being a practicing Muslim, sent her at age nine to a madrassa every Saturday, where she quickly came into conflict with her teacher. She had an irritating habit of questioning his rules. Why, she asked, couldn't girls lead the prayers? Where in the Koran did it say this? How did he know the Jews were plotting so much evil? Pressing too hard in her demand for evidence to justify his teachings about the Jews, she was expelled from the madrassa at age fourteen. Finding an English-language version of the Koran, she concluded it was an imperfect document with inconsistencies about the requirement for male dominance over women.

As a mature adult wrestling with the desire to retain her faith, she lashed out at "desert Arabia." She was unquestionably hostile to Arabs and especially Saudis. Saudi interpretations of the Koran, based on "desert tribalism," were spreading throughout the world, and she complained about Arab cultural imperialists. And she did not hesitate to criticize the United States for its failure to support advocates of human rights in its Arab client states.

One devout male Muslim whose work Manji admires greatly is Muhammad Yunus. Quite rightly, she sees his microcredit program as a means of empowering women. It fits neatly with her program to reform Islam. She argues for revitalizing Muslim economies by utilizing the talents of women—why should Muslim nations handicap themselves by neglecting the potential contribution of half of their population? She wants women to be entrepreneurs, to own television stations, to control wealth. To this end, the Grameen model can be of enormous assistance. With tiny loans, women across the Muslim world can be ennobled and begin as microentrepreneurs.

Manji's efforts have not gone unnoticed. Oprah Winfrey gave her the Chutzpah Award, Ms. magazine named her a Feminist for the Twenty-First Century, and she received a Simon Wiesenthal Award of Valor—presumably for continuing her efforts in the face of death threats. Salman Rushdie urged her to persevere. The Israeli government invited her to visit and see for herself how the country functions and how Israeli-Palestinian relations are managed. It was not disappointed: She contrasted Israel's "ferociously" free press with the controlled media of Muslim countries—and was excessively generous in her appraisal of Ariel Sharon.

Manji is not likely to make the short list for the Nobel Prize, but a woman with comparable views and a more subtle, scholarly way of expressing them, Shirin Ebadi, was awarded the Nobel Peace Prize in 2003. Ebadi, an Iranian lawyer, an advocate for human rights, especially for the rights of women and children, was the first Muslim woman to be awarded the Nobel Peace Prize. She had previously received the Thorolf Rafto Memorial Prize (2001) and has been commended by Amnesty International and Human Rights Watch.

Ebadi is married, has two children, and was Iran's first woman judge—before the Islamic Revolution that drove out the Shah and turned the country into a theocracy. Like Manji, she calls for *ijtihad,* but unlike Manji she does not focus on inconsistencies in the Koran. She professes to believe that the problem is not with the holy book, but rather with repressive Muslim regimes that fail to honor human rights as required by the Koran. She does refer disparagingly to a seventh-century view of women, but contends that rather than being incorporated into the Koran, it was rejected by the Prophet, who advocated equality for women. A devout Muslim, the Islam she speaks for is very similar to the reformed Islam endorsed by Manji.

Persistent issues for Muslim feminists have involved the treatment of female children as the property of their male relatives—who sometimes announce the girls' marriages at birth—the lack of legal equality of women before the law, and the conditions under which a marriage may be terminated. One of Ebadi's primary concerns was the legal age of puberty for girls in Iran. Under the Shah's regime it was raised to eighteen, presumably part of his top-down efforts at modernization, an attempt to offer young women protection comparable to that found in the developed countries of the West. After the revolution, the age was dropped to nine for girls (thirteen for boys). Ebadi and her colleagues failed to restore eighteen, but did succeed in raising the legal age for girls to thirteen. She continues her struggle to win equal rights for Iranian women, but there seems little reason for optimism. On the bright side, she has not been imprisoned lately.

Another promising sign was the formation in Malaysia in 1988 of the Sisters in Islam, a feminist network registered as a nongovernmental organization. It refers to itself as "a group of Muslim professional women committed to promoting the rights of women within the framework of Islam." Like Manji, they insist that Islam cannot be used to justify *cultural* practices that subordinate women and deem them inferior to men. They argue that the problem is caused by limiting the interpretation of the Koran to men. Their study of the holy text reveals that it calls for equality, justice, and freedom for women as well as men: It does not sanction the oppression of women.

The Sisters in Islam also contend that they are the true supporters of the revolutionary spirit of Islam, which they describe as a religion that *raised* the status of women when it was revealed in the seventh century. They point to the participation of women in support of the Prophet's activities during his lifetime. Leaping from history to the future, they warn that the social and economic development of the Muslim community requires the full participation of its women.

Others appear to have found the faith so oppressive that they might fairly be considered as Muslim by birth only—or perhaps as nonobservant. The Bangladeshi doctor, poet, and novelist Taslima Nasrin has certainly had a more difficult life than the Canadian Manji and, arguably, than the Iranian Ebadi. Her writings have gone beyond feminism to criticism of her fellow Muslims, of the Koran, and of religious-based law generally and have deeply offended Bangladeshis, allegedly fundamentalists. Her writings have been banned in her own country, fatwas have been issued against her, bounties placed on her head. She has been beaten and had her passport confiscated and has been threatened with imprisonment. It is not hard to understand why she now calls herself a secular humanist.

In 1993 she fled Bangladesh and was granted asylum in Sweden, where she now lives. She has been named Feminist of the Year by the American Feminist Majority Foundation and been awarded the Sakharov Prize and the UNESCO prize for tolerance and nonviolence. Much admired in the West—and in Hindu India—it seems doubtful that she has helped the women of Bangladesh as much as Yunus has.

In Pakistan, where she heads the Human Rights Commission, Asma Jahangir stayed to fight. The results have not been pleasant. In May 2005, a group of middle-class Pakistani women demonstrated in Lahore for equal rights. They were attacked by the police and hauled off to jail. Jahangir was singled out for special treatment: The police were ordered to strip her in public. She managed to keep her trousers on, but lost her shirt. The officer who targeted her was alleged to be an intelligence officer close to then-president General Pervez Musharraf.

Pakistan remains notorious for honor killings, with an estimated two women killed every day, and women who are raped (one every two hours) are as likely to end up imprisoned as their rapists. And there was the classic case of Mukhtaran Bibi, who was gang-raped on the order of a village council as punishment for her brother's transgressions. Originally imprisoned as a result of international pressure, the rapists were released in 2005 and *her* passport seized by the Pakistani government to prevent her from telling her story in the United States.

But Muslim women fight on—and sometimes they win. For more than twenty years, Lulwa Al-Mulla has been struggling to win rights for women in Kuwait. She and her fellow activists all too slowly chipped away at resistance by their country's political elite—ultimately prevailing with the help of pressure from the United States on the royal family. A royal decree called for equality in 1999, but was ignored by lawmakers. In May 2005, the Kuwaiti Parliament finally passed legislation allowing women the right to vote and to run for public office—provided they observe undefined "Islamic guidelines." It will be interesting to see what happens in future national elections.

My focus, however, is on the twentieth century, and upon two Egyptian women, Huda Sha'rawi and Doria Shafik, who pioneered the women's movement in the Muslim world. Margot Badran, one of the leading students of the interplay between feminism and Islam, sees stirrings of a demand for gender equality in late-nineteenth-century Egypt, before British imperialism interrupted the course of modernization. And, indeed, the women's movement in early-twentieth-century Egypt manifested intense nationalism, its earliest demonstrations targeting the colonizers rather than the patriarchal customs and laws of the society.

The issues that emerged a century ago in Egypt derived largely from dissatisfaction with marriage and divorce practices, but also from what has been called "harem culture." Upper-class Egyptian women were "protected" by their male relatives, usually denied an education, caged at home, and veiled outside the home. Activists demanded literacy, an end to child marriage, restrictions on polygamy, and more equitable divorce laws.

The story of the organized movement in Egypt begins with Huda Sha'rawi (1879–1947). She was born into a wealthy and powerful family. Her father, Mohammad Sultan Pasha, speaker of the House of Representatives, died when she was eight. At twelve she was betrothed to a cousin, Ali Sha'rawi, in a family real estate deal and married him at age thirteen. At fourteen she fled from the home of her husband and was allowed to return to the residence of her mother. At twenty-one, under pressure, she resumed her married life. In the intervening seven years, she appears to have been influenced considerably by her French chaperone, the wife of a leading Egyptian politician. She returned to her husband a grown woman, well-educated and determined to lead a useful life. Fortunately, he was receptive and may even have encouraged her activism. Certainly his wealth and the prominence he attained as a nationalist and diplomat facilitated her endeavors.

Huda Sha'rawi was quickly caught up in the nationalist and feminist ferment in Egypt during the early years of the twentieth century. Opposition to British imperialism was intensifying. In 1911 a series of feminist demands were placed on the agenda of the Egyptian National Congress. In 1918, Sha'rawi became the public voice of the feminist movement and in 1919, along with many of her colleagues in the movement, was an active participant in the nationalist revolution. In 1920 she was elected president of the Wafdist Women's Central Committee (WWCC)—Wafd ("delegation" in Arabic) being the name the nationalist movement took after the British refused to allow an Egyptian delegation to present its case at the Paris Peace Conference in 1919. Sha'rawi and her followers assumed that the men with whom they stood up against imperialism would support women's rights. They were quickly disabused of this assumption. Egyptian men had no intention of treating them as equals.

The great leap forward for the women's movement in Egypt came in 1923. Sha'rawi resigned from the WWCC and founded the Egyptian Feminist Union (EFU). An organization of upper- and middle-class women, it met for the first nine years of its existence in Sha'rawi's home. Pressing hard, it won important concessions almost immediately. In 1924 the marriage law was amended to raise the minimum age for girls from thirteen to sixteen. Ostensibly more important was the language of the new Egyptian constitution, which declared all Egyptians to be equal. Unfortunately that promise was eviscerated only weeks later when the new electoral law denied political rights to women. After that setback, the women's movement focused its energies almost exclusively on fighting against the prejudices of the patriarchal society at home. There was little point in fighting against the British if Egyptian women would fare no better in an independent Egypt.

In 1925, the EFU began publication of the magazine L'Egyptienne. Interestingly, it was written in French, an obvious reflection of the upper-class audience at which it was targeted. For years, Sha'rawi and the other members of the EFU pressed for state-funded education for women; equal opportunity in the schools and the workplace; and the reform of laws pertaining to marriage, divorce, and child custody. Sha'rawi and a few of the others represented Egypt at numerous international women's conferences. Winning the right to public secondary education, they pressed for admission to the universities, fighting discipline by discipline.

There were always complaints from traditionalists, whether devout Muslims or merely male chauvinists, that the feminist movement was a Western import—that its goals were contrary to the teachings of the Koran or to Egyptian culture. The women fought back in several ways. One was to demonstrate their national bona fides by condemning British imperialism, not only in Egypt but in Palestine, where they opposed Zionist inroads. Another was to point to Turkey, a Muslim country that had shed the hated imperialist capitulations *and* granted women the much-coveted right to vote. In Turkey for a conference in 1934, Sha'rawi pointedly praised Mustafa Kemal for his reforms, specifically those that empowered women. At home, rather than call for the blessings of secular democracy, she always insisted that women's demand for political rights was grounded in the sharia: It was consistent with Islamic teachings. Throughout her life, she tried to stay within cultural boundaries. Although she had ceased to wear the veil in 1923, she continued to wear a head scarf. It was never easy for her critics to tar her with the brush of Western influence—not for lack of trying.

Far more dramatic were the actions of and their ultimate consequences for Doria Shafik. Throughout her career, Shafik was extraordinarily bold and confrontational. She became an international celebrity and succeeded in outraging first the religious establishment and then, after the revolution of 1952, enraged the government of Gamal Abdel Nasser, for which she proved no match.

Born into a middle-class family in 1908, Shafik was considered to be a leader in the second generation of Egyptian feminists. She looked to Huda Sha'rawi for inspiration and won Sha'rawi's support in 1928—although the two women were markedly different in style and action. Shafik was twelve when her mother died, a painful experience aggravated by the discovery that her mother had arranged a marriage for her, to be performed when she was sixteen. When time for the wedding came, Shafik refused: she had other plans for herself. Her parents had provided excellent schooling for her, she excelled in French, and she wanted to go to France to further her education. She wrote to Sha'rawi, who invited her to her home and recognized in Shafik a potential feminist leader of the future. She agreed to finance her studies at the Sorbonne.

Off to Paris went Doria Shafik. Once there, she defied the representative of the Egyptian Ministry of Education, enrolled in a curriculum of her choosing (philosophy), and decided for herself where and with whom she would live. There seems little doubt that she felt liberated, that she was ecstatic about the freedom she was enjoying.

In 1932, after several glorious years in France, she returned to Egypt, only to discover that her father had arranged a marriage for her. The man came from a good family and was himself wealthy and well-educated—a good match. And initially, Shafik accepted the idea, but the concept of arranged marriage offended her. She begged off, regretting the pain she brought her father, and sailed off to France to complete her studies and resume her life as a modern woman, quite comfortable in cosmopolitan Paris.

Her father had accepted her decisions, and she returned home summers to see him, Sha'wari, and other friends in Cairo. In 1935, she threw down the gauntlet to the mullahs. For the first time, Muslim women chose to compete to represent Egypt in the Miss Universe contest and Sharik, by all accounts a very beautiful woman, decided to enter the competition. She did not win, but the woman to whom she was runner-up went on to win the Miss Universe title. Her biographer, Cynthia Nelson, explains that Shafik felt that she had proven herself intellectually among the male scholars in Paris and was determined to demonstrate that she lacked nothing in the way of feminine attributes: The New Woman represented the unity of beauty and intellect. According to the traditionalists, she had violated the tenets of Islam, and an uproar followed in the press.

Her behavior clearly did not alienate Sha'rawi, who lent her summer home for the marriage of Shafik to a prominent journalist and feminist friend of Sha'rawi's. Shafik and her friends exulted in the marriage, perceiving it as a prototype for modern Egypt—a power couple who saw each other as equals. Unfortunately, it did not last. Like too many male supporters of feminism, the groom's preference for independent women did not include an independent wife. And back to Paris Shafik went, determined to be celibate.

The beautiful intellectual continued her work in philosophy and simultaneously tried to manage her love life to protect her reputation from the gossip endemic among Egyptian students in Paris. She was apparently in love with a French poet, but understood that the life she imagined for herself back home precluded a foreign husband. In 1937 she married a younger cousin, also a student in Paris. She saw him as a bridge back to Egypt, her best chance of coming to terms with the very different life she would have to live when she returned. Her brother could bring home an English bride without paying a price, but she recognized that the standards for women were different.

Originally her thesis was to be on aesthetic attitudes in ancient Egypt. Although she completed that project, she also began a thesis on religion and women's rights, for which she turned to Sha'rawi for material on the early women's movement in Egypt and the social reforms it won. Her studies had gained her insight into Western secular humanism and she hoped somehow to reconcile Western liberalism with Islam. She was searching for the path to equal rights for women in Muslim, specifically Egyptian, society.

In 1939, before she defended her thesis—and just before the outbreak of World War II—Shafik returned to Egypt, eager for a public role. Both religious conservatives determined to preserve harem traditions and members of her own family pressed her to conform to accepted cultural practices. Presumably, that meant staying home and having children. However, she and her husband needed money. She liked—and bought—more beautiful things than they could afford, and he had a taste for gambling. She needed work and hoped for an appointment to teach philosophy at the national university. Without a degree, she had no chance of such a position; she settled for an appointment as inspector of French language teaching in the secondary schools.

Concern over the war in Europe unsettled Shafik, largely out of fear that her thesis defense would be postponed indefinitely. In February 1940, she resigned from her position and went to Paris to defend her thesis. It went well, and her argument that the women's rights she advocated were consistent with Islam impressed committee members. With degree in hand, she returned once more to Cairo, confident of an appointment to the national university. Once again, it was not forthcoming. The university authorities perceived her as too controversial, a potential troublemaker, both for her reputation as a feminist agitator and as a beauty pageant contestant.

The next few years were trying for Shafik. Her beloved France was overrun by the Germans. Her relationship with Sha'rawi deteriorated. She was convinced that her ex-husband had turned Sha'rawi against her, but at times she seemed to think it was others in Sha'rawi's EFU entourage who were determined to keep her at a distance, presumably to keep her from inheriting the leader's mantle. Shafik was not the kind of person to ask herself if she might have offended her former patron. And so she ended up working for the Ministry of Education once more, depressed by her inability to land a position commensurate with her education and ambition. On the brighter side was the arrival of the first of her two daughters in 1942.

At some point during the war she developed a relationship with a powerful Egyptian princess who enlisted her to edit a literary and cultural magazine, *La Femme Nouvelle*, in French. Its target audience was manifestly the region's educated elite. It was not a promising route to leadership of the feminist movement, but it was the only opportunity commensurate with her talent and energy. The experience proved useful and in late 1945 she was able to publish her own magazine, *Bint al-Nil*, in Arabic. It was designed for middle-class Arab women and, in addition to the usual fare of women's magazines—fashions, nutrition, child care—she slipped in her jeremiads on women's rights, toned down, at least initially, by a journalist who worked with her.

By the late 1940s, Shafik's demands became more strident, and she aroused hostility among Islamists, who perceived her as too Western and secular, and among leftists contemptuous of her palace connections and her bourgeois literary pretensions. Undaunted, she demanded legislation to protect the rights of women and insisted that those who denied equality to women—most men—were misinterpreting the Koran. She saw nothing in the holy book that justified denying women the right to vote or to hold public office, nothing that allowed men as many wives as they chose or granted them the right to repudiate their wives capriciously and unilaterally. She became convinced that the only way to protect women was to elect some of them to Parliament, where they could fight for the necessary legislation and publicize their cause.

To this end, she founded a movement that evolved into a political party, the Bint al-Nil Union, as a means to liberate Egyptian women. Its stated goals were political equality for women and the elimination of illiteracy among women, but Shafik became increasingly radical. Frustrated by the inability of men to understand that the participation of educated women in public affairs would contribute to the well-being of the nation, she took action to dramatize her cause.

In February 1951, she led fifteen hundred women in a magnificently executed operation to storm the Egyptian Parliament. She declared the legislative body illegitimate because it excluded women. She demanded permission for women to participate in the nation's fight against the remnants of British colonialism and in politics generally, the reform of personal status laws to limit polygamy and the freedom of men to divorce their wives, and equal pay for equal work. The women refused to leave the building until promised that the prime minister would meet with a Shafik-led delegation. He reneged on the promise and she, to her delight, was brought up on charges. She was becoming a celebrity in the international media and looked forward to the opportunity to defend her cause. Although Muslim conservatives were eager to see her punished, denouncing her and her followers as Bolsheviks, enemies of Islam, and agents of imperialism, the case was eventually dropped by the government, which preferred to bury the issue.

Before the end of the year, an anti-British insurgency erupted in Egypt. Shafik saw another chance to advance her cause. She called on Egyptian women to join the struggle and organized the first female military unit in the country. Although there seems to have been a lot of posturing, some of her followers insisted they wanted to fight alongside the men. In January 1952, Shafik and some of her "troops" surrounded Barclays Bank in Cairo and shut it down for the day.

Relentless, she demanded the right of women to vote and hold office, despite a fatwa that declared voting was degrading to women and against their nature. She applied to be a candidate for Parliament and her papers, not unexpectedly, were rejected by the government on the grounds that only men were eligible. She argued that the government and the clerics were misinterpreting the Koran, noting that women voted in Pakistan. No one less than the Grand Mufti entered the fray, issuing a fatwa condemning the feminist movement in general and Shafik in particular. A less bold creature might have been intimidated, but not Shafik. Unfortunately, the government was unyielding—and it rejected all political rights for women.

In July, a military coup threw out the decadent King Faruq. Shafik dared to think that the Free Officers movement that seized control of the government would be receptive to her program and appealed directly to its leaders. She won official recognition for Bint al-Nil as a political party, the first time an Egyptian government officially accepted a role for women in politics. For the next year and a half, she remained optimistic. Women were allowed into the National Guard in 1953, and her campaign against illiteracy among women appeared to have government support. But her hopes were dashed in 1954 when the committee formed to write the new constitution was exclusively male.

Inspired by Gandhi—pacifism did not seem to come naturally—Shafik went on a hunger strike to protest the absence of women on the committee. She was joined by eight other women and attracted, as she anticipated, widespread media attention. If Egypt was to be free, she argued, women had to be free—and they could contribute greatly to the nationalist struggle. Unable to persuade the women to give up their hunger strike, the government hospitalized them. But Shafik had succeeded, Nelson demonstrates, in gaining a prominent place for women's issues in the nation's consciousness.

Hundreds of other women demonstrated in Cairo, demanding that the government yield to the strikers. Religious leaders called the women whores and demanded that they beaten by their husbands—a requirement of the Koran, they insisted. Telegrams came from all over Egypt and from abroad, generally supportive of Shafik and her followers. The hunger-strikers were joined by an American journalist, and students at American University in Cairo petitioned the government, arguing that a modern state could not deny half its citizens political rights.

Bowing to international as well as domestic pressure, the government promised, in writing, that women would receive full political rights in the new constitution. Shafik ended the strike and a few months later began a world lecture tour. In India, she was the guest of Prime Minister Nehru. And, indeed, the constitution, when finally promulgated in 1956, gave women the right to vote—for the first time in the Arab world.

Shafik was not satisfied with the constitution, noting that it made voting obligatory for men and not for women and that it made it more difficult for women to run for office. She questioned the sincerity of the government, and there was ample evidence that she was right to do so. Gamal Abdel Nasser had emerged openly as the nation's leader and strongman, and he had no use for civil society. His regime targeted feminist organizations, including the EFU and Bint al-Nil, bringing them under the Ministry of Social Affairs, where they were used for purposes of the state. The government controlled the travel of women and, in a markedly retrogressive step, required them to obtain the permission of their nearest male relative as a condition for being granted an exit visa.

Nasser's dictatorship outraged Shafik to the point where she overreached. In 1957, she decided to undertake another hunger strike, demanding an end to the dictatorship, freedom for all Egyptians, women as well as men—and, for good measure, a nationalist fillip—a demand that Israel be forced to sur-render Egyptian territory seized in the Suez War of 1956. Aware that the government would not hesitate to force an end to her strike, she chose to conduct it in the Indian embassy. Nehru ordered the embassy to look after her and to provide diplomatic cover when she needed medical attention. The press in India and the West celebrated her courage once again, and Nasser was humiliated. Obviously, he had no intention of surrendering power, and his security forces could hardly wait to get their hands on her.

Fortunately, at least for the short run, Nehru—with whom Nasser had a good working relationship as co-leaders of states that chose neutrality in the Cold War—persuaded the Egyptian government to settle for putting her under house arrest when she left the protection of the embassy. Her hunger strike gained nothing and resulted in the destruction of all copies of her magazine and her private papers, as the police raided her offices. Her arro-gance and the ease with which traditionalists could label her as a product of Western influence facilitated Nasser's determination to crush her.

Shafik lived in near-total seclusion for the remaining eighteen years of her life. She was allowed to travel after Nasser's death and visited her first grand-child in the United States in 1971 and again in 1973, but it seems evident that being banned abruptly from the activities that had given meaning to her life resulted in depression. Even the easing of restraints in the 1970s did not end her despair. She committed suicide in 1975.

Conditions for women in Egypt, probably better than anywhere else in the Arab world, have progressed little since Shafik's death. However, the efforts of Sha'rawi and Shafik won some educational rights and public roles that were unthinkable in the nineteenth century and that, regrettably, remain unthinkable in some Arab countries. Moreover, they galvanized a feminist movement that gained considerable freedom and public roles for women, raised issues, and created precedents that keep the fight for equality alive in Egypt. Divorce laws were relaxed in 2000, making it easier for women to end their marriages. But in that context, Suzanne Mubarak, the wife of Egypt's president, complained publicly that women remained the most underprivileged members of Egyptian society in education, health, and job training. A year later, on the fiftieth anniversary of Shafik's invasion of the Egyptian Parliament, Fayza Hassan, writing in the *Al-Ahram Weekly* (Cairo), left no doubt that the goal of equal status for women was still out of reach.

One woman to whom a friend pointed as an important Muslim feminist is Thoraya Ahmed Obaid, under-secretary-general of the United Nations and executive director of the UN Population Fund. It is truly remarkable to see a Saudi woman, product of the most conservative Arab state, center of the tribal culture that Manji and other Muslim feminists decry, heading a UN agency focused on empowering women. She established the first women's development program in western Asia in 1975 and has built partnerships between the United Nations and NGOs on women's issues. She has fought worldwide for every issue on the feminist agenda and quite possibly accomplished more that any other advocate of equality for women. At no time has she surrendered her conviction that religion is important in the promotion of human rights.

It will probably come as no surprise to Manji or any of my readers to learn that Dr. Obaid was educated in the United States, at Mills College and Wayne State University—from which she received her PhD. Nor will they be surprised to learn that of the many awards and honors she has received over the years, none come from Saudi Arabia. Muslim feminists have a tough fight ahead of them and they are not likely to make many gains in my lifetime, but, for the record, there are none more worthy of our esteem.

PART III

RACIAL EQUALITY

Jack Greenberg, NAACP Legal Defense Fund, Library of Congress, NYWT&S Collection, Prints & Photographs Division, LC-USZ62-134438

CHAPTER 6

Jack Greenberg and the
NAACP Legal Defense Fund

Of all the men and women I chose to include in this volume, Jack Greenberg is the one with whom I can most easily identify. He is also the man who chose a path I wish I had chosen for myself—and might well have, had I had any idea it existed.

Both of us were born, ten years apart, to Jewish families in the Bensonhurst section of Brooklyn. We were bar mitzvahed but were never observant Jews. We graduated from Columbia College after being awakened to the life of the mind by Columbia's magnificent core curriculum. We rejected the careers we had originally considered—accounting for Greenberg, psychiatry for me. At different points in our lives we served as naval officers in the Pacific—and we both studied Chinese. He considered Asian studies, but chose law. I considered law, but chose Asian studies. In the end, I wrote more books than he did, but his was the greater moral vision. He, of course, did far more for humanity—or I would be writing my memoirs instead of this book.

One important difference was probably in our families, in the environment in which we grew up. In his memoir he wrote of his family's commitment to fairness and justice and of their concern for the disadvantaged. My parents had little reason to believe they lived in a fair and just world, they believed *they* were the disadvantaged, and, had they they ever heard of him, they would have shared Hobbes's perception: It's a jungle out there.

At the core of Greenberg's life was the thirty-five years he spent with the NAACP Legal Defense Fund (LDF), an organization he joined in 1949 as a twenty-four-year-old graduate of Columbia Law School. He met the LDF's director, Thurgood Marshall, while working on an LDF project at the behest of Walter Gellhorn, one of his teachers. Upon graduating from law school like many, conceivably most, of his classmates, Greenberg intended to make some money first, and then serve worthy causes. Things didn't work out that way: The good works came first, the big bucks never did. Marshall was looking for an assistant, Gellhorn recommended Greenberg, and he went to work to fight Jim Crow, "the major evil" of the America into which he was born. Ultimately, after Marshall became a federal judge, Greenberg directed the LDF for twenty-three years.

Greenberg perceived a resemblance between anti-Semitism and the black experience in the United States, but not all of his fellow Jews shared his convictions. One of Greenberg's earliest cases came in Baltimore, Maryland, where the NAACP found the local Jewish community unsympathetic. When Juanita Mitchell, a civil rights lawyer leading NAACP efforts in the city, turned to Marshall for help, he sent Greenberg. She was skeptical, accepted him grudgingly, and never had any cause for regret. And Greenberg became part of the essentially black world of the civil rights movement, sleeping in segregated hotels, eating in segregated restaurants, living and working with those blacks willing to accept a white Jew as a brother. In 1953, in Washington, D.C., the nation's capital, African Americans could join him to eat in only two places: Union Station and the YMCA.

Marshall was pleased with Greenberg's work and sent him to Delaware, where he joined the state's only black lawyer in a case challenging school segregation. Presenting evidence of the disparity in the condition of buildings, grounds, and equipment, and the difference in quality of books and teachers, the two men convinced the Delaware court that the only schools available to African American children provided them with an inferior education and were unacceptable. The court ordered the students to be admitted to hitherto all-white schools. The state appealed the decision to the U.S. Supreme Court, where it was merged with cases arising from four other states.

Incredibly, at the age of twenty-seven, Greenberg was then called upon to argue his first case before the U.S. Supreme Court—surely one of the youngest lawyers ever to appear before the Court. And the case was part of the most important civil rights case of the twentieth century, none other than *Brown v. Board of Education* (1954). The Court decided unanimously to accept his contention—and that of his six colleagues, led by Marshall—that segregation, "separate but equal," was always unequal—and unconstitutional. The decision was the beginning of the end of legal apartheid in America, despite bitter resistance in the South and President Dwight Eisenhower's disinclination to force acceptance of the Court's decision. The case became a precedent for all claims to equal treatment—by women, the elderly, and the handicapped, as well as people of color. Greenberg went on to argue more than forty cases before the Supreme Court and hundreds in lower courts in the battle for civil rights in the United States.

Not surprisingly, given his legal training and profession, Greenberg saw the courts as the central arena for achieving peaceful social change. Step-by-step he would chip away at the Jim Crow laws upon which segregation depended, until the whole edifice collapsed. He was unprepared for and uneasy with direct action—the boycotts, sit-ins, and Freedom Rides that began with Rosa Parks's refusal to give up her seat on a bus to a white passenger in Montgomery, Alabama, in 1955. But legal defense was often needed and there were very few black lawyers in the south—only one each in Delaware, Alabama, and Louisiana. Greenberg and the LDF adjusted quickly to offer support to the activists. In 1963, the LDF, led then by Greenberg, was chosen by Martin Luther King Jr. to handle all cases in which King's Southern Christian Leadership Council was involved. J. Edgar Hoover's perception of Greenberg as subversive was thus confirmed. When Greenberg saw his FBI file years later, he discovered that the agency was aware of a plot by white racists to assassinate him, but never bothered to warn him. None of the threats to his life seem to have intimidated him.

How did a young white lawyer become the director of the LDF? It was a question raised frequently, often hostilely, by blacks in the civil rights movement. Certainly Greenberg's proven ability contributed to the choice—made by Thurgood Marshall. In 1961, President John F. Kennedy appointed Marshall to the Circuit Court of Appeals. At the time, Marshall, angry at his deputy, Robert Carter, passed him over and nominated Greenberg as his successor. The appointment was approved easily by the board of the LDF, but it was clear that the board of the NAACP would have preferred a black lawyer. In the years that followed, Greenberg would often find himself under attack from black militants. Derrick Bell complained that Greenberg ran the LDF as a "penthouse plantation." He implied that Greenberg operated as if he was endowed with "hereditary superiority," based, presumably on the color of his skin. Years later, in 1982, Bell supported a boycott by black students of a course on race and the law that Greenberg and Julius Chambers taught at Harvard, ostensibly because Greenberg was white (although Chambers, who succeeded him as director of the LDF, was not).

There were others who would not share my admiration of Greenberg, among them radicals who saw him as an establishment liberal, a liberal integrationist, and leaders of Jewish organizations opposed to affirmative action. Marshall had resigned from the National Lawyers Guild in the late 1940s, fearful that the Guild's presumed adherence to the line of the American Communist Party would damage the reputation of the LDF. When Greenberg took over the LDF, the Guild sought to renew its connection, but Greenberg and his board chose to avoid any organization-to-organization connection—although the LDF continued to work with individual Guild lawyers. Later, Greenberg was unwilling to take the case of Angela Davis or to align the LDF with the efforts of the Black Panthers, to the dismay of many of his staff members. He considered the Black Power movement unhelpful to the cause of civil rights. Greenberg and Martin Luther King shared an approach as well as a vision—and Greenberg was viewed with contempt by the same radicals who lost patience with King.

From another corner, the American Jewish community, initially strongly supportive of the civil rights movement, began to splinter once legal segregation ended. Greenberg perceived segregation to be only a part of the misery inflicted on blacks in America. Educational and employment opportunities had to be created. Greenberg accepted the need for busing to integrate schools and affirmative action as the remedy for a century of discrimination in the workplace. Jews were no more (or less) accepting of busing than other white parents. But tensions between Jews and blacks began to grow in the late 1960s as blacks burned Jewish-owned stores in New York and struggled to win control over ghetto schools in Brooklyn from teachers who were predominantly Jewish.

Shifting Jewish attitudes were reflected in the pages of *Commentary*, a leading intellectual journal funded by the American Jewish Committee and edited by Norman Podhoretz—another Brooklyn-born and Columbia-educated Jew. Podhoretz, who had grown up in the transitional Brownsville neighborhood, where poor Jews encountered poor blacks, had no use for the black self-image of victimhood: He remembered being victimized by black toughs. To Greenberg's surprise, major Jewish organizations opposed affirmative action for blacks, perceiving the kind of quota system that had been used to limit the advancement of Jews. Eventually, although Podhoretz and *Commentary* remained hostile, the American Jewish Committee was won over to the cause of affirmative action. But Podhoretz's view won the support of the B'nai B'rith's Anti-Defamation League—which fought Greenberg and affirmative action every step along the way, contributing greatly to the embitterment of relations between Jews and blacks in America.

The 1960s were clearly the most momentous years for the civil rights movement and required expansion of the staff of the LDF. Fortunately in the 1960s, for the *first* time, the organization was able to obtain support from major foundations. The LDF's caseload nearly tripled by 1965, and Greenberg added a dozen lawyers to the original five. By 1970 the LDF had twenty-eight staff lawyers and hundreds of cooperating lawyers around the country. And they were successful time after time when fighting for equal access to public accommodations, forcing all but the most die-hard segregationists to surrender on the issue by the end of the decade.

One unintended consequence of desegregation that Greenberg had failed to appreciate was the damage to blacks-only hotels that followed the opening of all hotels to black patrons. Similarly, the black community was very uneasy about integrating schools, fearful that black schoolteachers would lose out. As he came to realize, some members of the black middle class were hurt by his successes.

The victories of the LDF and the larger civil rights movement did not come easily during the presidency of John F. Kennedy. Greenberg was horrified by some of Kennedy's court appointments. Perhaps consciously balancing his appointment of Thurgood Marshall, Kennedy appointed Harold Cox to the Circuit Court of Appeals. Greenberg called Cox "possibly the most racist judge ever to sit on the federal bench." Lyndon Johnson proved to be a better friend to the movement. He not only drove the Civil Rights Act of 1964 and the Voting Rights Act of 1965 through Congress but also agreed to clear all judicial appointments in the South with the LDF.

Greenberg's vision unquestionably transcended the need to end segregation: He never believed the fight for civil rights ended when blacks could join whites in restaurants, hotels, ballparks, or at the voting booth. Nor did he see civil rights as an issue of whites versus blacks. He insisted that civil rights were a human question, and he demonstrated his commitment to *human* rights again and again in the years that followed. Later in life he wrote that if he were starting anew, he would study international human rights law.

One source of discomfort for Greenberg was his decision to live in suburban Connecticut, where his children attended excellent and safe schools that were utterly lacking in diversity. It was a dilemma similar to that which American political figures of all backgrounds had to face when they came to work in Washington. President Jimmy Carter was among the few who sent their children to generally poor and largely black public schools in that city. The overwhelming majority chose to send their children to private schools, or chose to live outside the city in suburban Maryland or Virginia. Greenberg found solace in the fact that Thurgood Marshall sent his children to the elite Dalton School in New York, as did his black colleague and later great judge, Constance Motley. There probably are not many among us who would put our children at risk to showcase our principles.

At home Greenberg founded the Mexican-American Legal Defense Fund; represented Hispanics, Native Americans, and poor whites; and fought capital punishment. Looking abroad, he founded Asia Watch to try to improve the lot of hundreds of millions of people oppressed by rulers who insisted that Asians were different, that Asian values did not include Western conceptions of human rights. In 1978 he went to South Africa to set up an organization that would function like the LDF in the fight against apartheid. In 1983, he flew to the Philippines to investigate the status of human rights there after the murder of Benito Aquino. He was one of the original members of Helsinki Watch and traveled in Eastern Europe to assist human rights advocates in the fight against totalitarian oppression. Wherever men and women suffered, Greenberg was one of the knights who rode to their assistance, trying desperately to use the law to ameliorate their misery.

When he retired from the LDF in 1984 to accept a position at Columbia Law School, he was proud of the superb organization he was leaving and wistful about some of the goals he had failed to accomplish. He knew the problems he confronted in America and internationally would continue to exist, perhaps, as Thomas More once said, until all men are good—and that will not be for some long time. At Columbia he was able to establish a Human Rights Law internship, training young lawyers to carry on the fight. But he had been determined to end capital punishment in the United States—a practice that leaves the country in the company of some of the most sinister nations in the world—and he failed. He was also saddened by the divisions that had emerged between blacks and Jews, and troubled by the inability of the Anti-Defamation League to appreciate the importance of affirmative action to blacks. And perhaps most of all, he remained troubled by the continued horrors of life in the ghettos, by the continued existence of a black underclass.

No, Jack Greenberg could not work miracles, although the movie based on the work he did alongside Thurgood Marshall (in which Greenberg is played by Tobey Maguire of *Spider-Man* fame) might suggest otherwise. Nonetheless, the world is surely a better place for his efforts. I wish I felt as proud of my own.

Martin Luther King Jr., Library of Congress, Prints & Photographs Division, NYWT&S Collection, LC-USZ62-122993

CHAPTER 7

Martin Luther King Jr. and the Struggle for Racial Equality

Martin Luther King Jr. was a notorious womanizer and a serial plagiarist. How can I justify including him among my "profiles in humanity"?

The reader may have noticed that although we have reason to assume that Pope John XXIII abstained and that Gandhi was reasonably well-behaved, several of the others about whom I've written were more likely to view extracurricular sexual activity as an essential part of their mental and physical maintenance. Obviously, I align myself with those who do not consider private vice an obstacle to public virtue. As an academic historian, though, I find plagiarism much more troubling. Some years ago, writing about King's plagiarism, John Higham said, "The greatest American spokesman for rights failed a test of responsibility, from which no historian can grant exceptions." To be sure, I am not empowered to grant exceptions, but for my purposes, Higham's reference to the "greatest American spokesman for rights" is the operative phrase. And I can think of no one greater.

King's story is so well known that I considered omitting a sketch of his life and contribution, but concluded that I could not. No one did more to prick the boil of racial tension in the United States. No one was more successful in persuading white Americans of their guilt for centuries of discrimination against black Americans—and of the need for white America to end the travesty of segregation. He failed to end racism in his country and he failed to gain equality for black Americans, but the progress toward a more humane response to people of color in my lifetime has been extraordinary, however short the effort has fallen. And to the extent that majority support was necessary for forward movement in the American political system, it was King who forged that majority.

My own support for King and his goal was based on what I had learned in the summer of 1954, when I worked at a New Hampshire resort along with a troop of African American students from Hampton Institute. Only a few weeks earlier, the Supreme Court had condemned segregation in *Brown v. Board of Education*, but we lived in separate dormitories, segregated by race, and we were employed differently—whites in the dining room serving guests, and blacks, with the exception of a dishwasher, outside keeping the grounds. Contact between blacks and guests were minimal, but I had my first intensive encounter with black college students (although my fraternity at Columbia had been expelled from the national organization for pledging a black member just two years earlier). In brief, I developed a close friendship with one Hampton student. He and I and a white woman who had graduated Phi Beta Kappa from Boston University spent much of our leisure together. I became more than a little interested in her, but found to my astonishment that she had a long-standing relationship with my black friend. How could she choose a black man over me? And then it occurred to me: He was smarter, a better athlete, and better looking—why the hell not? For the first time, I understood the racism implicit in my question.

The United States has never lived up to Jefferson's words about equality in the Declaration of Independence, but it has inched closer over the centuries. Every year on the Fourth of July, speakers repeat those words and set a standard by which Americans must judge themselves. And in the years preceding the country's entry into World War II, most of us were proud to see a black American, Jesse Owens, triumph in the Olympics over which Adolf Hitler presided—and were delighted when Joe Louis, our "Brown Bomber," knocked out Germany's Max Schmeling. As a devout fan of the Brooklyn Dodgers, I was ecstatically happy when Jackie Robinson joined the team in 1947 and led it to a pennant. Baseball was being integrated: Maybe we were on our way to creating a more equitable society.

There was little in King's youth to foreshadow the role he would play in the late 1950s and 1960s. He grew up in a relatively privileged home with loving parents. His father was a highly respected minister and a stern disciplinarian. In a story King told frequently in later years, he claimed his first experience with racism came when he entered elementary school. A white boy with whom he had played as a preschooler was forced by his parents to end the friendship as the boys went off to their separate schools. King was hurt and angry at white people, as he came to understand what had transpired. Subsequently he tasted other bitter fruits of segregation, such as being forced to give up his seat on a bus to a white.

He was an able student; he graduated from high school at the age of fifteen and went on to all-black Morehouse College. At Morehouse, he quickly learned that his high school education had been poor and he could not easily work at college level. That may explain the temptation to plagiarize. His performance at Morehouse was mediocre, but the faculty seems to have sensed an innate ability and recommended him for graduate work.

To what extent his ideas and visions were shaped at Morehouse is not clear. In his autobiography, he remembered reading Thoreau's "Civil Disobedience" and becoming fascinated by the concept of nonviolent resistance. His classes and readings led him to question his religious education, as many of us did. But before he graduated he came to terms with biblical teaching, persuaded he could separate the truths from the myths. Ultimately he decided to enter the ministry and, at nineteen, went off to Philadelphia to study at Crozer Theological Seminary, an integrated institution.

In intercollegiate meetings while at Morehouse and again at Crozer, King had extensive contact with white students, and his anger at whites subsided. There were even reports that he fell in love with a white woman at Crozer but was persuaded that marriage would destroy both of them—and especially his prospects for getting a church. He recalled reading Walter Rauschenbusch and other theorists of the social gospel and moving on to the realism of Reinhold Niebuhr. He heard A. J. Muste lecture on pacifism—which he rejected—and Mordecai Johnson, president of Howard University, on Gandhi and nonviolent resistance—which he found appealing. Several of his biographers have been skeptical about King's recollections, suggesting he was less influenced by his studies—at which he was less than conscientious—than by traditions within the black church. Certainly his interest in Gandhi did not ripen until much later. Most likely, he responded to readings and lectures as most of us do, most of the time: He was attracted primarily to ideas that were consistent with the values that he had already internalized, inculcated by his parents and the church he had attended.

Nonetheless, it is evident that the books and articles he read at school and the lectures he attended enabled him to articulate those values and to conceive of means by which he might act upon them. Reading in the social gospel confirmed his sense that religious leaders had to be concerned about the social and economic well-being of their flocks, not merely their souls. Niebuhr reminded him of the existence of evil and of the ineffectiveness of pacifism in the face of evil. Muste could not persuade him to the contrary. As he looked for the means to combat injustice, he found the idea of nonviolent resistance promising, and attributing it to Gandhi gave it more weight.

After Crozer, from which he graduated as valedictorian, he decided to enroll in a PhD program at Boston University's School of Theology—seeking a degree in philosophy rather than theology. He may have contemplated an academic position, but more likely sought the cachet that a doctorate would give him, a means of distinguishing himself from the ordinary black preachers of the South. He was moving away from the emotionalism he associated with the black church, preparing for a ministry that would be more respectable intellectually.

At the university, he established himself as a leader among black students, behaving in the eyes of some as though he were a prince. He apparently had more money available than most, had his own car, and reputedly loved to party. He devoted a great deal of time to his social life and perhaps a lot less than he should have to his studies. Nonetheless, his inherent ability impressed his teachers, and they overlooked the fact that some of his papers had been plagiarized. He performed well on his doctoral exams and then accepted an appointment as minister to the elite Dexter Avenue Baptist Church in a middle-class black neighborhood in Montgomery, Alabama. There was still a dissertation to be written.

While still at the university, he met and, despite his father's reservations, married Coretta Scott, an Antioch graduate studying at the New England Conservatory of Music. She appears to have been his intellectual equal and she shared his concerns about racial inequality and the maldistribution of wealth in America. But she was not eager to return to the segregated South, and she does not seem to have been prepared for the role in which he cast her: as the stay-at-home mother of their children. And his friends have suggested that over time she was not able or willing to meet his sexual needs. But in September 1954, King began his pastorate in Montgomery.

Over the next several years, he attended to a very demanding congregation, emerged as a civil rights leader, and managed to complete a dissertation, parts of which were plagiarized from an earlier dissertation written for the same professor at Boston University—who obviously did not read it very carefully. The pressures on King in the mid-1950s easily explain why he chose to cheat—but they do not justify his actions. And this disgraceful behavior is aggravated by evidence that he had been guilty of plagiarism before. There can be no doubt that he knew what he was doing.

And then there was Rosa Parks, who on December 1, 1955, refused to move to allow a white passenger to take her seat on a Montgomery, Alabama, bus. Mrs. Parks was an NAACP activist, but her act had not been planned. She was simply tired that day and fed up with being pushed around. Her arrest and conviction for disobeying a segregation law triggered a massive movement in Montgomery—and Martin Luther King Jr. found himself pushed to the forefront of that movement.

On the eve of Mrs. Parks's aborted bus ride, King was a highly promising young minister whose principal aspirations were to demonstrate that he was a cut above other black ministers and that he was in full control of his church—and to finish his dissertation. There can be no doubt of his commitment to racial equality—he pressed his congregation to join the NAACP—or his leadership qualities, recognized by his classmates at Boston University. But he did not set out to be a civil rights leader and did not originate the idea of a bus boycott to protest segregation on the city's buses. The proposal came from E. D. Nixon, a Pullman porter who was past president of the Alabama NAACP. It was also Nixon and his associates who created the Montgomery Improvement Association (MIA) to manage the protest and negotiations with the city's white leadership. Perceiving in King an articulate, well-educated man who could both inspire local blacks and communicate with whites, they offered him the presidency of the Association. As one biographer, David Garrow, has written, leadership was thrust upon King.

King's first speech to the black community demonstrated the wisdom of the elders who chose him to speak for them. He knew he had to be sufficiently militant to arouse his audience to make the sacrifices necessary to bring the white power structure to heel. But also knew he had to couch his call to action in language that would not frighten whites. He spoke of democracy and the right of blacks to live in dignity, of the moral courage to stand up for rights promised by the Constitution—and of Christian love. He asked blacks to stay off the buses until a more equitable arrangement could be reached with the bus company and city leaders. To the dismay of the NAACP, King and his colleagues were not asking for the abolition of segregated buses, but merely for a few black drivers and a fairer allotment of seats, especially on buses that went through black neighborhoods. To King's delight the response of the black community was nearly unanimous compliance with the boycott. Hundreds trudged long distances to work. Black taxi drivers charged only bus fare, and car pools were arranged.

Despite the obvious moderation of the MIA demands, city officials would yield nothing. They did meet with King and other representatives of the MIA, but it was evident that they would countenance no challenge to absolute white authority. Day after day, week after week, month after month, the boycott continued. The bus company, sustaining hemorrhaging losses, was prepared to deal, but city officials would not allow it. The police began to harass the boycotters, forcing taxis to charge full fare and arresting and jailing King for speeding, but far worse were the threatening phone calls. And then one night, King's house was struck by a bomb. The threats had to be taken seriously: there were people out there willing to kill blacks who claimed equality, blacks who threatened the existing white monopoly of power. Friends found him shaken, but he believed God had chosen him for the role and he could not turn back.

An Alabama grand jury indicted King and other boycott leaders for violating an anti-boycott ordinance, and he was subsequently convicted. The case drew national attention and comparisons to Gandhi's nonviolent methods of attacking British imperialism in India. King expressed admiration for Gandhi, but at the time knew little about Gandhi's campaigns. He later claimed he had studied Gandhi for years, but the techniques used to fight segregation in Montgomery, the passive resistance to white power, were an obvious response of an otherwise powerless people—and were probably honed by outside opponents of segregation, such as Bayard Rustin.

It was soon evident in the course of 1956 that the Montgomery boycott had become a symbol of the fight against racism in America—and that an eloquent, charismatic young minister named Martin Luther King Jr. was becoming a national figure, the voice of that struggle. As anticipated, he had the ability, essential to the cause, to win over white audiences, to persuade a national majority that the Negro was entitled to all the rights of citizenship that inhered in the Constitution—at least as long as the movement was focused on the South.

In November 1956, the U.S. Supreme Court declared that a South Carolina law mandating segregated seating was unconstitutional. The Montgomery city administration persisted in its resistance to desegregation, rejecting bus company efforts to abandon segregation and employing all sorts of dubious legal maneuvers to avoid compliance. Finally, in December, the city fathers grudgingly surrendered and segregation on Montgomery buses ended, as did the boycott. A few days later, local racists acknowledged King's leadership role with a shotgun blast through the front door of his home.

King came to understand that the dangers to him were very great, that as he came to symbolize the movement for racial equality, he would become a prime target for assassination. That knowledge, added to the responsibilities he bore as a civil rights leader, changed the man. School friends who had not seen him for several years thought he had aged significantly. Of far greater import were revelations of tremendous moral courage, of a man who profoundly believed he was doing God's work and that his life was in God's hands. The sense that few men and women obtain of having been chosen for a mission that they alone can accomplish is exhilarating—and perhaps common to several of those of whom I write. Although he was never able to give up his lust for sexual activity, even when he knew his enemies were documenting his transgressions, he was no longer the Boston playboy and dishonest graduate student. Millions of black Americans knew his name, followed him, and counted on him, and he was prepared to give his life for them. Greatness had been thrust upon him, and he had transformed himself into the man who could carry that burden.

Over and over again, King told his followers that they had won a victory for democracy and justice—not a victory over the white man. They had appealed successfully to the consciences of those who had exploited them and demonstrated the value of nonviolent resistance. He never lost sight of the value of white guilt to his cause—and he never forgot that he needed white support to reach the movement's goals.

King's prominence irritated other black leaders, not least Roy Wilkins of the NAACP. The leadership of the NAACP preferred to progress through legal action and pointed to the success of its Legal Defense and Educational Fund, the work of Thurgood Marshall, Jack Greenberg, and their associates. The tactic of nonviolent resistance, of mass action, worried them. Not least, the NAACP and other black organizations were troubled by King's establishment of the Southern Christian Leadership Conference, fearing that the SCLC would draw funds away from them. Nonetheless, in 1957, the NAACP awarded him its top honor, the Spingarn Medal.

In March 1957, King was invited to Ghana to join in the celebration of that nation's independence. He began to see connections between the struggle of African and Asian peoples against imperialism and the civil rights movement in the United States. His followers, like the revolutionaries of color in distant countries, were seeking freedom and dignity. He may well have seen himself in a role similar to that of the Ghanian leader Kwame Nkrumah. He also was quick to recognize the problems the U.S. government would have when diplomats from black African countries began to encounter racial discrimination. He perceived that the success of the civil rights movement was essential to what came to be called American "soft power" in the ideological confrontation with communism.

For the next several years, King focused on building support sufficient to get a civil rights bill passed in Congress. Southern congressmen were able to block all such efforts, and the Eisenhower administration made no effort to push for legislation. Racial justice was not one of the issues that engaged the president. King and other movement leaders understood that they could not change the South until black Southerners were able to exercise their right to vote. When substantial numbers of blacks could vote, politicians were more likely to be responsive to their demands. Indeed, there were areas in the South where blacks were the majority and would be able to elect black officials or friendly whites. King and other black leaders finally won a meeting with Eisenhower in June

1958, but they left empty-handed and discouraged by the president's apparent ignorance of and disinterest in their issues.

King received a warmer reception in India, to which he was invited by the Gandhi National Memorial Fund at the initiative of Harris Wofford, a white civil rights activist and Gandhian—the first white to graduate from Howard University's law school—and subsequent adviser to John F. Kennedy. In India, Prime Minister Nehru invited the King party to dinner and expressed warm support for King's efforts. It was on this trip that King received intensive schooling on Gandhi's career and methods, in part from surviving members of Gandhi's entourage.

In February 1960, four black students from North Carolina A&T College demonstrated that King was far from the only American black inspired by the liberation movements sweeping Africa. Young blacks were growing restive, dissatisfied by the pace of change in the United States. These four students decided to sit down at a lunch counter in Woolworth's in Greensboro, North Carolina, and to demand service—and refused to leave when only whites were served. They were joined by other students the next day, and the sit-in movement spread across the city and into neighboring states. Neither King nor any other black leader had been consulted. They would have to run faster if they were going to continue to lead. King went to North Carolina to try to help the students coordinate their efforts. He lectured them on the theme that the struggle was against injustice, not against white people. It's unlikely that he convinced many of them, but when SNCC (Student Nonviolent Coordinating Committee) was formed, both the name of the organization and the invitation for King to serve as an adviser were hopeful signs.

King was trying to focus on the presidential election campaign, hoping to gain commitments to civil rights legislation from both parties. Initially he thought Nixon, with whom he'd had occasional contact, would be more supportive than Eisenhower had been—and certainly King's father leaned toward the Republican candidate. Kennedy's record on civil rights in the Senate had not satisfied King. But it was Kennedy who risked alienating white voters by indicating his support for him. The two men had met in June 1960, and King came away from the meeting better disposed toward the young Massachusetts senator. He thought Kennedy just might provide the presidential leadership needed to protect voting rights and push for equal housing for blacks. When King was arrested in Atlanta for participating in a sit-in and sentenced to four months in prison for violating parole, it was Kennedy who called Coretta and promised to help. Nonetheless, King refused to endorse Kennedy formally, as requested by several of the candidate's aides—although he left no doubt in the minds of his followers of his gratitude to Kennedy.

Papa King went further, declaring he would vote for the Democrat. In October 1961, Kennedy invited the younger King to the White House.

The Freedom Rides, organized by the Congress of Racial Equality (CORE) in May 1961, provided further evidence that young blacks in the civil rights movement were impatient with King's leadership. The original plan was for an integrated group to travel from Washington, D.C., to New Orleans, challenging segregated facilities at bus terminals along the way. CORE's leaders anticipated a violent response from hostile Southerners that would gain international attention and force the U.S. government to step in. After a relatively peaceful start, the first two buses were attacked in May in Anniston, Alabama. Some of the passengers were beaten and a bus set on fire. The remaining bus went on to Birmingham, where passengers were attacked as they left the bus.

The Freedom Riders were getting the attention they wanted, but they could not get a bus driver to carry them to their next destination. A new group set out from Nashville, Tennessee, for Birmingham and was arrested immediately upon arrival and run out of town by the soon-to-be-notorious police commissioner, "Bull" Connor. The next day, protected by state troopers, they were able to ride a bus from Birmingham to Montgomery, but there was no police protection upon their arrival and they were beaten by white thugs. At this point King flew back from Chicago to address a huge rally at a church—which was quickly surrounded by hostile whites. Conceivably, it was only the appearance of the National Guard, at the behest of Attorney General Robert Kennedy, that kept the mob from setting fire to the church. The next day the Freedom Riders decided to continue on to Mississippi and told King that he was morally obligated to ride with them. He would not—and seeing them off at the bus station did not assuage their disappointment. And when Robert Kennedy requested that the Interstate Commerce Commission (ICC) ban segregation at terminals for interstate buses, an order that did not become effective until November, King was ready to move on, even if CORE would not.

In December 1961, it was an action by SNCC in Albany, Georgia, that pulled King into a confrontation neither he nor the traditional black leadership there had sought. Despairing of the approach of the older local leaders, young SNCC organizers focused on black high school and college students in the community, ultimately forcing their elders to organize a test of the city's compliance with the ICC order. SNCC and the NAACP were competing to direct the civil rights movement in Albany. The arrest of Freedom Riders who arrived by train triggered demonstrations and more arrests. It was time to call in the cavalry. King agreed to come down.

Efforts to negotiate with city officials failed, and King saw no alternative to leading a march to city hall. After refusing an order to disperse, he and hundreds of marchers were arrested and jailed. Negotiations followed and a tentative agreement was reached for the release of all prisoners and the creation of a biracial committee contingent upon a sixty-day moratorium on demonstrations. The city's offer split the black activists, but they voted to accept. A local black leader announced that the city had promised to desegregate all terminal facilities, but the mayor quickly disabused everyone of that notion by announcing he had made no concessions and that there was no formal agreement. The city did not intend to bend in the slightest to the civil rights movement, and the episode at Albany was perceived widely as a defeat for the movement generally and for King personally. King, trying to make the proverbial silk purse out of a sow's ear, claimed valuable lessons had been learned. And by now the divisions within the movement were readily apparent.

In July 1962, King was found guilty of the charges for which he had been arrested in Albany the previous December and opted to serve forty-five days in jail rather than pay the fine. He was persuaded that accepting imprisonment would best serve the cause, but he was outsmarted by the mayor, who ordered his release, alleging that the fine had been paid by a nonexistent "well-dressed Negro." Albany's white leaders did not want King sitting in their jail attracting every civil rights leader in the country and provoking mass demonstrations.

But King did not go home, and the movement employed sit-ins, boycotts, and more demonstrations seeking to win concessions from the city. Unhappily the city won a federal restraining order against King and other black leaders, barring mass demonstrations. He felt he had to obey the injunction, further alienating younger black leaders. The SNCC staff in Albany demanded that the movement ignore what it deemed an unjust ruling and objected to what they considered to be his usurpation of leadership in the city. The movement's lawyers, however, persuaded an appellate court judge to dissolve the restraining order and King was free to resume his efforts. Unfortunately, before he returned from court, the arrest of a group of marchers triggered small-scale black violence, playing into the hands of the police.

After a day of penance for the transgression against his insistence on nonviolence, King resumed efforts to negotiate with the city and was again refused and arrested. Pressure began to build on President Kennedy to take action, and the president spoke out in favor of the movement's efforts to secure civil rights for its people peacefully. But hard-liners in the city leadership would not budge and the black community lost heart. Faith in King was diminished. In the absence of white-on-black violence, the movement's tactics proved ineffective.

King then turned his attention to Birmingham, Alabama. There he could count on Bull Connor to respond brutally to black pressures—and in Birmingham he and the SCLC would not be hampered by incessant squabbling with the NAACP and SNCC. The NAACP had been labeled a "foreign corporation" and banned from operating in Alabama. SNCC had no base there. But King also understood that his life would be in danger in Birmingham.

Connor responded to marchers and demonstrations as anticipated. King was jailed for refusing to obey an injunction against marching, high school demonstrators—the "Children's Crusade"—were driven off with dogs and fire hoses, and the movement attained the national media coverage it wanted. The president called Coretta to assure her that King was safe, and Robert Kennedy warned Alabama newspaper editors that King was their last hope for peaceful change. When the business community chose to meet the movement's demands, outraged segregationists bombed the motel where King had been staying. As violence escalated, the president sent in federal troops to maintain order. Nationally, black organizations came together, however briefly, to provide both moral and financial support. And contributions came to the SCLC from all over the world. Birmingham, thanks to Bull Connor and others of his ilk, gave King and the civil rights movement the impetus they had been denied in Albany. If there had been any doubters before, after Birmingham King was perceived nationally and internationally as the movement's leader.

In August 1963, King led the March on Washington at which he gave his "I have a dream" speech, which resonated across the country. He had originally intended the march to put pressure on the president, but in June, in response to Governor George Wallace's symbolic action to block two black students from enrolling at the University of Alabama, Kennedy gave a televised address calling for an end to racism and promising to propose a civil rights bill to Congress. King redirected his efforts toward Capitol Hill. The president left no doubt that he would prefer that the march be canceled and the NAACP came aboard hesitantly and grudgingly, unhappy about the preeminence of King and the SCLC. More than a hundred thousand people joined the march, many of them white. Afterward, King and other leaders, including Walter Reuther of the United Auto Workers, met with the president at the White House.

The success of the March on Washington and the belated national focus on issues of civil rights buoyed King's spirits—and the best was yet to come. *Time* chose him as its 1963 "Man of the Year." After Kennedy's assassination, President Lyndon Johnson asked King to support his "War on Poverty."

King was eager to improve the lives of poor whites, who would not otherwise accept affirmative action for blacks. In October 1964, he was awarded the Nobel Peace Prize. Accepting the award in Oslo he preached nonviolent resistance not only to racism but also in support of disarmament. He was a world-renowned figure, whose words would be heard on all the major issues of the day. It would have been hard for him not to see himself as chosen by his God to accomplish the tasks before him.

There were, however, numerous clouds threatening to rain on his parade. Coretta was not happy. He continued to shunt her aside to look after his children and was rarely home. Quite likely, she was aware of or at least suspected his womanizing. She was also disappointed by his refusal to keep any of the Nobel Prize money for the family. John F. Kennedy's assassination underscored the threat to his own life. The FBI, whose leader, J. Edgar Hoover, was intensely hostile to King, sent him a tape of a drunken orgy in which he had participated and suggested he commit suicide. Garrow quotes him as contending that "fucking's a form of anxiety reduction." Black Muslims threw eggs at him when he tried to address them. And he was constantly struggling with the NAACP and SNCC over money and tactics.

In the years that he had left, there was great progress on civil rights, especially in the South, but for King personally things went poorly. LBJ's war in Vietnam troubled him deeply, and he felt compelled to speak out against it. His venture into foreign affairs and his criticism of the administration's policies alienated the president, a Southerner with a profound commitment to support for King's fight against racism. Some of King's supporters, black and white, feared he was diluting his message and weakening the movement. Others had long believed he was too moderate. The black power movement was gaining momentum with young blacks, and any step King might take to reach out to them would likely increase tensions with the NAACP. His efforts to obtain jobs and decent housing for blacks in the North were constantly frustrated. The nation might support him against the brutality of Southern racists, but it was not prepared to follow him in a restructuring of the economic and social order or on Cold War policies in Southeast Asia or anywhere else. No wonder friends found him frequently depressed.

Perhaps his last great triumph came in Selma, Alabama, in 1965, when state troopers and police assaulted protestors and thugs attacked out-of-state reporters and photographers, providing the kind of attention upon which the movement thrived. The goal of the movement, once the Civil Rights Bill of 1964 had been passed and a sympathetic Lyndon Johnson had been reelected, was voter registration. Blacks had to be free to exercise their right to vote, unencumbered by needlessly complicated literacy tests or intimidation by the Ku Klux Klan and other white racists. Johnson seemed to be hesitant about introducing a voting rights bill, and movement leaders were determined to force his hand.

SNCC had been conducting a voter registration drive in Selma for several years, with minimal success and little national attention. In November 1964, a Selma activist urged the SCLC to come to Selma, claiming that SNCC's commitment was fading. King and his advisers decided to use Selma as a starting point for action across Alabama. The local sheriff, Jim Clark, was a notorious hot-tempered racist who could be expected to reprise Bull Connor's role, behaving viciously and intensifying support for the movement across the nation. He did not disappoint.

Early in January 1965, King appeared in Selma to launch the SCLC's voter registration drive. He had no expectation of gaining voting rights for Selma's blacks through marches or other nonviolent demonstrations. His purpose was to provoke white-on-black violence and generate moral outrage. Over the next several weeks, as marchers attempted to register to vote, cameras recorded Clark and his men beating protesters and roughly dragging them off to jail—where, as King noted, more blacks could be found than were registered to vote.

On March 7, six hundred demonstrators, mostly local blacks, led by SNCC's national chairman and an SCLC organizer, began a march from Selma to Montgomery to demand voting rights and an end to attacks on protesters. As they crossed the bridge over the Alabama River, they were met by state troopers and a posse raised by Sheriff Clark. Ignoring an order to disperse, they were immediately attacked with tear gas, billy clubs, cattle prods, and bull whips, and run down by horsemen. Some were thrown off the bridge. The film footage of the attack shocked television audiences across the country, and volunteers began to pour in to Selma.

King returned to Selma the next day and despite his misgivings, pleas from the Justice Department and Jack Greenberg of the NAACP-LDF, and a federal court ban, determined to lead another march on March 9. At virtually the last minute, he reached an agreement with President Johnson's representative to turn the marchers around after they crossed the bridge in return for an assurance that they would not be attacked. As they approached the troopers, King informed the troopers that his people would conduct prayers. Then they sang "We Shall Overcome" and turned back—outraging SNCC, further undermining that organization's trust in King's leadership. That night, several white ministers who had joined the march were attacked by local whites and one of them subsequently died from the beating.

Pressure mounted on the White House as pickets demanded federal intervention and sympathy marches were held in several Northern cities. On March 13, with Alabama governor George Wallace present, Johnson gave a press conference in which he declared his support for the Selma marchers. On March 15, on national television, he announced to the American people his intention to give the voting rights bill King and other movement leaders craved to the Congress. Selma, he declared, deserved to be ranked alongside Lexington, Concord, and Appomattox as a major battle in the fight for freedom in the United States. And he ended his address by promising that "we shall overcome" bigotry and injustice in our country.

On March 21, after the court had lifted the ban on marches, King led three thousand men and women from all over the country, including forty of America's leading historians, across the bridge from Selma to Montgomery. Several hundred completed the fifty-four-mile trip and were greeted by thousands of supporters when they reached Montgomery. It took several more months and more tragedy before Congress passed the Voting Rights Act, but the movement had achieved its goal and to most Americans, King was the symbol of its success.

The spring of 1965 was also notable for the assassination of Malcolm X. King and the charismatic Black Muslim leader were far apart in their approaches. King was troubled by Malcolm's preaching of hate toward whites and his anti-Semitism. Malcolm was contemptuous of King's willingness to collaborate with white liberals and his vision of an integrated society in which the promise of equality would be realized. But Malcolm's murder was a sharp reminder to King of his own mortality, and that was underscored by a warning from the U.S. attorney general of indications of plots against him.

In August, rioting broke out in the Watts neighborhood of Los Angeles. After rumors of police brutality swept the community, young blacks attacked the police and passing cars driven by whites. Stores were looted, cars and buildings set afire. It took nearly a week for the police and National Guard to restore order—and not before thirty-four people were killed, thousands injured, and hundreds of buildings destroyed. King flew out to Watts and was appalled by the damage and the attitude of the young men who had ignored his teachings of nonviolent resistance. Proud that they had stood up to the police, they were in no mood to listen to him. The hero of Selma and Montgomery was just another "Uncle Tom" to them. The striking gains that the civil rights movement had attained, especially during the Johnson presidency, struck militants as too little, too late. King had little if any influence over them. His time had passed.

In his remaining years, he pursued two intensely frustrating causes: opposition to the war in Vietnam and equality for blacks in Northern cities. His emergence as a major figure in the antiwar movement irritated the president, troubled members of his own board at the SCLC, and worried many of his supporters who feared his peace activities would prove detrimental to his civil rights leadership. He insisted there was a connection between his concern for the well-being of the poor, white as well as black, and his opposition to the war. Funds that could be used for Johnson's War on Poverty were being diverted and wasted in the sordid war in Vietnam.

His efforts to fight for social justice in the North accomplished little. He understood that Northern whites were quick to rally behind him when he was confronting the brutality of Bull Connor and Jim Clark, but they were not genuine believers in equality for blacks—certainly not in their backyards. And when he did win concessions from the likes of Chicago mayor Richard Daley, black militants accused him of selling out. He could not stop violent disruptions in the cities, and increasingly he found that he was not being taken seriously by his audiences. He was heckled, laughed at, and ignored by the very people he was trying to help.

Stokely Carmichael, the SNCC leader, began calling for "black power" and brushed aside King's fears of alienating white supporters. CORE turned against him. Desperately and unsuccessfully he continued to seek some way to satisfy black militants without losing the support of black moderates and whites. He was tired, losing confidence, depressed, and exhausted also by the FBI's efforts to intimidate him with threats to reveal his sexual escapades. Conceivably, Coretta had had enough of his extracurricular activities and was pressing him to desist.

He soldiered on to Memphis to support the striking black garbage collectors. His associates thought he had been buoyed by the response to his last speech on April 3, 1968. The next night, he was shot and killed by James Earl Ray.

Martin Luther King Jr. became a great moral leader accidentally. He was in the right place at the right time, and he was pushed into a leadership role. He knew the cause was just and he came to believe he was serving God's will—which gave him strength he never knew he had. Like most great men and women, he was no saint. He never had the willpower to refrain from activities he believed sinful. He atoned for his sins by persuading white America to begin to provide justice for black Americans. They have not yet reached the Promised Land, but no one else in his time could have led them as far in that direction as he did.

Donald Woods, used by permission of AP Photos/Fiona Hanson

CHAPTER 8

Donald Woods, Bram Fischer, Helen Suzman, and the Fight against Apartheid

There were, of course, white South Africans who opposed apartheid in their native land. Many, especially among English speakers, simply voted against the National Party. Most went on with their lives, troubled by living in a country widely perceived as a pariah among nations, but having jobs to do and families to support. The fight against apartheid was not their ultimate concern.

A few whites found apartheid unbearable. Some of these left. Some stayed at home and fought it as best they could. The efforts of the writers Nadine Gordimer and Alan Paton are well known. Three less-well-remembered opponents of the apartheid regime were Donald Woods, Bram Fischer, and Helen Suzman.

Woods is doubtless more familiar to American and European readers because of the 1987 film *Cry Freedom*, focused on the life and murder of his friend Steve Biko, leader of the Black Consciousness Movement, in 1977. Woods fled South Africa in December 1977, addressed the UN Security Council in 1978, and spent much of the next fifteen years lecturing in Europe and North America and writing in opposition to apartheid. He played an important role in keeping the issue in view in the West.

Woods was born in the Transkei, South Africa; grew up among blacks; and as a young man, accepted the "need" for white supremacy as essential to the safety of whites and the stability of the country. In later life, he claimed that it was in the midst of his legal studies that he realized that a race-based system of justice was a travesty. After a very brief spell as a country lawyer, he began writing for the East London (South Africa) *Daily Dispatch*, and he ran for Parliament in 1957 on the ticket of the Union Federal Party, a minor party opposed to apartheid and supportive of black participation in the political process. He never had a chance of winning.

Journalism became his career of choice, and in 1959 he headed off to England, then Wales, and then Canada, writing for different papers. He returned to South Africa just before the Sharpeville massacre of 1960 and resumed writing for the *Daily Dispatch*. Racial issues clearly consumed him, as they did white liberals in South Africa generally. He interviewed black leaders and senior police officials and, after becoming editor in 1965, began recruiting black journalists and publishing a weekly supplement in Xhosa—a language he had spoken along with English as a child.

His editorship became a cat-and-mouse game with the security forces. He criticized the regime, and government agencies tried to intimidate him. Thanks to his legal training, he managed to avoid prosecution. He had a sense of how hard to push and how to use the law to protect himself. However much the police might subvert the rule of law when dealing with blacks, a white man could still count on the likelihood of justice in South African courts. The press had considerable freedom, and Woods pushed against the boundaries but was careful not to cross them. He even got away with calling attention to the prime minister's wartime record of Nazi sympathies.

In 1973, he met the charismatic young black leader Steve Biko. He did not like what Biko had to say. Biko stressed black self-reliance and was contemptuous of Mandela, the African National Congress (ANC), and any blacks working toward a multiracial society. Woods smelled racism and challenged him. Biko was dismissive of Woods's ideas, as he was of white liberals generally. Bram Fischer, the communist leader, then serving a life term for his efforts to fight apartheid, was the one white man Biko admitted to admiring. Biko was willing to fight and die for black freedom—were white liberals? Despite their differences, Woods and Biko became friends.

The friendship with Biko was a turning point in Woods's life. Biko was anathema to the Afrikaner security forces. He challenged them constantly and they harassed him constantly, breaking into his offices and arresting him several times. Woods used his newspaper to push back—and went further than the authorities would tolerate.

In 1975, after Biko's office was broken into, Woods accused the police and demanded that those he believed responsible be charged with a criminal

offense. The government demanded to know the source for his information—presumably someone on the police force or someone to whom the
offenders had boasted. He refused and was sentenced to six months in prison,
suspended while the judicial system considered his appeal.

In 1977, Biko died in police custody, tortured and beaten to death. The
official report was that he had died on a hunger strike, but the condition of
his body left little doubt as to what had actually happened. Woods demanded
an investigation, published details of Biko's death, and was a major contributor to the public outcry. The security forces had had enough; a month
later, Woods received a banning order. He could no longer write, not for his
newspaper nor any other publication. He could attend no meetings, nor meet
with more than one person at a time who was not a family member. He was
required to report to the police weekly.

Confining as the conditions were, Woods might have been able to cope
with them. He began to write a biography of Biko with the hope of being
able to publish his work eventually. But his children received chemical burns
from T-shirts they received in the mail, and he was convinced the police
were sending him a message—that his family was not safe. In December
1977, disguised as a priest, he fled South Africa, settling eventually in England and devoting the rest of his life to fighting against apartheid, and for a
free press in South Africa. In 1997, five of the policemen complicit in Biko's
murder confessed before South Africa's Truth and Reconciliation Commission, and Woods named the three others who were still alive. All would go
free, but their lives would be very different in a South Africa ruled by representatives of its black majority.

Bram Fischer did not live to be vindicated. As he lay dying of cancer in
1975, he was released from prison grudgingly by the apartheid regime. His
fellow political prisoners noted that his jailers treated him more viciously
than any among them. He was, after all, the very worst sort—an apostate, a
traitor to his Afrikaner heritage, and a communist to boot.

Fischer was born in 1908, into an exceptionally prominent Afrikaner
family. His grandfather had been prime minister of the Orange River Colony
and had held several cabinet posts after the creation of the Union of South
Africa. He may be remembered best for his efforts to send all Indians back
to India, an effort in which the opposition was led by Gandhi. Bram's father,
a Rhodes Scholar, became a highly successful lawyer. Bram was to win a
Rhodes himself, to marry a niece of General (and sometime Prime Minister)
Smuts, and to establish his own well-regarded law practice. It was not an
obvious lineage or experience for a revolutionary. Stephen Clingman, author

of a superb biography of Fischer, notes that he was probably the only Rhodes Scholar to be awarded the Lenin Prize by the Kremlin.

At the university in South Africa, Fischer began to question the white supremacist assumptions that he had internalized in his youth. The influence of one of his teachers, Leo Marquard, an outspoken white liberal, seems to have had a catalytic effect on his attitude toward race issues. Through Marquard he met educated blacks whom he came to respect as his equals. By the time he graduated, Fischer was arguing against racial segregation. And then he went off to Oxford on a Rhodes Scholarship.

In England, his politics appear to have drifted left—at least as far as sympathy for the British Labour Party. Fischer was not a communist and did not join the Communist Party, but he and some friends did visit the Soviet Union during the summer of 1932 and were favorably impressed. The following year he observed the rise of Hitler in Germany. He foresaw a conflict between communism and fascism and, given that choice, had no reservations about wishing the Soviets well. While clear-sighted in his estimate of the Nazis, his critical faculties do not appear to have served him well when evaluating Stalin and his works. Too many left-leaning intellectuals allowed themselves to be deceived by what they were shown and told in the Soviet Union in the 1930s.

Upon his return to South Africa, Fischer began his legal practice, specializing in mining issues and representing mine owners. At some point in the late 1930s—he said 1938—he joined the Communist Party. It is conceivable that his wife, Molly, joined before him. Their friends agreed that she was the more radical and the more confrontational of the two. Fischer would not have been the first or last man radicalized by his wife. Together they were determined to resist the rise of fascism in South Africa. During World War II, Fischer declared his party membership openly and stood successfully as a communist for election to the Johannesburg Bar Council. Soviet resistance to Hitler allowed little room for anticommunism in the early 1940s. Shortly after the war ended, Fischer was elected to the party's central committee.

In addition to Soviet opposition to fascism, the Communist Party appealed to Fischer as the only multiracial party in South Africa. He shared its commitment to racial equality. Unfortunately, many blacks mistrusted the communists—especially the white ones. Mandela and his colleagues controlling the ANC Youth League were hardly different than the Pan-Africanist Congress (PAC) black nationalists in their initial unwillingness to work with communists. And the Comintern, with its usual doctrinaire insensitivity to local conditions, ordered the South African party not to work with the

ANC, which it labeled bourgeois. Mandela's suspicion of the Communist Party persisted for some time, but he could not deny the sincerity of the support he received from Fischer and Joe Slovo, the party's leader.

Despite his membership in the Communist Party, outlawed in 1950, and despite his known opposition to apartheid, Fischer was appointed King's Counsel in 1951. Clingman suggests that the appointment had been cleared by several members of the prime minister's cabinet. Whether the Nationalists were trying to co-opt Fischer or the cabinet ministers had been neglectful in approving the appointment, the government soon had reason to regret it. Fischer defended the ANC leaders in 1952 when they were convicted of "statutory communism." In the months that followed, his activities on behalf of communist-front organizations provoked temporary banning notices late in 1953.

Apparently Molly took over some of Bram's party work, traveling through the Communist bloc in 1954 and arriving in Beijing in time to share in Mao Zedong's celebration of the fifth anniversary of the establishment of the People's Republic of China. She returned, delighted by the "success" of Mao's revolution, accepting uncritically what she was told in China. Neither she nor Bram appears ever to have questioned the line from Moscow or Beijing, even when it changed.

In 1958, Fischer joined the legal team that was defending Mandela, Slovo, and other dissident leaders against charges of treason. The accused were acquitted when the judge ruled that the prosecution had failed to prove that they had attempted to overthrow the state—or that the ANC's Freedom Charter was a communist document. To some black leaders, Fischer's role was inspirational—perhaps enough whites out there would support racial equality. From his fellow Afrikaners, he elicited anger and disgust. He was betraying his race and his class.

Mandela went to prison in 1962 when he was caught reentering the country after leaving illegally to rally support for guerrilla operations against the government. In 1963, a government raid on the headquarters of his military high command in Rivonia led to the "Rivonia Trial." Papers incriminating Mandela and the rest of the leadership were found there, and all were brought up on charges of sabotage. The prosecution indicated its intent to seek the death penalty. Fortunately Fischer, who visited the headquarters frequently, was not present at the time of the raid. He was available to lead the defense.

This time, conviction was inescapable. The government had evidence that Mandela and his colleagues were planning a campaign of sabotage.

Fischer's goal was to keep them from the gallows, and he succeeded. But Mandela and the others went off to Robben Island for life, and the trial proved to be Fischer's last hurrah.

The blow from which he never recovered was the death of Molly a few months after the trial ended. She was killed in a car accident in which he was driving. No matter who was at fault, few men could escape the plague of guilt that would follow inexorably. And in Fischer's case, it meant losing a woman who was his partner in far more than the traditional sense. Molly seems to have been the driving force in his life.

Fischer was serving as acting head of the clandestine Communist Party of South Africa. Shortly after Molly's death he was arrested for belonging to an outlawed party and brought to trial in November 1964. In the midst of the trial, while out on bail, he decided to flee, imagining he could rally the party and carry on the fight against apartheid underground. And he tried. Disguised and in hiding, he wrote letters to newspaper editors, white liberals, and Afrikaners he thought might be receptive. Mandela was proud of him. But Fischer was not a self-contained man, and his need for companionship gnawed at him. Some friends tried to help with calls and visits, exposing themselves and, ultimately, Fischer. One of these friends broke down under interrogation and revealed Fischer's hiding place. The police seized him in November 1965, less than a year after he had fled. Tried and convicted, he was sentenced to life imprisonment for sabotage. At the trial he invoked the right to reject the validity of laws that were immoral, laws passed by a legislature that represented but a fourth of the nation's people. In 1967, the Soviets awarded him the Lenin Prize.

Eighteen years later, ten years after Fischer's death, Nelson Mandela gave the first Bram Fischer Memorial Lecture in Johannesburg.

On January 1, 2009, Helen Suzman died in Johannesburg. The obituaries reminded me of what an extraordinary woman she was. For much of her career, she was the lone voice against apartheid in the South African Parliament, the one consistent vote in opposition to the Nationalist government's increasingly brutal efforts to suppress the country's black majority. Undeterred by sexist and anti-Semitic jeers from many of the other 164 members of Parliament (MPs), by government harassment, or by death threats, she became what a *Washington Post* reporter called "a one-stop shopping center for anyone seeking justice from an evil system." Another journalist called her the regime's worst nightmare: "an articulate Jewish woman with an attitude and a following abroad." In 1966, when the deck seemed stacked against her reelection, her victory was hailed by the *New York Times* with the suggestion that as the sole voice for all the people of color denied the right to vote, it was possible that she represented more South Africans than all other MPs combined. This was the woman to whom Alan Paton, the great South African writer, dedicated his book *Save the Beloved Country*. And in 1996, it was Helen Suzman who stood at Nelson Mandela's side when he signed the constitution as South Africa's first black president.

Suzman was born in Transvaal, South Africa, in 1917 to Lithuanian Jewish immigrants. Her mother died when she was two weeks old and she was raised primarily by an aunt. She was educated in a Catholic convent at a time when Anglican schools were considered inhospitable to Jews, and often attributed her tenacity to the nuns who taught her that losing was unacceptable. She studied economic history at the University of the Witwatersrand, but at nineteen dropped out to marry thirty-three-year-old Dr. Moses Suzman, who became one of South Africa's leading physicians. She returned to the university to obtain her degree several years later, after the birth of her first child.

From 1941 to 1944, Suzman worked as a statistician for the War Supplies Board and then returned to Witwatersrand University, where she lectured in economic history from 1945 to 1952 and joined the South African Institute of Race Relations on that campus. In her memoirs, she indicated that her opposition to apartheid stemmed from her study of racial laws. Her father, Sam Gavonsky, does not appear to have shared her views.

In 1948, the Afrikaner-dominated Nationalists won control of the government on an apartheid platform, and Suzman joined the opposing United Party (UP), generally considered pro-British. She and her friends assumed that the Nationalist victory had been a fluke, and they expected the United Party to regain control in 1953. She was persuaded to be a candidate for a safe UP seat in Houghton, a wealthy suburb of Johannesburg, with a large Jewish population. Once she won the nomination, she was elected without opposition. But the Nationalists trounced the UP in most of the rest of South Africa, increasing their majority, and Suzman found herself a member of the Official Opposition.

She gave her maiden speech to Parliament on women's rights and later argued for a woman's right to an abortion, but her ultimate concern was always racial discrimination. To her dismay, most of her fellow UP MPs voted with the Nationalists on race questions. Only about a dozen of them, the "liberal wing," worked with her to oppose the government's racist policies. Fortunately, one of them was Harry Oppenheimer, son of the wealthy head of the Anglo-American Corporation. Oppenheimer helped her to learn the ways of the legislature and, after he left Parliament to take over his father's business, became a major financial contributor to her campaigns.

In 1959, Suzman and eleven of her colleagues resigned from the UP in protest against its support of racist laws and formed the Progressive Party. They received support from Oppenheimer. But in 1961, the government called an early election in which all of the Progressives except Suzman lost their seats. For the next thirteen years she was the lone Progressive Party member in the South African Parliament. She was also the first MP since 1910 to be elected on a platform rejecting racial discrimination.

Her years as a one-woman opposition party were often lonely—there were no colleagues she could join for lunch in the parliamentary dining room, and she usually ate by herself in her office. The other MPs did not deign to hide their hostility, meeting her critiques of the policies they supported with charges that she was betraying the country, working for the communists, and plotting to turn the country over to the blacks. But Suzman had a sharp tongue and a quick wit and easily held her own. Accused of embarrassing the country when she questioned its laws, she replied it was not her questions but the government's answers that embarrassed the country. When P. W. Botha, her bête noire, an "obnoxious bully" who became prime minister in 1978, remarked on the floor that it was well known that Suzman did not like him, her response was "Like you? I cannot stand you." When she was given the UN Prize in the Field of Human Rights on the thirtieth anniversary of the signing of the Universal Declaration of Human Rights, Botha announced that she was going to New York to receive an award from the enemies of South Africa. Another Nationalist prime minister, B. J. Vorster, was generally acknowledged to be her only equal, as intelligent and quick-witted as Suzman—and he seemed to enjoy sparring with her. On one occasion he said that she was worth ten UP MPs. Recording this quote in her memoirs, she wrote, "I thought this an understatement."

Given the brutality with which the regime crushed its enemies, Suzman's survival was extraordinary. The government tried various forms of electoral chicanery that narrowed her winning margins significantly, but she always won. Clearly, parliamentary immunity protected her remarks on the floor. The government had no legal recourse. But Botha, who accused her of complicity in the assassination of his predecessor, and other officials often threatened to "get her." Dissidents not infrequently died in mysterious accidents or received letter bombs. One possible explanation for her survival is that she had cultivated the foreign press and diplomats and quickly became a prominent international figure. Perhaps no one in the security forces imagined it would be as easy to escape recrimination for killing her as it was for murder-ing Steve Biko or any other black leader or communist. Perhaps, as some of her critics on the Left imagined, she was useful to the regime: Allowing her to fulminate "harmlessly" against apartheid enabled the government to pose as a democracy that permitted free speech.

One parliamentary privilege that Suzman demanded was the right to visit prisoners. The government always quickly approved her requests for permis-sion to visit prisons for whites, but usually stalled on her requests to inspect those for blacks. She had to wait seven years between visits to Robben Island, where Mandela was being held. She probably did not help matters much by remarking on the floor of the legislature that she could have more intelligent conversations with black prisoners "than with many members of this House." On another occasion, one of those members suggested that she would give South Africa to the blacks—and then move to Israel.

Suzman understood that prison conditions were always improved on the eve of her appearance, but despite the presence of wardens, she was often able to uncover evidence of mistreatment. By all indications she was successful in obtaining remedies in almost every case. It was on one of these visits, in 1967, that she met and came to admire Mandela, although she remained uneasy about the ANC. At Robben Island the other prisoners insisted that she speak with him, their leader. He later credited her with having the most vicious of the guards removed. He knew who she was, and was impressed when she ap-peared at his treason trial; his lawyer, Bram Fischer, spoke of her with awe and admiration, inconsistent with his usual attitude toward white liberals. When Fischer was himself imprisoned years later and dying of cancer, Suzman led the appeal that won him release to spend his last days at home.

The Progressives gained strength in the 1970s. In 1974, Suzman was joined by seven additional Progressive Party MPs. In 1977, merging with the Reform Party, the Progressive Party became the Progressive Federal Party. With the disintegration of the United Party, the Progressives became the Official Opposition. Suzman no longer had trouble finding companions for lunch.

There were issues on which Suzman's positions were at variance with those of the black leaders she supported—and with those of radicals such as Bram Fischer. Unsurprisingly for an avowed liberal and parliamentarian, she insisted on peaceful change and would not condone guerrilla warfare or acts of terrorism. Much like Jack Greenberg, she pursued legal means of ending apartheid, abolition of the laws that provided the underpinning for South Africa's system of racial discrimination.

The stand for which Suzman was most strongly criticized was her opposition to international sanctions against South Africa. To black activists at home and abroad, it appeared that she was defending the interests of the wealthy white liberal businessmen who supported her. Many of her friends in the West were also troubled. She argued cogently that isolating the country was the wrong way to reform the apartheid regime—the Nationalists already exhibited a bunker mentality and would become even more defensive. Worst of all, sanctions would hurt the poor blacks they were intended to help. When the economy contracted, blacks would surely be the first to lose jobs. When foreign firms withdrew from South Africa, their policies of preparing blacks for management positions, their "social responsibility programs," went with them.

If Suzman was right, how would one explain the changes that did occur in South Africa in the late 1980s and 1990s? If the Nationalists did not reverse course under the pressure of sanctions, why did they? As the apartheid regime disintegrated, she contended that the demise of communism in the Soviet Union and Eastern Europe deprived the Nationalists of the threat they had wielded so successfully, of their claim that a white South African government was the West's only bulwark against the communism that otherwise would sweep over black Africa. But more importantly, she insisted it was the resistance of blacks and others of color that forced the change that brought universal suffrage and majority rule to South Africa. As a supporter of sanctions at the time, I'm still not convinced she was right—but sanctions haven't helped much with Burma.

When it became evident that apartheid was doomed and a black majority government was on the horizon, Suzman concluded it was time to retire. She won her last election in 1987, but perceived that liberals had become irrelevant. The people for whom she'd fought all her adult life no longer needed her. She resigned in 1989 after thirty-six years in Parliament. Her service did not end immediately: She was invited and agreed to sit on the Independent Electoral Commission to oversee her country's transition to majority rule.

She remained concerned about the escalating criminal violence in the country, fearful that the ANC would inherit an ungovernable country. Regrettably, that problem has yet to be remedied. And after the black majority came to power, Suzman did not hesitate to call it to account when she perceived wrongdoing. She was especially critical of Thabo Mbeki after he succeeded Mandela as president of South Africa. She found him as much given to cronyism as Zimbabwe's Robert Mugabe, and she was outraged by his absurd refusal to accept scientific evidence of the causes and means of managing HIV/AIDS.

And then she was gone, leaving no one as fierce, witty, and articulate to stand up to the government. The *Guardian* once called her the "brightest star in the liberal firmament." A Nationalist MP who opposed her on every issue conceded years ago that it was not likely that there would ever again be "anyone in the history of the country who would do as much for human rights" as she had. South Africa's loss is irreparable.

Helen Suzman and Nelson Mandela, used by permission of AP Photos/John Parkin

CHAPTER 9

Nelson Mandela: Grace in Victory

Of all those of whom I write, Nelson Mandela is second perhaps only to Gandhi as an iconic figure, as a symbol of moral authority. Like Gandhi's ultimate triumph over British imperialism, Mandela's extraordinary success in negotiating the peaceful transfer of power from an oppressive white minority to an impoverished black majority was one of the great feats of the twentieth century. His subsequent impressive leadership of South Africa stands in marked contrast to the horrors inflicted on their country by other African "liberators" such as Idi Amin, Joseph Mobutu, or Robert Mugabe.

In 1918, as the victorious powers arranged to meet at Versailles to hammer out the treaty that would end the First World War, delegations of subject peoples—Koreans, Vietnamese, and Africans among them—traveled to the site of the conference in the vain hope that Woodrow Wilson's promise of self-determination for all peoples applied to them. One such group was the six-year-old ANC, seeking freedom from British colonialism in southern Africa. The year 1918 was also the year of Nelson Mandela's birth.

Mandela was born in Transkei, home of the Xhosa nation, now part of South Africa. His father, a hereditary chief, had four wives and, eventually, twelve other children. His mother was a Christian who had him baptized in the Methodist Church and, when he was seven, sent him to a local mission school where his British education began. His father died when he was only nine, but Mandela acquired a powerful sponsor, the Thembu regent. The regent was indebted to Mandela's father, and young Nelson was himself a minor royal, the great-grandson of a nineteenth-century Thembu king.

Mandela's British—and Methodist—education continued through secondary school, from which he graduated in 1938. He subsequently attended the only black university in South Africa, as one of a handful of blacks to receive such an elite education. In their recollections, classmates suggest Mandela was a little arrogant and, as a prince, accustomed to a degree of deference. They concede, however, that he showed respect for commoners who were his intellectual superiors. He was well on his way to acquiring the status of an educated Englishman when, as a representative of his fellow students, he stood up to the university authorities on a seemingly common and trivial difference over the food served in the cafeteria. He was unyielding on what he took to be a matter of principle. The contretemps resulted in his expulsion.

Young Mandela was already exhibiting some of the qualities for which he would be known in the years ahead. He manifested a sense of entitlement and righteousness. He was stubborn. His peers recognized him as a leader—and he did not hesitate to learn from those wiser than he was.

His expulsion from the university outraged the regent, who decided it was time for him to assume the responsibilities of adult life and arranged a marriage. Mandela was not willing to settle down to a life as a tribal official and fled to Johannesburg, further angering the regent. It was 1941, in the midst of World War II, and there was a shortage of white labor. Mandela found work as a night watchman in a mine.

Before long, the fact that Mandela had lied about having the regent's permission to travel became known, and he was fired from his job at the mine. As he bumbled about the city, exploiting vague contacts, he eventually found his way to the office of Walter Sisulu, a realtor, also from Transkei, who specialized in finding properties that blacks were allowed to buy. Mandela explained his circumstances to Sisulu—omitting the part about the regent—and Sisulu found him a job as a clerk in the office of a Jewish lawyer, Lazar Sidelsky. Sidelsky appears to have been free of the racism that afflicted white-black relations, and Mandela admired him. He was, Mandela later said, "the first white man who treated me as a human being."

The next few years were enormously fruitful for Mandela. He completed the requirements for his university degree through correspondence courses and was allowed to begin legal studies at the University of the Witwatersrand. Through Sisulu, who became his mentor, he found the ANC and decided on a life dedicated to overthrowing white supremacy. He participated in a bus boycott in 1943 and, in 1944, joined Sisulu and his Fort Hare schoolmate, Oliver Tambo, on the executive committee of the ANC's Youth League.

These were also years when he had his initial contact with communists. In his autobiography, he claims their ideology had little appeal to him. His Methodist education had provided religious armor against the teachings of Marx and Lenin, and he did not see class conflict as the critical issue in South Africa. Although there were communists among the ANC members, he and his colleagues in the Youth League kept them out. Youth League members were very much black nationalists, unwilling to work with whites, South Asians, or communists. Nonetheless, Mandela attended communist lectures and developed close friendships with several, most notably Joe Slovo, who later led the Communist Party of South Africa and was deeply committed to racial equality. Mandela could not help but be impressed by the multiracial social events to which the communists invited him.

The events of the next few years forced Mandela to be less fastidious about whom he would accept as allies. After the war, conditions for black Africans and Indians worsened rapidly. Jan Smuts, prominent military leader of the World War I era, serving his second tour as prime minister from 1939 to 1948, was committed to a vision of a South Africa led by white settlers and their descendants. In 1946 he ordered the ruthless suppression of striking African mine workers—whom he and many other whites perceived as dupes of a communist conspiracy. Presumably blacks were not smart enough to form a union and organize a strike by themselves. If the oppressive white minority saw the communists as aiding the black population, it was only a matter of time before blacks would accept communists as comrades in their struggle for equality.

Soon afterward, Smuts's government passed the Asiatic Land Tenure Act, limiting the right of Asians to buy land. Mandela and his colleagues were tremendously impressed by the Gandhian tactics of passive resistance with which the Indian community fought back. Mandela began to study the successes of Gandhi and Nehru in India, but he was uncomfortable working with Indians in South Africa. He appears to have perceived them as better educated and more sophisticated than ANC members, specifically himself, and he feared they might dominate the ANC. Moreover, he considered Indian shop owners in South Africa to be exploiters of black labor. Nonetheless, they confronted a common enemy, and the ANC supported resistance to the Land Tenure Act. India's successful struggle for independence from the white minority that had dominated that country for nearly a century was inspirational—and Nehru urged Indians in South Africa to support the ANC. Slowly and grudgingly, Mandela conceded the value of uniting with Indians and other "coloreds."

Worse, of course, was yet to come. Mandela's hope that somehow Anglo-American liberalism, the British Labour Party, and the promises of the United Nations would ameliorate conditions in South Africa evaporated with the Afrikaner-dominated National Party's electoral victory in 1948. Led by Daniel Malan, the Afrikaners were in the process of reversing their Boer War losses and gaining control of the country. They had no intention of sharing it with black Africans or other people of color. There were few liberals among them.

The Youth League, predictably more radical than the traditionalists in the ANC, began to press the parent organization to undertake mass action, paralleling the passive resistance of the Indian community. In 1949, the ANC tried: It organized boycotts, strikes, and demonstrations and called for civil disobedience. In June 1950, Mandela was appointed to the National Executive Committee, recognition both of his growing personal stature and of the increased influence of the Youth League. A few days later, the ANC sponsored a National Day of Protest.

Mandela was thirty-two years old, and life was treating him well. In addition to his growing stature within the ANC, his law practice was beginning to take off. He had money, he had a car, and he could afford good clothes. Despite his marriage to Evelyn Mase, Sisulu's cousin, in 1944, he had a reputation as a man about town, perhaps even a womanizer. He was tall, good-looking, athletic, and, by most accounts, arrogant. The Thembo prince was "making it" in the white man's city. But it was still the white man's city, and in 1950 the Afrikaners reified their plans for apartheid.

The Population Registration Act forced everyone in South Africa to register by race. The Group Areas Act determined where races could live. Once an area was designated for white residence, blacks had no right to live there and could be driven out. In the same year, the government outlawed the Communist Party.

Mandela wanted to fight apartheid but was uncertain about the appropriate means. The ANC leadership stepped up its training for passive resistance. Mandela accepted nonviolence as a tactic, although he was never willing to rule out the use of force if it proved necessary. He recognized that Gandhian practices that had been effective against the British in India and Africa might not work against the Afrikaner nationalists. However, given the government's monopoly of military power, there was no immediate alternative.

Another important issue was whether to cooperate with the communists. Mandela mistrusted them, but noted the support their May Day demonstration had received from black workers. He was increasingly impressed by the personal sacrifices that communists were willing to make on behalf of equality for black Africans. He began reading communist literature—Marx, Lenin, Stalin, and Mao—as well as the writings of black nationalists such as Kwame Nkrumah and George Padmore. He was aware that Marxist-Leninists favored national liberation movements and that the Soviet Union was aiding many colonial peoples in their struggles for independence. Just as he was persuaded that it made good sense to cooperate with Indians, he gradually accepted the value of working with the communists. Black Africans needed all the allies they could find—and there were not many choices available.

In June 1952, the ANC, the Communist Party, and the Indians joined forces in a "Campaign of Defiance against Unjust Laws," which received widespread publicity. Membership in the ANC rose sharply. It was also the year in which Mandela was jailed for the first time—for a curfew violation. But the government was uneasy about the growing strength of the opposition, especially the cooperation between blacks and Indians. It's uncertain whether the government's fear of communist involvement in the anti-apartheid movement was genuine or merely a cover, in the early days of the Cold War, for its efforts to impose its will on the black majority.

It was clear, however, that the government had Mandela and other leaders of the Defiance Campaign in its sights. In July they were arrested and charged with violating the 1950 Suppression of Communism Act. Twenty-one of them were brought to trial in September. Supporters, white as well as black and Indian, used the trial to mobilize massive demonstrations and packed the courtroom. Mandela and his colleagues were found guilty of "statutory communism," a term that covered virtually any kind of opposition to the government. They were sentenced to nine months at hard labor, but the judge, noting that the campaign had not resulted in any acts of violence, suspended their sentence.

The government was not to be deterred, however, from its determination to restrain its critics. Shortly after the judge ruled, the minister of justice issued a "banning" order against Mandela and fifty-one other opposition leaders. Mandela called banning a kind of "walking imprisonment." For six months, he was not permitted to make any speeches or attend any meetings, political or otherwise—including his son's birthday party. He was allowed to speak to only one person at a time. For Mandela it was only the first of frequent bannings that were to plague him until he was sent to prison and deprived of all freedoms. He could still function and occasionally evade the restrictions, but his actions were unquestionably hampered and the psychological effect was depressing. Recognizing the government's intention to stifle the ANC, its leaders began to organize an underground network of cells and a system for secret communications.

When the banning expired in 1953, Mandela delivered a speech that reflected his frustration. He questioned whether nonviolent resistance would work to dismantle apartheid and suggested that it might be time to change tactics. Although he was reprimanded by the ANC's executive council, the idea of resorting to force continued to evolve in his thinking. The ANC began to establish contact with foreign communists, first in Europe, then in China. When Sisulu went to Beijing, Mandela persuaded him to ask the Chinese for guns. Although supportive of African nationalism generally, Mao warned against premature armed struggle, and Sisulu came back empty-handed. Mandela's authorized biographer, Anthony Sampson, sees Mandela evolving into a revolutionary in the 1950s. His speeches were increasingly inflammatory, incorporating much communist-style anticolonial rhetoric. He also began writing for *Liberation*, a notably leftist publication. In effect, he was taunting his tormentors, the enforcers of apartheid.

Over the next several years, Mandela and other ANC leaders worked on what became the Freedom Charter, their image of what a democratic South Africa would look like. The critical component, anathema to the Nationalist regime, was the call for one man, one vote. Were it to be accepted, it obviously would mean the end of white minority rule in South Africa—and perhaps a calling to account of those whites who had abused their authority. In June 1955, a "Congress of the People" was called to adopt the Charter. Three thousand representatives of various dissident organizations attended, roaring their approval as each section was read to them. At the moment final approval of the entire document was to be voted, the police interrupted, confiscated all documents, surrounded the delegates, and announced that they were suspected of treason. Mandela, knowing he would be jailed if caught, was able to slip away as the police recorded the names of the participants.

Despite police intimidation, Mandela was able to continue both his legal practice and his anti-apartheid activism for another year and a half before the government concluded the ANC was too dangerous and decided to imprison its leaders. Perhaps seeking to counter regime contentions that he and the ANC had fallen under the influence of their communist supporters, he wrote a disclaimer in *Liberation* in 1956. Although the Freedom Charter openly called for a redistribution of wealth and a return of the nation's resources to its people (i.e., black Africans), Mandela declared that he was not a socialist and that in the country the ANC envisioned, there would be private enterprise and ample opportunity for African entrepreneurs to utilize their skills.

In December 1956, Mandela and 155 other dissident leaders, mostly from the ANC, were arrested and charged with "high treason," with being part of a communist conspiracy to overthrow the state. Mandela noted wryly that in prison the anti-apartheid leaders were able to hold the longest unbanned meeting in years. As the proceedings began, the defendants were released from prison on bail. The preparatory examination and the actual trial went on for more than four years, without a verdict until March 1961.

In the interim Mandela's marriage unraveled. In brief, he was a wretched husband. His wife, a nurse, received little attention. The ANC was his first love and she could not compete. She had reason to believe that when he was not preoccupied with the fight for black equality, he was involved with other women. She turned to religion for solace and became a Jehovah's Witness. He became enamored of a beautiful and vivacious woman who, shortly after he divorced his wife, became his second wife, Winnie Mandela.

In 1958 he enhanced his radical credentials with an article in *Liberation* attacking American imperialism, noting American support for its allies who forcibly retained their colonies in Africa. The Soviet suppression of the Hungarian uprising in 1956 does not seem to have aroused comparable indignation. His article provided the government with one more piece of evidence of Mandela's participation in a communist conspiracy, and added to its case against the ANC as it tried to justify its efforts to destroy the organization in the court of world opinion.

Suddenly, in 1959, the ANC was upstaged by the creation of the Pan African Congress (PAC), whose leaders declared their intention to overthrow the apartheid regime and replace it with a black, socialist, and democratic government. Unlike the ANC, the PAC refused to collaborate with Indians or whites. In particular, it rejected communist support. Mandela saw the PAC as a spoiler, undermining the efforts of the ANC. He was specifically disdainful of its avowed anticommunism, which he saw as a bid for support from the Western press and the U.S. government. But he appears to have underestimated its appeal to black intellectuals.

The South African regime was gradually becoming an international pariah, notwithstanding its support for the West in the Cold War. In 1960, seventeen former colonies in Africa won their independence. The British prime minister, Harold Macmillan, came to South Africa and delivered a speech in which he focused on the "winds of change" that were sweeping across the continent. The government in Pretoria had no intention, however, of being swept aside.

In March 1960, PAC organized a demonstration in Sharpeville as part of its campaign to do away with the system of "Native passes," internal passports all blacks were required to carry. The pass system was designed to control the movement of blacks around the country—and to keep track of potential troublemakers. In December 1959, the ANC had voted to hold countrywide demonstrations against the system, but PAC was not interested in a sub-ordinate role and operated separately. In the town of Sharpeville, several thousand peaceful demonstrators surrounded the police station. The police panicked and opened fire on the demonstrators, killing sixty-nine of them and wounding hundreds of others, including women and children, many shot in the back as they fled.

The international response to the massacre was everything PAC and the ANC could have hoped for. The South African government was condemned widely. The United States and the United Nations protested. The ANC responded by calling for a day of mourning, and Mandela and other leaders burned their passes. Hundreds of thousands of black South Africans stayed at home in protest.

The regime reacted harshly. It declared a state of emergency and insti-tuted martial law. Both the ANC and the PAC were declared illegal. On March 30, Mandela, still out on bail during the treason trial, was arrested and detained for five months—without access to his lawyers. His release came sufficiently early, however, to allow him to testify at the trial and to use the opportunity to denounce imperialism and the commercial exploitation of black Africans, sounding increasingly like the communist he never was.

To the delight of right-thinking people across the world, the treason trial ended in an acquittal of all those charged on all counts. The judge ruled that the prosecution had failed to prove that the defendants had attempted to overthrow the state or that their Freedom Charter was a communist docu-ment. Justice was still possible in South Africa, although Mandela was not satisfied. He concluded that the defendants had been fortunate to have the trial presided over by a good and fair judge, but that more often than not the state would manipulate the legal system for its own ends. He knew he had been targeted by the government, and before the trial ended, he decided that if freed, he would go underground.

Shortly afterward, the ANC decided to take a major action and, in a se-cret meeting, debated whether to call a general strike with supporters taking to the streets to demonstrate or to simply have them stay home and fail to report for work. Mandela, arguing for the stay-at-home strategy, prevailed. If the people were out in the open, they were vulnerable to attack by the po-lice. Another Sharpeville was to be avoided. But the government did what it could to intimidate potential strikers and sympathizers in the press. It carried out intensive raids against opposition leaders and, two days before the strike was scheduled, mobilized the military and the police. Tanks and helicopters appeared in the black townships. Hundreds of thousands stayed home none-theless, but Mandela and the other ANC leaders were disappointed by the numbers and called off the strike on the second day. To Mandela, passive action seemed a dead end in light of the state's willingness to use its massive coercive powers.

In June 1961, Mandela argued for creation of a military auxiliary to undertake guerrilla warfare against the South African government. He ran into stiff resistance, not least from the ANC president, Chief Albert Luthuli, a committed pacifist. More surprising was opposition from the communists, who contended that the time was not ripe for violence. Mandela criticized the communists for being doctrinaire, pointing to Fidel Castro, who did not wait for the ideal historical moment to achieve success in Cuba. The Cuban revolution excited him. Luthuli, who was awarded the Nobel Peace Prize later that year, was tougher to counter, but he ultimately acquiesced in the creation of an organization that would be nominally separate from the ANC. Under Mandela's leadership, it was called "Spear of the Nation," better known as just MK—and he was authorized to recruit white fighters as well as blacks.

Mandela had begun to study guerrilla warfare, reading about Algeria, China, Cuba, Israel, the Philippines—even the Boers—anything he could get his hands on. He sent four of his men to China for training. He decided that MK would start with sabotage and try to minimize violence to individuals ("collateral damage" in the jargon of the U.S. military). He slipped out of South Africa and traveled around the continent and eventually to London to raise funds for his operations and to establish contacts. He noted that several African leaders as well as potential supporters in the West were uneasy about the ANC's links to communists and realized he had a public relations problem to deal with. He had already recruited his friend Joe Slovo, a prominent communist, for his high command. He concluded it would be best to have ANC represented only by blacks at international conferences. Finally, he went to Ethiopia for military training, excited to be in a country run entirely by black Africans.

Mandela's months as a roving ambassador for his guerrilla movement, dismissed by his authorized biographer as "romantic and unrealistic" in the face of the government's powerful military and security forces, came to an end in August 1962. He was caught reentering South Africa and charged with leaving the country without a passport and incitement to violence. He decided to defend himself and to use the trial for political theater. He wore traditional African costume to underscore the fact that he was a black African appearing in the white man's court. Buoyed by news that the UN General Assembly had voted sanctions against South Africa, he argued that he had chosen to follow his conscience rather than the law in an unjust society. He was sentenced to five years in prison. His performance won him international attention, but not an escape from his sentence.

Foreign criticism did not deter the Nationalists from transforming South Africa into a police state. To them, Great Britain and the United States were the only countries that truly mattered, and they assumed that Cold War considerations would prevail in London and Washington. The Afrikaners imagined themselves as part of the West's struggle against communism and the West's most reliable ally on the continent.

In July 1963, after Mandela had served nine months in prison, he and several of his colleagues were brought to trial under new charges of sabotage, guerrilla warfare, and terrorism. The police had captured important ANC documents that served to incriminate the organization's entire leadership. If convicted, they faced the death penalty. Much of the state's case against Mandela was based on his handwritten notes on various communist, guerrilla, and revolutionary writings, not easily refuted. And one of his men testified against him and the other defendants.

Again, Mandela chose to use the trial to condemn the apartheid state and to portray his actions as a just response to oppression. In a speech that his biographer Anthony Sampson called the most effective of his career, he spoke of his ideals, of the democratic state of which he dreamed, of a multiracial nation in which no one would be discriminated against because of color or ethnicity, in which opportunity for all would be equal. He stood before the court as the representative, indeed the leader, of all opponents of apartheid. It was a vision for which he would continue to fight as long as he lived—and for which he was prepared to die. Two days before the court was due to rule, the UN Security Council called for an end to the trial and amnesty for the accused. Neither the government nor Mandela was surprised when the United States and Great Britain chose to abstain. The court sentenced him to life imprisonment, very likely sparing him because of the international pressure and widespread multiracial demonstrations in South Africa, as well as the efforts of Bram Fischer.

Mandela spent the next twenty-six years on Robben Island. There were obvious deprivations, beyond the actual confinement. Some of the guards delighted in brutalizing and humiliating prisoners, preaching white supremacy. There were no newspapers or radios. The inmates were not allowed watches or clocks. They were denied contact with the outside world, initially permitted to send and receive only one five-hundred-word letter, to and from relatives only, every six months. They worked in the blazing sun without sunglasses. Black prisoners were not fed as well as coloreds or whites.

However, some of the guards proved to be decent human beings, willing to ameliorate conditions. And there were cycles during which discipline was relaxed, however temporarily. The prisoners' struggles for better food, sunglasses, long pants, and study privileges succeeded. Thanks to the Red Cross, Mandela was able to continue his legal studies in a correspondence course with the University of London. He taught a course on political economy—although his grasp was clearly limited to a vaguely Marxist approach. In general, he was treated better than most prisoners, perhaps because of his brief international fame, perhaps because of his bearing and demeanor.

Mandela changed perceptibly during the early years in prison, helped in part by the presence of Sisulu, who continued to serve as a mentor. He learned to control his temper and was soon preaching against confrontational behavior with the guards. The ANC leadership on Robben Island agreed to try to educate rather than confront the guards, with remarkable success. Mandela claimed to pity rather than hate them.

Old acquaintances among the prisoners found him less arrogant. They marveled at his forbearance and his capacity for forgiveness. He quickly became a model for other prisoners, exuding confidence, demanding to be treated with dignity. His avoidance of confrontation allowed no room for servility. As the years passed, he was able to extend his influence over guards as well as other prisoners.

When Mandela arrived at Robben, there were more PAC prisoners than ANC, but after 1967, arrests of ANC members put his people ahead in that grim contest. Disagreements between the two organizations continued in the prison. PAC members remained adamantly opposed to working with communists, whites, Indians, and coloreds. Theirs was truly a black nationalist movement. Mandela, however, was increasingly convinced that the apartheid regime could not be toppled without appealing to all races, including liberal Afrikaners. After 1969, prisoners were allowed to receive books, and Mandela appears to have been influenced by the writings of Nadine Gordimer, whose novels suggested widespread support among whites for Mandela's cause.

In the late 1970s, young Africans caught up in the Black Consciousness Movement (BCM) began to join the ranks of prisoners on Robben Island, siding with the PAC members in the debates with the ANC. Mandela was uneasy about the approach of the young militants and seems to have had modest success in persuading some—but certainly not all—of those associated with the PAC and BCM of the importance of working toward a multiracial society. Most saw him as too moderate and suspected him of selling out. He was not amused.

One part of the debate was over the relationship of the ANC to the Communist Party of South Africa. Mandela's efforts to persuade anticommunist PAC members that the ANC, while delighted by the support of communists, was independent of them and by no means a front organization for the Communist Party, were compromised by his own MK warriors. Those trained in communist countries did not distinguish between communism and the ANC and often parroted propaganda lines they had learned in their host countries. Mandela had to disabuse them of this practice as well, but he himself perceived that the communist countries were the strongest supporters of national liberation movements. No less than other political prisoners, Mandela was hostile to the United States as the indispensable bulwark of imperialism worldwide. Even when the American government became supportive, Mandela was at best ambivalent toward Washington and was more responsive to those he considered true friends, such as Castro.

By the late 1970s, violence in South Africa had increased significantly. Negative international attention was focused on the country and economic pressure intensified. The Soweto Uprising of June 1976, in which thousands of students protested a government effort to force them to learn Afrikaans—the language of the oppressors—precipitated riots across the country. By comparison, the imprisoned ANC elders were increasingly perceived as relatively reasonable by government officials. The authorities became more responsive to their demands, ending the manual labor requirement in 1977, for example.

Mandela was sixty in 1978, and he had emerged as the spokesman for political prisoners and someone with whom Pretoria might be able to deal. Of course, the apartheid regime hoped to be able to fracture the opposition, and to use Mandela if it could to decrease violence within the country and pressure from without.

Perhaps because of his birthday and the many years he had spent in prison, Mandela received renewed international attention in 1979. He was given the Nehru Award for International Understanding, and a "Free Mandela" campaign erupted in several parts of the world. The UN Security Council called for his release. The government was not willing to be pushed, but it was maneuvering to find a useful way to free him. In 1981, the minister of justice reported to his colleagues that Mandela had all of the qualities necessary to be the number one black leader in South Africa. He suggested that Mandela had been strengthened in prison, that he exuded a sense of having been called to his leadership role. He was impressed by Mandela's charisma, his idealism, and his apparent lack of bitterness.

The inauguration of Ronald Reagan as president of the United States in 1981 gave Pretoria a little breathing room. The white supremacist government knew it had little to fear from the Reagan administration and it moved slowly. In 1982, it moved Mandela, Sisulu, and several other prominent ANC leaders to Pollsmoor, a prison on the mainland, where their living conditions—space, food, and access to news—were improved greatly. Mandela suspected the authorities merely wanted to separate the leaders from the followers, but more likely it was an attempt to improve the government's image. In 1984, the year Bishop Desmond Tutu won the Nobel Prize and the anti-apartheid struggle was in the headlines, Mandela was allowed to meet with foreign journalists and to receive a delegation from the British Commonwealth.

One interesting discussion Mandela had with foreign journalists involved reporters from the right-wing *Washington Times*. American conservatives generally perceived him as a communist and a terrorist, swallowing the South African government line. But some of Mandela's words and actions had given substance to the charge. To his visitors he insisted he was not a communist, and he tried to assure them that his vision for the future was a multiracial democracy. They pressed him on the ANC's use of violence, demanding to know why he could not emulate Martin Luther King—hardly a hero to the Right at home—and Mandela distinguished between tactics King might use in the United States and the tactics necessary to combat a ruthless police state.

Just as King had gained acceptance in America when young blacks concluded he was irrelevant and became more radical and violent, so Mandela increasingly was perceived as moderate by the Afrikaner elite as violence spread through South Africa. The government was looking for a safe way to release him, especially when he needed prostate surgery in 1986 and there was fear of losing him. The minister of justice visited him and proposed talks. Both Mandela and the regime feared the eruption of a full-scale civil war—and they talked. Perhaps not surprisingly, Mandela perceived himself negotiating from a position of strength—the government was running scared. Other ANC leaders were less confident, fearing the regime would succeed in its transparent effort to drive a wedge between Mandela and the organization. Obviously, they need not have worried.

The talks went on without progress. By 1988, when Mandela's seventieth birthday drew worldwide attention, he had been given a suite of rooms in the prison, had his own personal cook, and was guarded by men whose orders were to be sure his life was comfortable. He was being taken out for drives around the city. He obviously enjoyed the perquisites, which he recognized as preparations for his release, but brushed aside the government's terms for a deal. The ANC would not renounce the use of force in its struggle against apartheid and it would not reject collaboration with the Communist Party. Most importantly, Mandela and his colleagues would never abandon their commitment to the principle of majority rule—black African rule over the country. There was, however, some indication that the ANC might prevail on that issue: The minister of justice asked what constitutional guarantees Mandela envisioned for minorities in a black-run South Africa.

As the position of the Pretoria regime deteriorated at home and abroad, in July 1989 Mandela was brought before President P. W. Botha, a man deeply committed to the maintenance of apartheid. Botha had resigned as leader of the National Party, but remained head of state. Mandela was determined to meet the president as an equal (he demanded a new suit for the occasion) and determined not to tolerate any racial condescension—and he was pleased to find that he was met with respect. Each man, despite their intensely held and conflicting views, appeared to conclude that the other was trustworthy.

But Botha, who had suffered a stroke, was jostled aside by F. W. de Klerk a month later. Neither Mandela nor any of the other leaders knew much about the new president—and what little they knew suggested that he, too, was a staunch advocate of apartheid. Quickly, however, came clear signs that change was in the air. Bishop Tutu was allowed to lead a peaceful march against police brutality. In October, Sisulu and several other ANC leaders were released from prison without the imposition of any bans. They were allowed to speak as officers of the ANC. Mandela concluded that de Klerk was not an apartheid ideologue, that he was a man with whom he might be able to strike a deal. He asked for and obtained a meeting in December 1989.

The conversation with de Klerk confirmed Mandela's sense that South Africa was on the cusp of a major step toward the end of apartheid. The man actually seemed to listen when Mandela told him what needed to be done and of his own vision for the future. Several weeks later, on February 2, 1990, de Klerk announced that the government was lifting its ban on all political organizations: The ANC, the PAC, and even the Communist Party would be able to work in the open, legally. He suspended capital punishment, generally reserved for blacks, and committed his administration to releasing all political prisoners who had not been convicted of violent crimes. Mandela would be released unconditionally.

A week later, Mandela and de Klerk met again. The president informed Mandela of his intention to have him released the next day. De Klerk was probably surprised when Mandela asked to delay his release for another week, to allow the ANC to prepare a reception and to give him a few days to review what he wanted to say to his followers, to white South Africans, and to the rest of the world that would be listening. De Klerk's advisers thought that allowing the ANC to organize some sort of welcoming celebration might bring nationwide disruptions. Mandela was allowed to choose the place at which he would be freed, but not the time. Two days later, on February 11, 1990, a triumphant Mandela left prison and was delighted to find that he was cheered on his drive out by whites as well as blacks. There could be no doubt that South Africa had changed during the nearly thirty years he had been incarcerated.

But if Mandela, Bishop Tutu, and all the others who had struggled so many years against the apartheid regime thought the Nationalists were prepared to step aside, they were quickly disabused of that notion. Black-on-black violence increased rapidly after Mandela's release from prison, as Chief Mangosuthu Buthelezi led his Zulu warriors of the Inkatha Freedom Party against the ANC with encouragement from elements within the government—and from foreign right-wing groups such as the Heritage Foundation in the United States.

Mandela was convinced he could work with Buthelezi, but the younger generation in the ANC wanted to fight. The young men in the organization considered Mandela too moderate, too conservative, in his dealing with both Inkatha and the government. They complained that he spoke to government officials more often than he spoke to them. They had little use for his message of peace and reconciliation and found his call for forgiveness of their white oppressors beyond comprehension.

Holding the ANC together was Mandela's first major task after he gained his freedom. Explanations for his success always point to his moral authority—and certainly that gained him important international support. Also important was the skill with which he played the leader's role. He was aware of his charisma and the symbolic value of his years in confinement—and of the value of his aristocratic bearing and the quiet power he exuded. He understood the necessity of not departing from the ANC line on most issues, but within the organization he did not hesitate to impose his will. Too important a figure internationally, too well respected by the white holders of real power, Mandela could not be pushed aside.

With the ANC behind him, Mandela could press the organization's case with de Klerk. The critical problem was the unwillingness of the Nationalists to accept majority rule, to accept an electoral system in which they would be swept away by the black Africans upon whom they had inflicted so much misery for so many years. In May 1990, Mandela noted that de Klerk had not delivered on his promises. The right to vote had not been granted to Mandela or any black African—and years were to pass without that situation being remedied.

Unable to make progress at home, Mandela took advantage of his new freedom to travel abroad to muster support and to increase pressure on Pretoria. In June, he began a six-week tour of Europe and the United States—whose president, George H. W. Bush, had been the first head of state to congratulate him upon his release. In Washington, he addressed a joint session of Congress. The American media was effusive in its praise. At each stop, despite de Klerk's entreaties to the contrary, he encouraged his audience to maintain sanctions against South Africa. He was convinced that sanctions were essential to his cause. Absent that pressure, the apartheid government would be very slow to grant majority rule—if ever.

After he returned to South Africa, Joe Slovo, the Communist Party leader and Mandela's close friend and ally, proposed that the ANC end its armed struggle, as a means of removing Pretoria's excuse for delaying negotiations. Mandela was hesitant, but once persuaded, pushed Slovo's initiative through the organization. Mandela stressed that the ANC was *suspending* the use of force, not ending it. Much would depend on the government's response.

Unfortunately, the violence intensified as the security forces facilitated Inkatha attacks on ANC members and their supporters. Mandela was unable to persuade de Klerk to pacify the situation. Very likely de Klerk feared an insurrection among his supporters—and a loss of his power—if he did take the action necessary to restrain Inkatha. There is no doubt that he was under pressure from Afrikaner extremists. Dissatisfaction with Mandela's approach increased within the ANC; in May 1991, he was forced to suspend negotiations with the government. He had been out of prison more than a year, but the prospects for majority rule remained remote.

Both Mandela and de Klerk understood that neither side could prevail by force. A full-scale uprising doubtless would bring a bloodbath. But they could not find a way to progress. The whites who had ruled the country for a century were unwilling to relinquish power and feared the tyranny of a long-brutalized black majority. Black South Africans, for the most part, were unwilling to settle for anything less than complete control of the instruments of government.

Nonetheless, late in December, serious negotiations resumed in Johannesburg. A Convention for a Democratic South Africa was organized to conduct formal negotiations between the government, the ANC, and lesser political parties. The PAC refused to participate in what its members perceived as an effort to create a multiracial government—as opposed to the black-only regime they advocated. Buthelezi also held back. But when de Klerk, playing to his right, launched an intemperate criticism of the ANC, tension erupted between Mandela and de Klerk, torpedoing the meeting.

The legitimacy of de Klerk's concerns was confirmed a few weeks later when a National Party candidate was defeated in a by-election in a Nationalist stronghold by a candidate of the Conservative Party, a militant right-wing party opposed to any concessions to blacks. De Klerk gambled and held a nationwide referendum of white voters and won overwhelming support for negotiations—but whether out of fear or conviction, he persisted in demanding some kind of de facto veto power for whites over the actions of any black majority government. He replied to Mandela's demand that he stop Inkatha violence by insisting he lacked the power to do so.

The ANC responded with what it called "rolling mass action"—strikes, demonstrations, and boycotts—culminating in a tremendously successful general strike in August 1992. Rising tensions forced Mandela and de Klerk to meet again. In September, the government accepted the idea of a constitutional assembly, elected by all South Africans regardless of color, to adopt a new constitution and serve as an interim parliament. A few critical details remained undecided, however: In particular, they did not reach agreement on the size of the majority that decisions of the constituent assembly would require. Would it be so large as to give the whites the veto they wanted?

Once again it was Joe Slovo who rose to the occasion. He proposed what author Anthony Sampson calls a "historic concession," in which the ANC agreed to "sunset clauses" to allow white civil servants to retain their jobs—to provide for an interim government of national unity, Afrikaner Nationalist ministers serving alongside ANC ministers—and an amnesty for security officers. Mandela pushed the proposal through his executive committee. With the obvious proviso that whites would not have a veto over legislation, his colleagues could swallow the concessions.

Talks resumed with the government in December, and agreement was reached on a five-year multiparty government, with parties polling over 5 percent proportionately represented in the cabinet. After five years, the government would be selected by a simple majority. It took six more months, until June 1993, for an interim transitional committee to agree to schedule a one man, one vote election for the following April. Before the year was out de Klerk and Mandela were awarded the Nobel Peace Prize. By then the two men had grown to dislike each other, but had not allowed their feelings to interfere with the essential task. Neither was happy about having to share the prize with the other.

In the election campaign, Mandela modeled his people's forums after the town meetings Bill Clinton had staged in his successful 1992 run for president. He proved to be a terrific campaigner and fund-raiser. De Klerk later said that Mandela was overrated as a statesman but underrated as a politician. He played his audiences magnificently. For older blacks, he came across as the stately and dignified chief. For younger, more volatile blacks, he was the guerrilla leader and revolutionary. For white audiences, he was their longtime prisoner, willing to forgive them.

Inkatha boycotted the elections and Mandela worried continually about the Afrikaner right. He understood that the military and the security forces could sabotage the election. Shrewdly, he called on ex-president Botha, assuring him that reconciliation and not revenge was his agenda. He assumed Botha still had influence with the most conservative Afrikaners, and conceivably, the tactic was decisive in gaining the acquiescence of the generals to the election. Very likely they were sufficiently confident of their power to be able to adopt a wait-and-see approach to a black majority regime.

In the election, the ANC won 62 percent of the vote. The major disappointment was the failure to win the support of coloreds—who, fearing black rule, voted for de Klerk and the Nationalists. In May 1994, Nelson Mandela was sworn in as president of the Republic of South Africa. His cause had prevailed. The framework of apartheid had been dismantled, and black Africans had regained control of their land.

As president, Mandela understood the need to continue to assuage the fears of the white elite, but he also had to restrain the black majority without losing its support. He chose to play the role of father figure, presumably above the political fray. He used his promise of forgiveness as an element of his power, a means to divide whites and shrink the radical white opposition. The bloody revolution so many Afrikaners dreaded did not come, and after a few months into his presidency, there was probably a collective sigh of relief. Life went on and a degree of stability the country had not known in years was established. In 1997, Mandela stepped down as president of the ANC and in 1999, after five years as president of the nation, he concluded that his mission of peaceful reconciliation, if not completed, was safely on track. It was time to move aside and allow the next generation to lead.

Mandela, although hardly a humble man, never succumbed to the egomania and kleptomania that led to the wreckage of so many other Third World liberation movements. He was well aware of the failures of other African revolutionary leaders and determined to avoid their mistakes. He lived simply and contributed a substantial part of his income to charity. Most frequently criticized over the years was his loyalty to colleagues who proved to be corrupt or ineffective in office. He enjoyed exercising his powers of patronage, but was reluctant to recognize unfortunate appointments. Frequently authoritarian in the domination of his cabinet, hypersensitive about criticism, he nonetheless genuinely believed in democracy and led primarily through the exercise of his moral authority. He was described as chiefly, princely, aristocratic—but never dictatorial.

He had been slow to realize that the socialist tracts that had informed his thinking about economic affairs had been discredited by the collapse of the Soviet economy. He had spoken of allowing private enterprise and encouraging black entrepreneurship, but he left prison still thinking in terms of state ownership of essential industries. His Chinese and Vietnamese friends had trouble disabusing him of these ideas, as they explained their own reasons for liberalizing their economies. Apparently, attendance at the World Economic Forum at Davos in 1992 opened his eyes to the need for South Africa to participate in the international economy. He continued to admire the ideal of a classless society, but as president spent an inordinate amount of time with Harry Oppenheimer—probably the country's wealthiest citizen and longtime Mandela supporter—and his rich friends. They doubtless contributed to his ultimate conviction that the ANC had to remain on good terms with big business for the nation's economy to thrive.

Mandela's record as diplomatist may well have eroded some of his moral authority. His penchant for loyalty was a bit of an albatross. It was not easy to reconcile his insistence on the centrality of human rights in international relations with his friendship with Muammar al-Qaddafi of Libya, Saddam Hussein, and Castro. But it was Mandela who ultimately persuaded Qaddafi to hand the Lockerbie bombing suspects over for trial, and it was Mandela who led the attack on Nigeria's Sani Abacha when Abacha executed a dissident poet.

Like that of many men and women consumed by the struggle for worthy causes, Mandela's family life suffered. His second marriage, to Winnie, also ended in divorce. She had provided staunch moral support while he was in prison, but she had also been involved in questionable activities, some of an apparently criminal nature. As a young and vigorous woman, it was not unreasonable for her to choose not to be celibate over the nearly three decades of their separation. Differences between them after his release from prison, political as well as domestic, could not be resolved. Mandela was saddened by the awareness that his mother, his wives, and his children had been cheated. In his autobiography he wrote that it "seems to be the destiny of freedom fighters to have unstable personal lives."

Mandela was no saint, but he was a brilliant actor on the political stage of his country and he earned the moral authority with which he was credited. Perhaps his greatest wisdom was to accept the advice of men he knew to be wiser—especially Sisulu, Slovo, Tambo, and Tutu. They were a formidable team, and Mandela's charisma and forbearance enabled them ultimately to prevail in the struggle for freedom for all South Africans. Perhaps Mandela's greatest accomplishment was to hold together his nation, his people of all colors, after liberation—and to avoid the tragedies that afflicted so much of the rest of the continent.

PART IV

HUMAN RIGHTS

Clockwise from upper left: Sister Sara Salkahazi, courtesy of the Sisters of Social Service, Budapest; Hiram Bingham at Marseille, courtesy of the United States Holocaust Memorial Museum Photo Archives; Georg Duckwitz, courtesy of the United States Holocaust Memorial Museum Photo Archives; Father Pierre-Marie Benoit, "Father of the Jews," used by permission of the Department of the Righteous, Yad Vashem, Jerusalem

CHAPTER 10

Holocaust Rescuers

When I returned to Michigan State in 1966 after two years in Taiwan, I made a new friend, Hsu Dau-lin, an older Chinese intellectual who had been hired to teach advanced Chinese language courses for social science majors. I learned, mostly from others, that he had had a very distinguished career in China, both as an official and as the tutor of Chiang Ching-kuo, Chiang Kai-shek's son and heir apparent. Hsu's father had been a minor warlord in the turbulent days of the 1920s. I understood that he was humiliated to be reduced to teaching his own language, having had no training and little interest in linguistics. But he needed to find work to stay in the United States, where his young wife was studying for a PhD in mathematics.

In due course, Hsu lost his job, my efforts to the contrary notwithstanding, but his wife got a teaching position at Central Michigan University and they managed to make ends meet. Not surprisingly, he was depressed and talked of wanting to go back to China to die. And then one day, the INS decided to send him back and he grudgingly agreed to fight the deportation order.

I was sitting in the Asian Studies Center one afternoon when an attractive older woman marched in with her partner, a prominent immigration lawyer, to demand my help in keeping Hsu in the United States. She turned out to be Kate Wilhelm, the ex-wife of Hellmut Wilhelm, who had taught me Chinese history at the University of Washington—and she had a very interesting story to tell.

I guess I had known that Hsu had been educated in Germany in the 1920s or 1930s. I'm not sure that I had known that Wilhelm and Franz Michael, both leading German-born sinologists in the United States, had been his classmates. At some point in the late 1930s, perhaps early 1940s, Hsu was serving as Chinese consul in Rome and he arranged to get his Jewish friends, most notably Wilhelm and Michael, out of Germany, with visas to China. Kate Wilhelm insisted that he had saved their lives and that such a man deserved a place in America. And her companion would serve pro bono.

Unlike his colleague, Ho Feng-shan, consul general in Vienna, who issued thousands of visas to Jews, Hsu probably does not deserve a place at Yad Vashem. I had no sense that he put his own life in danger to save his friends or that he was involved in any larger effort to rescue Jews, but I don't know that. I never asked him how many Jews he saved. He was, however, the only one I've ever known personally who saved Jews from the Holocaust—and I thought of him for the first time in many years as I began to write about the "Righteous among the Nations," the men and women who risked their careers, more often their lives and those of their families, to save Jews from the Nazis and their collaborators.

Yad Vashem, devoted to keeping alive the memory of the Holocaust, is a complex of gardens, museums, archives, and monuments in Jerusalem. In 1963, it launched a project designed to honor non-Jews who risked their lives to save Jews from the pogroms and concentration camps that resulted in the deaths of six million in Europe. Within the complex is an Avenue of the Righteous among the Nations, along which two thousand trees have been planted to honor the rescuers. The names of all so recognized, approximately twenty-two thousand, have been engraved on marble plaques in the Garden of the Righteous among the Nations. Doubtless many more names would be listed if their bearers had not been caught and killed—either by the Germans or by hostile neighbors—for protecting Jews. Countless others went unnoticed because those they aided did not survive or come forward to testify to the heroism of their benefactors.

The most obvious point that emerges from examining the list of the Righteous and reading their stories is that many more Jews could have been spared if more people cared. In every country in Europe, Germany included, men and women chose to take the risk of saving Jewish friends, neighbors, and even strangers whose desperation affected them—while others participated in the murders or facilitated them, welcomed them, or stood by indifferently. All classes of people stepped forward to attempt to save the lives of otherwise doomed Jews: doctors, lawyers, and clerics; tradesmen, fishermen, and peasants; social workers and sewer workers; politicians, students, and housewives; and even German soldiers—including some members of the

Nazi Party. Most appear to have acted out of a sense of human decency, based primarily on Christian values.

It's evident that where clergy actively opposed anti-Semitism, the people were more supportive and Jews fared better. So many Catholic priests and nuns, especially in France, risked their lives to save Jews that one cannot help but wonder what would have happened if the pope had ordered priests in Poland, Latvia, and Lithuania to preach against pogroms—how many more Catholics in those countries might have resisted the temptation to commit atrocities—how many more Jews might have survived. When French cardinals and the pope belatedly, after ninety-three thousand Jews had been deported from France, opposed a Vichy law to facilitate further deportations, the law was not passed. There is also some indication that the Vatican did intervene successfully in Slovakia at the behest of two Sisters of Social Service in Budapest—one of whom, Sister Sára Salkaházi, murdered by anti-Semites, was declared a saint in 2006. In Poland, the bishop of Bialystok did appeal to his priests to help Jews, and at least one persuaded his parishioners to save a family they had never met. In Lithuania, however, while one priest saved approximately two hundred Jews from the Kovno (Kaunas) ghetto, Archbishop Vincentas Brizgys, head of the country's Catholic Church, rejected a petition to help Jews for fear it might jeopardize the church's standing with the Germans. And there is also evidence that Vatican officials tried to limit the efforts of the bishop of Assisi, who used monasteries and convents to hide hundreds of Jews. (One convent in Assisi was alleged to be the only one in the world with a kosher kitchen.)

In France, Bishop Pierre-Marie Théas and Archbishop Jules-Géraud Saliège wrote pastoral letters condemning the deportation of Jews. They directed that their letters be read from pulpits under their jurisdiction, contributing to widespread opposition to Vichy anti-Semitism. Pierre-Marie Benoît, a Capuchin monk, came to be known as "Father of the Jews" for his efforts to help Jews escape to Spain and Switzerland. His pleas for help from the pope went unheeded. Working in Rome, he probably saved four thousand Jews by obtaining forged documents from Hungarian, Romanian, and Swiss diplomats. Countless other priests and nuns formed a network to organize escapes. The efforts of Father Jacques de Jésus (Lucien Bunel) to save Jews at the religious school he directed were portrayed by Louis Malle in his film *Au Revoir les Enfants*—the last words of Father Jacques to his students as he was led away after being betrayed to the Gestapo. And Protestant pastors played equally important roles in rescuing Jews fleeing deportation. The most prominent of these was André Trocmé of Le Chambon-sur-Lignon, who turned the region into towns and villages of refuge. The people of the region are believed to have saved several thousand Jews.

Equally striking were the efforts of leading Bulgarian and Greek prelates. Metropolitan Stefan, head of the Bulgarian Church (a division of the Greek Orthodox Church), reprimanded his king for allowing Bulgarian Jews to be deported. The church had opposed anti-Semitic laws and the mistreatment of Jews from the outset. Dr. Mordecai Paldiel, former director of the Department for the Righteous at Yad Vashem—and himself a survivor of the Holocaust thanks to a French priest—has written that in all of Europe, the Bulgarian Church was the sole mainline church to oppose government plans to hand the country's Jews over to the Germans. In Greece, Metropolitan Chrysostomos of Zakynthos prevented the deportation of any of the island's Jews. Metropolitan Damaskinos saved approximately ten thousand Jews by colluding with the head of the Athens police to issue false identification cards and instructing priests to aid Jews and open convents to them. Again, evidence of what could be accomplished when the Church played an active and positive role.

Diplomats, especially those representing neutral countries—or countries allied with Germany—may be credited with saving thousands, perhaps hundreds of thousands, of Jews. In the late 1930s, before the outbreak of war in Europe, they could issue visas permitting fleeing Jews to travel to or through their homelands. During the war, Per Anger and Raoul Wallenberg of Sweden together saved more than a hundred thousand Hungarian Jews. Anger was serving in the legation in Budapest when Adolf Eichmann arrived in 1944 to organize the murders for which he later was found culpable. Anger issued protective passes to any Jews who came to his office, identifying the bearers as Swedish citizens. Calling for help from Stockholm, he gained the services of Wallenberg, among others. In addition to issuing passes, they set up safe houses, hospitals, and soup kitchens disguised as Swedish offices. They won agreement from the Hungarian government to honor their passes and had marked success bluffing and intimidating the Germans. It was Anger who subsequently publicized Wallenberg's life and pressed the Soviets to release his colleague—now believed to have been killed by the KGB in 1947.

Before the war, there was ample opportunity for American and British diplomats to aid endangered Jews, but the countries they represented had little interest in sheltering those seeking to flee Germany or Austria. Anti-Semitism was rampant in both the British Foreign Office and the American State Department. It was Ho Feng-shan of China who facilitated the escape of thousands of Austrian Jews, despite orders to the contrary from the Chinese ambassador in Berlin. One British official, Francis Foley, an MI6 agent working under cover as Chief Passport Control Officer in the Berlin embassy, finessed the issue after Kristallnacht by giving out thousands of visas enabling German Jews to leave for various distant parts of the empire, such as Palestine and Rhodesia.

Even after the war started, even after the fall of France, key officials in the U.S. Department of State opposed the rescue of European Jews. In 1996, Warren Christopher, then secretary of state, went to Yad Vashem to apologize for the role his department had played in obstructing the rescue of Hitler's victims. Nonetheless, one American diplomat, Hiram Bingham IV, posted in Marseille, ignored his superiors and worked closely with other Americans, including Varian Fry and Waitstill and Martha Sharp, to move Jews out of occupied France. He secretly issued more than 2,500 visas to Jews fleeing the Gestapo, hiding some in his home, providing disguises, and arranging travel. His actions cost him his job, as the men in Washington preferred not to offend the Vichy regime in France. More than sixty years passed before the U.S. Department of State praised him posthumously for "constructive dissent."

Similarly occupied, in Bordeaux, was the Portuguese consul general, Aristides de Sousa Mendes. In November 1939 he was instructed by the foreign ministry not to issue visas to Jews without prior approval. He, too, ignored his orders and continued to issue transit visas. After the fall of France, Bordeaux was overrun by Jews fleeing the Nazis. Sousa Mendes provided visas for all who sought them and when he was overwhelmed by the desperate refugees, he invited a rabbi friend to assist him. Together they stamped thousands of passports with Portuguese visas. In addition, he ordered the consul in Bayonne to issue more. His reward, in 1941, was dismissal from the diplomatic service without his pension. He died in poverty and he, too, was not "rehabilitated" until many years later.

In Lithuania, where American diplomats chose to withhold even the allowable quota of visas, a Japanese diplomat came to the rescue, saving thousands of Jews at the cost of his career. Chiune Sugihara, a Russian specialist who had converted to Greek Orthodox Christianity, was sent to Kovno to open a consulate in late 1939. When the desperation of Jews fleeing the Nazis from Poland became apparent, Soviet authorities on the scene indicated they would allow people to cross the Soviet Union en route to Japan. Without authorization from Tokyo, Sugihara began issuing visas. In one three-week period, assisted by his wife and a yeshiva student, he awarded at least two thousand visas to heads of families, saving an estimated six thousand Jews—while preparing to leave when Moscow decided to annex Lithuania. Sugihara worked closely with the acting Dutch consul, Jan Zwartendijk, who issued visas for Curaçao and Dutch Guiana, Caribbean colonies out of German reach. Those who were their beneficiaries, mostly Polish Jews (including my friend the late Abe Brumberg, who became a leading American specialist on Russian and East European affairs), were able to escape before the Nazis invaded in June 1941. Sugihara left the diplomatic corps after the war, probably involuntarily. On the hundredth anniversary of his birth in 2000, he was honored posthumously by the Japanese Ministry of Foreign Affairs—which now proudly displays his story on its website.

Two Turkish diplomats, Selahattin Ülkümen, consul general on Rhodes, and Necdet Kent, a consular official in Marseille, liberally gave Turkish citizenship to Jews who claimed Turkish descent. On one occasion, Kent boarded a train headed for Auschwitz and persuaded German guards to release seventy Turkish Jews. It took almost fifty years for the two men to be honored by their government—and Israel.

One of the more interesting "diplomatic" rescuers was an Italian, Giorgio Perlasca, who fought on the side of Franco's fascists during the Spanish civil war. At the end of the war, Franco's government gave him a certificate that read, "Dear Brother-in Arms, No matter where you are in the world, you can turn to Spain." Working as a businessman in Hungary in 1944, Perlasca chose not to return to Italy as ordered by his government and, fearing arrest when the Germans invaded in March 1944, took his certificate to the Spanish embassy. After several trying months, the Spanish ambassador gave him a Spanish passport and a letter for the Hungarian government approving Perlasca's request for Spanish citizenship. The ambassador then employed Perlasca to deal with Jews who claimed Spanish descent and had been placed in safe houses—often attacked by anti-Semitic Arrow Cross gangs. When the ambassador left for Switzerland as the Soviet army approached, Perlasca chose to remain behind as the de facto representative of fascist Spain in Budapest—unbeknownst to the authorities in Madrid. For seven weeks, until the Red Army arrived, he continued to protect Jews and to hand out protective passes, occasionally driving off Hungarian Nazis or Arrow Cross gangs single-handedly, always posing as the representative of the Spanish government. A few years before his death in 1992, Italy honored him.

At least as surprising as an Italian fugitive posing as a Spanish diplomat emerging as a rescuer of Hungarian Jews was the role played by Georg Ferdinand Duckwitz, German maritime attaché in Copenhagen. The story of the dedication of the Danish resistance to saving their country's Jews, including the king's threat to don a yellow star if his Jewish subjects were so tormented, is probably well known. On the eve of the Nazi roundup, 7,200 Danish Jews were ferried across to Sweden. Only a few hundred were caught by the Germans. Duckwitz was the man who made this feat possible. He learned when the Germans planned to strike and alerted contacts in the Danish underground. Then he persuaded a sympathetic German naval commander to keep his patrols at their docks and moorings on the critical night. The Danes did the rest, with the acquiescence of Swedish authorities. Duckwitz survived the war to serve a Hitler-free Germany in several major ambassadorial posts.

Asked why they acted as they did, why they risked their careers—and possibly their lives—to save Jews, all of these men gave essentially the same answer: How could they not do what they did? Aware of the misery of their Jewish supplicants, in most cases having witnessed abuses if not atrocities, they could not conceive of not providing the relief that was at their disposal. And yet most of their colleagues in embassies and consulates across Europe turned their backs on thousands, perhaps millions they, too, might have saved. Why does one man live with the imperative to do the right thing and another feel nothing of the sort?

Doubtless I should not have been surprised that there were Germans, even a few who had joined the Nazi Party, who were horrified by the mistreatment and ultimately the murder of Jews—and risked their lives to save them. I knew, of course, about Oskar Schindler and his list, even if I never saw the film. But there are over four hundred other Germans listed among the Righteous at Yad Vashem, and surely many more who belong there. At times, more than ten thousand Jews may have lived underground in Berlin, suggesting massive assistance from Berliners.

The Schindler story is interesting because Schindler was not a man with a profound commitment to justice or human rights. He was a member of the Nazi Party. He was—and remained to the end—a hustler, an entrepreneur out to maximize his profits. With the help of the SS, he bought a Jewish-owned factory in Kraków for a fraction of its value. Cheap labor in the form of Jews at the mercy of the Nazis served him well. And yet, he came to see these hapless creatures as human, worthy of his compassion and beneficence. The plight of his workers humanized him, and he did what he could to save as many as possible, over a thousand, risking his life and his fortune along the way. As the Holocaust evolved, as he became cognizant of the German atrocities, he appears to have undergone a moral transformation. He came forward as a courier for Jewish aid organizations and helped get out the word about what was going on at Auschwitz. In the last months of the war he saved his workers by moving the factory to Czechoslovakia—where he had served earlier as a spy for the Nazi regime—and feeding them with his own money. His story had to be made into a film, a classic story of the thug with a heart of gold.

Another Nazi Party member who saved some of his workers was Karl Plagge, who oversaw a vehicle repair shop in Vilna, Lithuania, while serving as a major in the Wehrmacht. Plagge had been disillusioned by the Nazis after they came to power, appalled by anti-Semitism at home, and subsequently horrified by the massacre of Jews in Poland. He saved Jews by issuing work cards to unskilled intellectuals, professionals, and their families, as well as artisans, by claiming they had skills necessary to run his facility. He treated his slave labor as humanely as possible, keeping them fed and frustrating SS efforts to kill them—although the SS murdered most of the children while Plagge was on leave. In the closing months of the war, he warned his workers to flee when he learned of an SS plan to massacre them all before the Red Army arrived. More than two hundred survived. He appears to have been a less complicated man than Schindler—no spying, no alcoholism, no mistresses—and there will never be a movie about him. He never saw himself as a hero, but explained later that he had to do what he did to keep an image of himself as a decent human being.

Similarly, Albert Battel was a Nazi Party member, an officer in the Wehrmacht stationed in Poland, who used army troops to stop the SS from seizing Jewish workers for deportation to the death camps. He argued that the murders and deportations were undermining the work of the army. An investigation by the Gestapo determined that he had had Jewish friends before the war—and he was transferred to the Russian front. Himmler put his name on a list to be arrested as soon as the war was over—assuming Germany emerged victorious.

Anton Schmid, an Austrian serving in the Germany army in Vilna, sheltered Jews in his home while Germans were murdering them in the streets. He won the freedom of Jews on their way to killing sites by claiming they were needed for army work. He hid Jews in his office and conspired with Jewish activists to transport fleeing refugees to safer places. Unlike the others, he was arrested and executed in April 1942.

Berthold Beitz was neither a Nazi nor a womanizer, but despite being less dramatic than Schindler, performed essentially the same acts. He was appointed business manager of an oil company in Boryslaw, Poland (now Ukraine), where almost all of the Jews had been killed by Germans and local Ukrainians. He saved hundreds, many without usable skills, by employing them and their families. Some he rescued from deportation roundups, keeping them out of the death camps. He warned them when raids were impending and hid some in the attic of one of his buildings. His wife was alleged to have sheltered Jews in their home. To Beitz, who did not consider himself anti-Nazi, saving people from being murdered was simply the right thing to do.

Otto Weidt used similar techniques. He employed 165 handicapped Jews in his brush and broom workshop and supported more than 50 living underground, who were given shelter by other Berliners. He bribed and cajoled Gestapo agents with great success until October 1943, when a Jewish Gestapo informer called attention to his activities. Weidt talked his way out of jail after his arrest, but had little success rescuing the Jews he had been protecting.

Other Germans saved Jews out of religious conviction or a commitment to the anti-Nazi cause. Several were executed for their actions. Some acted spontaneously in response to Nazi barbarism or the pathetic condition in which they found those they saved. One woman was outraged when Nazis denied grapes to Jewish children and vowed to help the next Jew she met—and did. Some helped Jews for whom they had worked before the war or who had been their friends. One case of unusual interest, sufficient to have spawned a film, was that of Elizabeth Hurst. She had a husband in the army and had given birth to four sons, for which she received bonuses from the German government. She fell in love with a Jewish woman who later was caught by the Gestapo and is presumed to have died at Auschwitz. Subsequently she sheltered several other Jewish lesbians.

The Jews of Poland, Lithuania, and Ukraine historically had lived in uneasy proximity with their Christian neighbors. When the German army arrived early in the war, the natives were only too quick to contribute to the massacre of Jews, often without prompting from the Nazis. In Poland, Jews who fled into the forests to escape German murderers too often found the Polish resistance equally murderous. Most of the Jews who died in the Holocaust died in Poland. And yet, the largest numbers of Righteous memorialized at Yad Vashem were Poles. Despite the survivor stories of Ukrainians who hoped to curry favor with the Germans and win their independence by killing Jews, more than two thousand Ukrainians are listed. Nearly seven hundred Lithuanians, although far fewer than those who collaborated with German execution squads, nonetheless stepped forward to save Jews. Obviously, in Poland, Ukraine, and Lithuania there were more opportunities to save Jews, but there were also greater risks. Anti-Semitism in these lands was so great that a number of the rescuers were murdered by their neighbors when their actions became known after the war; many more were harassed, and all lived under the gravest threat that their acts of mercy would be reported to the Gestapo or local gangs that hunted Jews.

Some of the Poles who risked their lives knew the Jews they helped—had either worked for or with them before the war. Jan Zabinski, a zoologist who had had many Jewish friends in school, hid hundreds of fleeing Jews in the

Warsaw Zoo, as many as fifty at a time, twelve in his own home. One Polish woman discovered to her horror that she was married to a Jew. After her initial outrage, she began to help Jews fleeing from the Sandomierz ghetto and opened her home to those in need. Another, in Auschwitz for political offenses, fell in love with a Jewish woman he met in the camp and they escaped together. They made it back to his home village but his family, not happy to see him with a Jew, sent her elsewhere, then told him falsely that she had died. They met again in 1983 in America, under extraordinary circumstances, an incredible story of a Polish nanny in America telling her Jewish mistress of a Polish TV program about the escape.

But most of the Poles who saved Jews simply acted out of human decency. They saw people—other humans—being treated like animals, and worse, and could not turn them away when they sought help. Some didn't wait for the Jews to be in extremis but pulled them out of the ghettos, warned them of impending pogroms or massacres, and saved them. Polish peasants, nurses, nuns, policemen, and social workers risked their lives to save people they didn't know, people who were despised by their neighbors, because it was the right thing to do. Jan Karski, a young would-be diplomat sent to the Warsaw ghetto by the Polish government-in-exile, was so shaken by the hopelessness of the situation, the imminent massacre of three million innocents, that he spent the rest of the war in a fruitless effort to get Roosevelt and Churchill to rescue Polish Jews. For black humor it would be hard to top the story of the plastic surgeon who donated his services to remove signs of circumcision—as well as reconstructing "Jewish" noses.

In Lithuania, one of the more fascinating stories is that of a Polish nun, Anna Borkowska (Sister Bertranda), mother superior of a Dominican convent near Vilna. She not only hid Jews in the convent but also volunteered to fight alongside Jews in the Vilna ghetto uprising. The leaders of the uprising used her instead to smuggle in grenades and other weapons. To her dismay, her efforts to serve as a liaison with Polish resisters failed when the Poles refused to supply weapons to Jews.

Jonas Paulavicius, Jaroslavas Rakevicius, and Mykolas Simelis were native Lithuanians who took enormous risks to save Jews. Both Paulavicius, derided by his neighbors as the "Father of the Jews," and Simelis were murdered by their fellow Lithuanians, outraged by their efforts. Rakevicius, a simple peasant, could not bear watching Kovno Jews being massacred by his countrymen on the eve of the German occupation. He regularly drove his wagon ninety kilometers to Kovno to rescue fleeing Jews and saved about thirty, including the future president of the Israeli Supreme Court. His friend Jonas Mozuraitis, a poor peasant, hid some of them in a bunker under his house.

Both Rakevicius and Mozuraitis hid their benevolence as well as the Jews from their neighbors and survived.

Murderous anti-Semitism seemed rampant in Ukraine, where roving militias simplified the task of would-be Nazi executioners. A few Ukrainians who had been helped by Jews at some time sheltered their benefactors. Others were moved by an ordinary sense of decency to prevent murder. Most striking was the role of Ukrainian Baptists, who saw Jews as God's chosen people and saw it as a religious duty to save them. Some Jews knew this and sought out Baptist families in their flight. And then there was Anton Sukhinski, the "village idiot" of Zborów. The Germans killed the several thousand Jews they found in the town, but Sukhinski, who opposed killing any of God's creatures, saved seven. When his neighbors found out, they extorted money from the Jews and killed one in an eventual shoot-out. The other six fled, but when they were forced to return, Sukhinski hid them in a hole beneath his basement until the Red Army arrived.

In contrast to the suffering inflicted on endangered Jews by Poles, Lithuanians, and Ukrainians is the extraordinary role played by Danes and Albanians and, to a significant extent, by Bulgarians and Greeks. In Denmark, where almost all the Jews were saved by being transported secretly to Sweden, thanks to the warning by Georg Duckwitz, the Gestapo caught the leader of the rescue operation, Henry Thomsen, and he died in a concentration camp at the age of thirty-eight. The Bishop of Copenhagen had not hesitated to condemn the German plan to deport his country's Jews. The record in Albania was equally extraordinary. The Nazis controlled the country directly for only a year, but their effort to exterminate its Jews was thwarted by the Albanian people, who, according to Mordecai Paldiel, "rallied as one man to save the Jews in their midst." Every Jew who sought shelter found a hiding place with peasants or estate owners. In Bulgaria, not only the Church but also some political leaders, including Dimitar Peshev, vice president of the parliament, argued against the deportation of Bulgarian Jews, alerting Church leaders to the deal the government had worked out with the Germans. In Greece, the Germans succeeded in destroying the ancient Jewish community of Salonika, but many Greeks, including Princess Alice, sheltered Jews in their homes, on their farms, or in nearby forests and mountains. And Church leaders were responsible for saving many more.

I found a number of rescues or rescuers especially interesting. There were three Dutch organizations, two composed of university students, who worked together to save over a thousand Jewish children from the gas chambers. Students in Utrecht contacted others in Amsterdam with a plan to spirit children at risk from German roundups in Amsterdam to Utrecht. They quickly found safe homes for seventy and provided food, clothing, and forged ID cards. Soon they were moving a truckload of Jewish fugitives out of Amsterdam every week, finding safe houses all over the country. Female couriers registered babies as their own and claimed ignorance about fathers. The Catholic Church, especially the Archbishop of Utrecht, provided funding. Unfortunately, German agents penetrated the Utrecht end of the operation and betrayed its members. Several were caught, tortured, executed or sent to concentration camps, such as Belsen-Belsen, where one of the leaders died.

Another Dutch hero executed by the Nazis was the pacifist, anarchist, and evangelical Christian Johan Westerweel. He and his colleagues smuggled more than seventy young Jews across the Pyrenees into Spain. He led one group from the Netherlands, through Belgium and France, all the way to the Pyrenees. But he was betrayed and arrested by the Nazis at the Dutch-Belgian crossing point—and killed. He told the Jews that he was helping them not as Jews—he would do the same for any people—but in the name of justice.

Nearby, in Belgium, there was a château in the Ardennes woods, owned by the Queen Mother and run as a home for retarded children. Sixty Jewish children were hidden there in March 1943. Overall responsibility rested with a princess in Brussels, but the headmistress, Marie Taquet-Mertens, was credited with saving eighty Jewish children—several of whom testified that she kissed them all every night. In general, Belgians, like Danes and Albanians, seemed determined to protect their fellow citizens from the invaders.

The Swiss government was notorious for its appeasement of Hitler's Germany and its hostile policy toward Jews fleeing the Nazis. Nonetheless, there were Swiss citizens who refused to turn their backs on Hitler's victims. One of these was Paul Grüninger, a border guard who defied orders to send refugees back to Germany. He falsified the entry date on police seals on their passports so that it appeared they had entered Switzerland before the March 1938 deadline. He even bought clothes for some of those whose entry he facilitated. Eventually, the Gestapo located the leak across the border and persuaded the Swiss authorities to dismiss him from his post and try him for his "crimes." The Swiss prosecutor charged that he had allowed 3,600 illegals into the country. He was found guilty, fined, and denied his pension. Astonishingly, an effort to "rehabilitate" him in 1985 failed. It was not until 1995, many years after his death, that the Swiss government finally conceded that Grüninger had acted appropriately.

The previously mentioned Americans Varian Fry and the Sharps, Waitskill and Martha, were sent to France and Prague respectively by organizations determined to save refugees from the Nazis. The Sharps, initially sponsored by the Unitarian Service Committee, concerned primarily with

Unitarians fleeing the Nazis, were forced to leave Czechoslovakia as the Gestapo closed in on them in August 1939. In June 1940 they returned to Europe, this time to France, where they joined forces with Fry and Bingham to assist the escape of French intellectuals, mostly Jews and anti-Nazi activists. Eleanor Roosevelt had pushed the Department of State to allow two hundred of them to enter the United States, but Fry succeeded in getting as many as two thousand out of France to Spain, Cuba, Martinique, and North Africa—including Hannah Arendt, Marc Chagall, Max Ernst, Arthur Koestler, and Jacques Lipschitz. One amusing ploy that he used to get his charges into Spain was to obtain Chinese visas that unbeknownst to the Spanish border guards were stamped "no entry permitted" in Chinese. Martha Sharp, on her own, rescued twenty-seven children, nine of them Jewish. In August 1941, with the approval of the American embassy, Fry and the Sharps were thrown out of France by the Vichy regime.

Fry was a journalist and Waitskill Sharp was a Unitarian minister. A more unusual savior of Jews was Nikolai Kislev, a partisan commander of Belarusian origin. Drafted into the Red Army and captured by the Germans, he escaped and organized former Soviet soldiers for guerrilla warfare. He was ordered to collect escaped Jews and stop them from raiding local farms for food. He found hundreds in the forest, women and children as well as men, all of whom had been brushed aside by other partisan groups who perceived them as a burden or wanted nothing to do with Jews. He decided to lead them all to safety, behind Soviet lines. For nearly three months, he led this ragtag group, some sick, hundreds of miles through German lines, sometimes under fire, and put them on trains for the interior.

In Romania, Traian Popovici, the mayor of Cernauti, was appalled by the willingness of the country's dictator, Ion Antonescu, to order the deportation of fifty thousand Jews, half the population of his city. He asked the governor of his province if he wanted to be remembered by historians as responsible for more deaths than Robespierre. The answer, apparently, was yes. In July 1941, the Romanian army entered the city and killed six hundred Jews. Soon afterward the Germans came and killed over two thousand more. Until he was removed from office, Popovici succeeded in blocking the deportation of twenty thousand Jews, hiding some in his own home. Contrary to orders from the governor, he paid pensions to Jewish employees of the city government. He visited the ghetto to try to comfort those confined there. Under his successor, four thousand more Jews were sent to death camps. Popovici's career came to an abrupt end, but as he later insisted, he had no regrets. He had come from a long line of priests and knew what human decency required of him.

I found two other stories especially touching, one from Bosnia and one from Croatia. Mustafa and Zejneba Hardaga, Muslims in Sarajevo, sheltered Jewish neighbors, and sent food to the prison when the father was arrested and to Mostar after he escaped and assembled his family there. In the 1990s, when Bosnia was racked by the horrors of ethnic cleansing, Slobodan Milošević's war, those members of the Hardaga family who survived were brought to a safe haven in Israel. Zejneba died in Israel. Her daughter converted to Judaism and now works in the archives at Yad Vashem.

In Croatia, leaders of the Jewish underground hoped to join forces with Tito's partisans to fight the Germans and the dreaded Ustaše, Croatian fascists. They sent their women and children to Topusko, a town in which there were Ustaše supporters—and the refugees were not welcomed. One seventeen-year-old boy, Ivan Vranetic, chose to help, finding shelters, caring for the sick, warning the Jews when Ustaše raids were expected. In the process, he fell in love with a young widow, six years his senior. When the war ended, he proposed marriage. The woman's mother was adamantly opposed to her daughter marrying a Catholic—even one who had saved her life—and the Jewish family moved to Israel. There the woman remarried and had children. Ivan remained in Croatia, caring for his parents. In 1963, he visited Israel and found that the woman he had loved was divorced. He returned a year later to care for her and her children. As I write, he is the president of an organization that looks after Yad Vashem honorees who choose to live out their lives in Israel. Surely there's another motion picture here.

Explanations for why people were motivated to save Jews from the Holocaust rightly stress compassion and unwillingness to tolerate injustice. Most of the rescuers, especially those who lived in communities where anti-Semitism was rampant, appear to have met David Riesman's definition of "inner-directed." They acted in accordance with their principles. They followed their own moral compass, often, but not always, consistent with what they believed to be Christian values. Sometimes they were driven by hostility to the German invaders and sometimes by friendship with or love for individual Jews. A few may have been naïve, but the overwhelming majority of them knew they were taking extraordinary risks. And many suffered death, torture, imprisonment, and ostracism for their good deeds.

The sad addendum to this story involves the mistreatment of Christian rescuers in Israel, the ingratitude of some of those saved, and the disappointment of some of the Righteous in what they consider Israel's betrayal of the principles for which they risked their lives. Ivan Vranetic has expressed concern about racism in Israel. Several Christian rescuers who moved to Israel have complained about Orthodox Jews demanding that they leave the country. One had his house stoned by Jews chanting "Goy, goy, go away, goy." Another had swastikas painted on his house while his tormentors urged the goy to go back to Bulgaria. Worst of all was the disenchantment with the state of Israel: How could Jews turn around and mistreat Arabs on the West Bank and the Gaza strip? Gay Block and Malka Drucker in their book, *Rescuers: Portraits of Moral Courage in the Holocaust*, interviewed Maria Countess von Maltzan of Berlin, who saved many Jews during the war, including the man she married. The countess refused to go to Israel to accept a medal from Yad Vashem because Israel did not stand for her ideals. She referred specifically to Israeli complicity in the massacre of Palestinian refugees at Sidon in Lebanon.

What lesson was to be learned from the Jewish experience in the Holocaust if Jews can become oppressors? Who now are the Righteous?

Pope John XXIII, used by permission of L'Osservatore Romano, Città del Vaticano

CHAPTER 11

Pope John XXIII and Catholic Humanism

Although I grew up in a predominantly Catholic neighborhood in Brooklyn, New York, my interest in Catholicism did not begin until, as an undergraduate, I became fascinated by the writings of St. Augustine, St. Thomas Aquinas, and Miguel de Unamuno. At approximately the same time, I was appalled by what I learned about the vicious anti-Semitism of the "radio priest," Father Charles Coughlin; of Pope Pius XII's callous indifference to the fate of the Jews of Europe; and of the reactionary rantings of Francis Cardinal Spellman of New York. My attitude toward the Church was ambivalent, at best—until the election of Pope John XXIII.

The man responsible for my admiration of the role of the Roman Catholic Church was born Angelo Giuseppe Roncalli in northern Italy on November 25, 1881. His parents were poor peasants who already had three children and produced still another when Angelo was eighteen months old. Unable to care for them all—ultimately there were thirteen—his parents put Angelo in the care of a bachelor uncle. Uncle Zaverio raised the boy for the next ten years before enrolling him in a seminary in 1893. Angelo appears to have had little contact with his father and only a little more with his mother and siblings. The Church became his home and his family.

At the age of fourteen, young Roncalli began to keep a journal, published after his death as *Journey of a Soul*. Given the portly pope the world met in 1958, the least surprising of his early entries is his confession that he liked to eat. More surprising is his fear of being tempted by women. He determined to avoid their company and all talk of sex. He promised Mary, Mother of

God, that he would guard against impure thoughts, and he contrived a way to sleep that might keep his hands from straying and result in wet dreams. There seems little doubt but that at some point in his youth, a woman had aroused—and frightened—him. His concern about temptation did not pass until he was in his sixties.

As a teenager, he judged himself lacking in humility. He perceived his greatest failing to be excessive self-esteem. Having been passed off to an uncle as an infant and sent off to the seminary as a child does not appear to have left him feeling unloved or unworthy. Perhaps a psychologist would suggest he overcompensated, seeing himself as part of a divine plan, confident of his ability and virtue. He believed that God had a purpose for him and demanded absolute virtue of him, wanted him "entirely holy." Somehow he had to rid himself of a tendency toward pride and arrogance and of the desire for others to recognize his wisdom and virtue. When his parish priest died in 1896, he left the boy his copy of The Imitation of Christ, and Roncalli, according to several biographers, was greatly influenced by the book, finding in it guidelines for the spirituality he sought.

Philosophically, some of the ideas that illuminated his years as pope were nurtured by the milieu in which he was raised by his uncle and by the Church. His uncle was involved with Catholic Action, an organization committed to helping the working poor, to ameliorating the lives of the victims of industrialization. In 1891, two years before Roncalli entered the seminary in Bergamo, Leo XIII issued the encyclical Rerum Novarum, denouncing the evils of laissez-faire capitalism, focusing on the suffering of the poor, demanding that the state protect the rights of workers, and defending their right to organize. Leo was attempting to reverse the course of his reactionary predecessor, Pius IX, hoping to align the Church with the workers in their efforts to gain social justice.

Similarly, Bergamo in the 1890s was blessed with a bishop sympathetic to the victims of strikes and lockouts and determined to follow Leo's lead. The church in that small city was dedicated to social action on behalf of the poor. Roncalli's uncle and his bishop, as well as the pope, focused on social issues, suggesting to the young seminarian that there was more to his calling than theology, that the pastoral role of the priest was paramount. In 1899, he met and admired Giacomo Radini-Tedeschi, a member of the Roman Curia and a noted activist in the Church's quest for social justice—further reinforcement of the tendencies all around him.

Unsuppressed ambition to rise in the Church was spurred by the award of a scholarship to attend a seminary in Rome in 1901. In Rome he found fulfillment by working in soup kitchens, continuing to serve the poor as he had in Bergamo. He was drawn immediately into Radini-Tedeschi's orbit, but in November his contentment was suddenly shattered by a draft notice.

Not yet a priest, Roncalli served for a year as a common soldier, confronted by a world he had never known. He was unprepared for and horrified by the blasphemy and lewdness of barracks talk. He had apparently known lust himself, but the openness, the crudeness with which his fellow soldiers discussed sexual activity, real or imagined, shook his faith in the goodness of ordinary people. It must have been a very difficult year for a young man preparing himself for a life of celibacy—but he survived and was better prepared for military life when Italy went to war in 1914.

A more serious setback for Roncalli's vision came with the death of Pope Leo in 1903. Churchmen hostile to Leo's "modernism"—his attempt to bring Church practice into line with the realities of the new industrial world, his support for workers against capitalists, and his leanings toward democracy—prevailed in the selection of his successor, Pius X. Pius quickly repudiated Leo's teachings and began a purge of "modernists" in the Curia. Radini-Tedeschi's operations were eliminated and he was reined in, at approximately the same time as Roncalli's ordination as a priest in 1904.

By 1905, Radini-Tedeschi was no longer welcome in Rome, and he was sent to Bergamo as bishop. Not surprisingly, he took Roncalli along as his secretary. The two men were an odd pair: Radini-Tedeschi stiff-necked, authoritarian, unwilling to accept the Vatican's reversed course; Roncalli warm, friendly, accommodating, more willing to compromise to achieve their shared ends. The younger man served his bishop well, arguing in defense of historical criticism in a lecture at the seminary in 1907 and supporting Radini-Tedeschi's use of church funds to aid strikers at a local textile factory in 1909. But at a retreat in 1910, he professed to see the wisdom in the pope's efforts to root out "modernist errors" among the clergy. Perhaps moments like that were sufficient to mute criticism and spare him from Rome's purge of modernists.

His most difficult assignment was to work with the Committee of the Union of Italian Catholic Women. He was still not comfortable in the company of women, still fearful of temptation. In his journal he acknowledged that it would be dangerous to rely on his own powers: He needed help from Jesus. He was equally troubled by the fact that he was getting fat, but does not seem to have sought heavenly guidance in coping with this issue. Eating too well was not a sin—at least not of the same magnitude as thinking about sex.

In 1914 Italy went to war, and Roncalli was called to duty again in 1915. As an ordained priest, he served first as a medic and then as a chaplain. The horrors of war and his own relative maturity allowed him to view his fellow soldiers more charitably than he had on his first tour. Their stories and language no longer shocked him, and he ministered to their physical and spiritual pain with the warmth and empathy of an experienced pastor. Of enduring importance was his conviction that he and the Church had to work harder for peace.

When the war ended, Roncalli returned to Bergamo as spiritual director of the seminary. Radini-Tedeschi had died on the eve of the war, and life in Bergamo was much the poorer for his absence. Roncalli was now in his late thirties and beginning to doubt that his ambition to rise in the Church hierarchy would ever be realized. Frequently he berated himself for his frustration, for his desire for promotion, for opportunities to do more with his spiritual energy. He longed for honors and distinctions, but kept telling himself these were mere vanities. He would not attempt to persuade his superiors to find a better position for him.

Roncalli's hope that the Church would take a more active role in temporal affairs, specifically in the protection of the poor, was satisfied to a considerable extent by Benedict XV, who led the Church from 1914 to 1922. Under Benedict's guidance, the Vatican authorized the formation of the Partito Popolare Italiano (PPI) to advocate the interests of peasants and workers in Italy. Roncalli was delighted, believing as he did that the gospel held answers to the evils of industrial society.

At last, in 1921, he received the call to Rome, to serve in the office of the Propaganda Fide. There he could make valuable connections and learn to master the maneuvers necessary for success in the politics of any organization. But whatever dreams he had of advancing in the hierarchy of a church dedicated to social reform were dashed by the death of Benedict in 1922. Once again, the pendulum swung to the right. The new pope, Pius XI, rejected his predecessor's vision of the Church's role in society and abandoned the field to the fascists.

Roncalli proved to be a little less flexible than he had imagined himself to be. His own experience and the teaching of Radini-Tedeschi, of his beloved popes Leo and Benedict, and of his uncle led him to oppose the direction in which Pius XI was taking the Church. His reputation from Bergamo and his enthusiastic support of the PPI did not go unnoticed by the Curia, as evidenced by his next assignment: apostolic visitor to Bulgaria.

The Roman Catholic Church had not been faring well in Bulgaria, where the Orthodox Church was dominant. Roncalli's predecessor had been treated

with disdain by both civil and religious authorities. It was not a choice posting, but he was elevated to bishop before he left and named archbishop of
the Church in Bulgaria. His anxieties about being shipped out into veritable
exile were assuaged by assurances that he would not be in Bulgaria for long
and that his next assignment would be Argentina—a highly desirable position, whose papal legate might reasonably expect to be on track to become
a cardinal.

Alas, the call to Buenos Aires never came, and Roncalli spent ten difficult
years in Bulgaria. He had not expected to find his work easy, but he was surprised to find that most of his "trials" were caused not by the Bulgarians, but
by the Roman Curia. In his initial role as a diplomat, he found negotiating
with the ecclesiastical administration to which he reported far more irritating than his dealings with local authorities. Working with the leaders of the
Orthodox Church, in a country where those faithful to Rome were a minority, gave Roncalli a sense of the value of ecumenism, which he never lost.

As the years passed and he wondered if he would ever be recalled from
Bulgaria, he told himself that the Lord was testing his patience. Though he
much preferred pastoral work to diplomacy, he would do the Lord's work to
the best of his ability. He was determined to impress all with whom he worked
with a sense of dignity and to radiate loving-kindness. Again and again he
had to persuade himself to be content with his position, not to bemoan the
fact that he was little appreciated, perhaps even forgotten by his superiors in
Rome. Of course, he suspected that he was being punished for his support of
the PPI specifically and social reform generally, and he probably understood
that rumors he would be named archbishop of Milan were groundless.

At long last, in 1935, after ten years in Bulgaria, he received a new posting. Any dreams he might have had about Argentina or some other predominantly Roman Catholic country were quickly shattered. He was sent to
Ankara as papal representative for Turkey and Greece.

Ever ready to come to terms with his fate—God's will—he chose to see
the assignment as a reward, a reward for not complaining about being left in
Bulgaria for ten years. He thanked God for getting him through the years in
Bulgaria. He kept trying to convince himself that he didn't care about the
fact that he would never advance in the Church hierarchy. He told himself
that he didn't deserve to be promoted. But from time to time he allowed
himself to acknowledge that perhaps his career progression had been slowed
by differences with Rome, as when he was reprimanded for introducing a
few words of Turkish into his service. He was hurt by Rome's unwillingness
to accept his "on the spot" analyses of issues, but determined to continue
to speak truth to power—although gently, without complaint about having

been wronged personally. "Above all," he wrote in his journal, "I wish to continue always to render good for evil, and in all things to endeavor to prefer the Gospel truth to the wiles of human politics." He struggled hard to be content, not to lust for worldly honors or promotions. His was the philosophy of a saint, but one not likely to bring fulfillment of the ambition he could not quite suppress.

Roncalli did well in Ankara and became fond of the Turks. He was sensitive to Turkish nationalism and to the bounds of Mustafa Kemal's insistent secularism. He found his mission in Greece less satisfying, especially after World War II began and Greek suspicion of Roman Catholics was aggravated by hostility to the Italians who tried to overrun them. But he kept trying to reach out to all—not only to Catholics but also to Orthodox Christians, Muslims, and Jews. He perceived a need to tear down the walls Rome had built between Catholics and non-Catholics and saw himself doing it brick-by-brick. He found it easy to befriend the British embassy's Anglican chaplain. They were two Christians in a sea of Muslims, and Roncalli did not hesitate to pray in the Anglican chapel. In 1939 he became the first Roman emissary in nine hundred years to meet with the Orthodox patriarch of Constantinople.

As he approached sixty, Roncalli felt that his internal demons were coming under control. Women tempted him less: The impulses of "carnal desire" were withering. He claimed to be pleased that his body had ceased to respond to "the temptations which disturbed it in the years of my youth and vigorous maturity." He seemed at peace with himself, confident that body and mind were under control, and aware that he was unlikely to reach the higher echelons of the Church hierarchy no matter what he did.

The war troubled him, of course. Fond of France, he was particularly unhappy with Mussolini's decision to invade that country. But as the horrors of Hitler's atrocities against the Jews became apparent, saving Jews became his cause. Strangely enough, he appears to have been aided in his effort by friendship with Hitler's ambassador to Turkey, Franz von Papen. He later claimed von Papen helped him save twenty-four thousand Jews—a claim that may have kept the Nazi diplomat from a death sentence at the Nuremberg War Crimes Trial.

Roncalli received no help from the Vatican. When he forwarded a request from the Jewish Agency for assistance in gaining temporary asylum in Portugal and Sweden for endangered Jews, the Vatican refused—although funding would have been provided by Americans. In particular, Rome did not want to see Jewish refugees fleeing to Palestine, where they were perceived as a threat to Christian Holy Places: Palestine must not belong to the Jews. Despite his own reservations about sending Jews to Palestine, Roncalli signed transit visas enabling thousands of Slovakian Jews to leave Bulgaria for Palestine and forwarded immigration visas for Palestine to Vatican diplomats in Hungary and Romania, winning thanks from the grand rabbi of Jerusalem. Rumors that he issued certificates of baptism to Jews on request were dismissed by Peter Hebblethwaite, the best of his biographers. Nonetheless, one can scarcely imagine how many lives might have been saved had Pius XII been as caring as Roncalli was for all God's children.

One other thought took root in Roncalli's mind in the course of the war. To his long-standing belief that secularism was an evil poisoning the world, he added the conviction that nationalism was equally poisonous. World peace, for which Radini-Tedeschi had prayed on his deathbed in 1914, was obviously as important as social reform. The poor were the most likely victims of war as well as of laissez-faire capitalism. Peace would require the muting of nationalist fervor, the ability to see peoples of different nations as human, as equals. The war had enlarged Roncalli's view of his pastoral mission.

At the end of the war, the Vatican, which had aligned itself with the collaborationist Vichy government in France, faced a tense situation in that country. Socialists and communists had played major roles in the French resistance, and Pius XII was fearful of the spread of communism in Europe. On the other hand, Charles de Gaulle, leader of the victorious Free French, wanted the Church in France purged of those who had collaborated with Vichy or the Nazis. Although de Gaulle had little sympathy for the Left, in 1945 he was less troubled by communism than by Church leaders perceived as friendly to fascists. He demanded that the papal nuncio be replaced.

However reluctantly, the pope acquiesced and offered the post to his representative in Argentina. When he declined on grounds of ill health, the pope turned to his second choice, sixty-four-year-old Angelo Roncalli. Perhaps Roncalli's friendship with von Papen had misled the Roman Curia into assuming that Roncalli had outgrown his reformist tendencies.

After twenty years in Sofia and then Ankara, Roncalli may well have imagined Paris to be the last stop this side of heaven. He loved France, and he was delighted by the assignment. And the move reawakened dreams of becoming a cardinal, a promotion that usually followed the posting to Paris. He had to assure himself anew that promotion in the hierarchy was a matter of indifference to him.

Although he denigrated "the superabundant cunning and so-called skill of the diplomat " and prided himself on his ability to prevail by befriending all, Roncalli's task in Paris demanded every ounce of diplomatic skill he had acquired. Rome mistrusted the clergy who had been active in the resistance and was appalled by many of the "leftist" ideas of French intellectuals, both in and out of the Church. Many French priests were openly contemptuous of the Vatican and determined to reform the Church. Clever though he was, Roncalli was not prepared to enter the intellectual life of Paris. But he did understand the need for reform, given the alienation of French workers from the Church, and many of the reforms demanded echoed those of Radini-Tedeschi. Somehow he had to improve relations between France and the Vatican.

Roncalli served the Vatican loyally, never openly questioning its policies. Most French priests assumed he shared the views of the Curia, as when he persuaded de Gaulle to back off from his request that three clerics who resisted occupation authorities be elevated to cardinal. But the French clergy filled him with ideas for reforming the church, for aligning it with the realities of the postwar world. He was sympathetic to the priests who came out of the concentration camps determined to bring the workers back into the Church by modernizing rituals and teachings and using everyday French if necessary. Their ideas were anathema to the pope, but Roncalli succeeded in protecting the worker-priest movement as long as he was in Paris. He worked quietly with members of the French left, keeping the peace when they were vilified by the pope. He even developed a relationship with the Soviet ambassador to France, which could not have been explained easily to Rome.

Somehow, Roncalli succeeded in easing tensions between France and the Vatican, and his reward, in 1953 at the age of seventy-one, was the long-coveted promotion to cardinal. Now his greatest fear was that he would be assigned to the Roman Curia, to the administrative work he hated. Happily, he was offered the position of patriarch of Venice, where he imagined he would spend his remaining years doing the kind of pastoral work that gave him the greatest satisfaction.

There can be no doubt that Roncalli's vision was not congruent with that of Pius XII or the majority of the Roman Curia. His long years in the wilderness are ample evidence of that fact. However, the call to Paris and the elevation to cardinal indicated that he had never strayed so far from the course dictated by Rome that he was considered dangerous or incorrigible. Perhaps most important was the presence in the Curia of the able Giovanni Battista Montini, a highly regarded and influential priest who shared many of Roncalli's views and did what he could to protect him and to further his career. Unfortunately, after surviving thirty years in Rome, Montini offended powerful conservatives and was sent off to serve as archbishop of Milan. The dominant clerics in the Curia were less threatened by dissenters, however prominent, serving outside of Rome than they were by competitors for power and influence in the halls of the Vatican.

Nonetheless, Roncalli was thriving in Venice. He told himself that he had never imagined or desired so great a position, but was probably not convinced. He prepared for death while frequently noting his excellent health. Above all, he was having a wonderful time. He was the first patri-arch of Venice to attend the city's modern art biennial, and he lifted the ban against attendance by the clergy. He invited the avant-garde composer Igor Stravinsky to conduct the premiere of his *Sacred Canticle in Honor of St. Mark the Evangelist* in St. Mark's Cathedral, Venice's great landmark. And he angered Rome by welcoming the Thirty-second Congress of the Italian Socialist Party to Venice.

In 1956, Roncalli, conceivably under orders from Rome, did criticize the Christian Democratic Party for its "opening to the Left," its expressed willingness to collaborate with the socialists. And yet it was clear that he did not share the Vatican's inability to distinguish between socialists and communists. Moreover, he, like Montini, was troubled by the intensity of the Church's anticommunism. Both men appear to have believed the Church was pushing the Christian Democrats to the right and allowing the party to ignore the need for social justice—their ultimate concern. Roncalli's long-standing ties to Catholic Action notwithstanding, he was profoundly dis-turbed by the organization's emphasis on anticommunism to the detriment of its historic identity with the needs of the poor.

Central to Roncalli's sense of his God-given mission was the task of bring-ing people together. Initially, he conceived of his role as bringing lapsed Catholics back to the Church, especially alienated workers—thus, his support for the worker-priest movement in France. Gradually, he began to envision the possibility of bring all Christians together—certainly the Orthodox and, perhaps some day, the Protestants. Increasingly, he saw the need to reach out and recognize the humanity of others, even of Jews and communists.

And then in 1958, Pius XII was dead and Roncalli was called to Rome to participate in the selection of the next pope. Despite his determination to be humble and suppress ambition, he quickly realized that he was a contender, and he maneuvered skillfully to improve his chances. As usual, the central tension was between the Roman Curia and the outsiders, es-pecially the French cardinals. The perennial issue of the Curia's control of the Church, substantively as well as administratively, its determination to defend that power, and the desire of many cardinals outside Rome to have a greater voice in Church affairs, would be fought out in the selection of a new pope. Roncalli met with the key players on both sides, eager for each of the contending forces to see him as their best bet. His diplomatic experience served him well.

Many of the cardinals, perhaps even a majority of them, were looking for a man who would be very different from the cold, aloof, autocratic Pius XII. They were looking for a pope they would find accessible, a man who could reconcile the Church to the realities of the modern world, a man who could unite all classes of society, who might have appeal beyond the West, across the world. Some dared to hope for a pope who could reach out to communist leaders and bring peace to the world and an end to the persecution of Christians. Their first choice was probably Montini.

Montini, however, frightened the Roman Curia, and he was never in contention. The Curia's representatives at the conclave were resolute in their determination to keep him in Milan. Roncalli, however, was not perceived as threatening. He may have shared many of Montini's views, but he was an easygoing old man of questionable intellect who could be managed. Of the candidates who might satisfy the would-be reformers, the seventy-seven-year-old Roncalli was the least troubling to the Church's conservative bureaucrats.

And so, after eleven ballots, Angelo Giuseppe Roncalli became pope on October 28, 1958, and declared himself John XXIII. The reformers did not see him as their man, but the French cardinals who knew him believed he would support efforts to modernize the Church. Conservatives probably perceived him as a caretaker whose persona would satisfy those looking for a warmer, more accessible pope, but whose unfamiliarity with the ways of Rome would leave the bureaucracy in control. They would have time to regroup, to reorganize, to ward off the winds of change, to devise some means of keeping Montini out of the Vatican.

There was little to trouble the Curia in John's initial actions. He appointed as secretary of state Domenico Tardini, a conservative member of the Curia with whom he had invariably disagreed when their paths had crossed over the years. This was both an admission that he was unfamiliar with the workings of the Vatican bureaucracy and a signal that he wished to avoid confrontation with it. (In the months that followed he had reason to regret that decision, as Tardini proved to be less flexible than John had hoped.) In his first public address the pope spoke out against communism while calling for world peace. To be sure, he called for Christian unity and went on a bit about the wastefulness of the arms race, but these themes were too commonplace to arouse apprehension.

Only two days after becoming pope, John named a host of new cardinals, twenty-three in all, with Montini and Tardini at the top of his list. A student of urban machine politics in America would have recognized the balanced ticket immediately. In addition, he reached out to the developing world, naming the first black African cardinal and the first Filipino, Indian, and Mexican cardinals. The Italians remained dominant, but John's Church was reaching out to the rest of the world.

His style was unquestionably different from that of his predecessor. Not at all reclusive, he went out among the people of Rome, emphasizing his conception of the pastoral role of the city's bishop. On Christmas Day he visited a children's hospital and a prison. He advised the Curia that as a pastoral pope, he needed a pastoral Curia. The papal bureaucrats may have been contemptuous, but he was not challenging their power or meddling in theological questions for which they suspected he was intellectually ill-equipped.

And then, in January 1959, came a major jolt to whatever complacency members of the Curia might have enjoyed. John announced his desire to convene a Vatican Council, a meeting that—if not managed with excruciating care—could result in radical change. If possible, he would have to be dissuaded. If he persisted, the Curia would have to oversee the invitations and the agenda with the greatest attention. It would have to act as necessary to retain control of everything that occurred at the council. But that was not what John had in mind.

By all accounts he had no agenda of his own, but he was determined to have an open meeting with the broadest possible participation to consider new ideas, to consider ways in which the Church might serve mankind a little better. He wanted to invite observers from other Christian orders, praying for the reunification of all who called themselves Christians. And he was determined to avoid the inquisitional tone that seemed to pervade the Curia. He wanted to bridge the gap between the Curia's fixation on doctrinal issues and the needs of the local churches. In addition to ecumenism, he thought it would be useful to discuss the issue of clerical celibacy (which he favored) and the use of the vernacular in church liturgy (which he also favored). He seemed to realize he was traversing a minefield, but he was old, preparing to die, and he saw no need to be overly cautious.

As the most powerful conservatives in the Curia geared up for battle, John chose to avoid confrontation, demonstrating his lifelong ability to compromise, to settle for less than the whole loaf, for incremental change.

Tardini's hand was always evident in John's public statements. Would-be reformers were troubled, unsure of where the pope was headed, uneasy as they
perceived indications of the Curia's continued dominance. Montini feared
disaster, especially after he was excluded from the initial preparations.

An optimist might have gleaned reason for hope in some of John's activities. Not only did he roam out of the Vatican more than his predecessor had,
but he also met with foreigners as disparate as Queen Elizabeth II, Princess
Grace (Kelly) of Monaco, the Japanese prime minister, and several presidents of Muslim countries. He invited non-Catholic clerics to St. Peter's.
One day he was talking with an American Episcopal bishop and then, for
the first time in centuries, the Archbishop of Canterbury was received at the
Vatican. John began making small but significant changes in ceremonies,
modifying prayers to leave them less offensive to people of other faiths,
especially Jews. He dropped the reference to "perfidious" Jews in the Good
Friday service, hoping to begin the process of eliminating historic Catholic
anti-Semitism—despite intense opposition from within the Curia. In his
journal he wrote, "The whole world is my family."

A pessimist, however, would have perceived that John was not in control
of either the Curia or the Italian cardinals. Led by Tardini and Alfredo Cardinal Ottaviani, the Curia's response to John's desire for a more open and
inclusive Church was to become more repressive, throwing thunderbolts at
journalists and theologians who appeared emboldened by John's words. The
most powerful Italian cardinals, men chosen by Pius XII, remained true to
Pius's vision of the Church's role. In particular, they were determined to
keep anticommunism in the forefront of Church teaching and found John's
performance wanting.

For several years, leaders of the Christian Democratic Party in Italy had
been uneasy about the party's drift toward the right, toward what they feared
was neofascism. One party leader, Aldo Moro, was eager to broaden the
party's base through alliance with socialists, as a means of demonstrating
concern for workers. The idea was opposed vehemently by Giuseppe Cardinal Siri of Genoa—Italy's equivalent of Cardinal Spellman—with the support of the Curia. Such was the power of the Church in Italy that Moro did
not dare act without its approval.

John was troubled on two counts. He believed the Church should not
be interfering in secular politics—that the Vatican had long since accepted
the principle of separation of church and state. But even more important
was his dissatisfaction with the reactionary impulses that drove Siri and his
colleagues. John had worshipped Leo XIII, considered him the "light and
guidance" of his youth, the model of his priesthood, and he was determined

to carry on Leo's legacy of identifying the Church with labor. His record in Bergamo and in Paris demonstrated his commitment.

With support from Montini, John acted to neutralize Siri and the Curia. Montini fired the clerical editor of the Milan newspaper that had attacked Moro, and John saw to it that the Vatican's official paper held fire. Then the pope received Amintore Fanfani, Italy's Christian Democratic prime minister who was committed to Moro's opening to the Left. He publicly endorsed the concept of separation of church and state, indicating that the Church would not interfere in Italian politics, would not attempt to impede Moro's efforts. Indeed, John subsequently gave Moro an audience. Not surprisingly, Cardinal Siri saw John's pontificate as "the greatest disaster in recent ecclesiastical history."

A month later, he issued one of his most memorable encyclicals, *Mater et Magistra*, in which he expressed with great intensity his commitment to social justice, to helping the poor, to meeting the needs of farmers and workers. He noted that the right to private property was essential to freedom, but that right could not be protected to the detriment of the less fortunate members of society. Pay for work could not be left to the dictates of the market: It had to be just and equitable. Unregulated competition, "despotic economic power in the hands of a few" was as contrary to Christ's teaching as was the Marxist call for class struggle. John praised systems of social security and the welfare state's efforts to avoid mass unemployment, insisting only that the state not deprive the individual of his freedom of action. His principal fear was that in a weak or indifferent state, the weak would be exploited by the strong.

Looking beyond Europe, John expressed his profound sadness over the subhuman conditions in which millions of workers on entire continents were forced to live. He recognized how many countries were struggling to develop, but argued that economic progress had to be accompanied by social progress, so that all could share in any improvements. He praised the efforts of the International Labor Organization (ILO) to obtain economic justice and protect the rights of workers, and the work of the Food and Agriculture Organization (FAO) to alleviate hunger. He endorsed cooperatives and progressive taxes, and he called upon the great powers to give aid to developing countries without political strings.

Toward the end of the encyclical, John spoke to the international political situation. Predictably, he called for international understanding and cooperation. He addressed the arms race with surprising sophistication, explaining it in terms of what political scientists call the "security dilemma": each nation feared the other planned to attack and armed to defend itself, frightening the other and forcing it to increase its war-making capability, thus stimulating an endless arms race. He recognized the ideological roots of the mutual mistrust but questioned the need for so much defense spending, without suggesting that responsibility lay with the Soviets.

On many issues, birth control for example, John never strayed from the positions laid out by his immediate predecessors. There was little to warm the hearts of advocates of family planning or feminists. He certainly never questioned the Church's traditional priority of saving souls, but he stated explicitly that concern for "man's daily life, with his livelihood and education, and his general, temporal welfare and prosperity" were also essential to its mission. His was a mid-twentieth-century version of Leo's vision of the role of the Church. The differences between *Mater et Magistra* and the words of Pius XII were noticed around the world, even in Moscow.

But John's vision found little resonance in the various reports of the commission established to prepare for the council. Dominated by the Curia, which excluded liberal theologians and all lay men and women from its workings, the commission was obviously determined to defend the program of Pius XII. On the periphery, however, brilliant Catholic intellectuals, such as John Courtney Murray, SJ, and Hans Küng fought back. Léon Joseph Cardinal Suenens of Mechlin, Belgium, complained directly to the pope, and John encouraged him to criticize the preparatory texts publicly. Augustin Bea, SJ, upon whom John forced a cardinal's hat in 1960, is portrayed by Hebblethwaite as John's agent within the preparatory commission and credited with the maneuvers that allowed John to put his stamp on the council. Bea's principal focus was ecumenism, and his secret negotiations with Moscow succeeded in gaining the participation of bishops from communist countries and representatives of the Russian Orthodox Church. Ultimately, to bring about open debate and the modernization of the Church that John hoped would be his legacy, his bishops were forced to repudiate the work of his preparatory commission.

Almost immediately after the council convened in October 1962, the bishops attending voted to have members of the council's various commissions chosen in free elections, denying the Curia the power to appoint them. Ottaviani and his colleagues were in for a fight, the outcome of which might determine the role of the Church for years to come. And it was quickly apparent that the conservatives did not have the pope's support. In his opening address to the council assembly, John rejected the negative, inquisitional approach of the preparatory commission and invited critiques of its texts. He argued that the validity of Church doctrine would have to be determined by modern scholarship: Challenges could not be condemned merely on the basis of tradition. To the disgust of Ottaviani, he appointed Karl Rahner, SJ, a critic of the preparatory commission's texts, as the council's official theologian. As the tide shifted against him, Ottaviani is alleged to have declared his wish to die before the end of the council so that he might still die a Catholic.

Men like Rahner, Montini, Küng, and Suenens drove the council in the directions John had envisioned: toward greater cooperation with the non-Roman Christian churches, toward greater responsiveness to the needs of the laity, and away from obsessive anticommunism and anti-Semitism. John wanted and would get a Church that was alive to the realities of the 1960s, ready to move beyond the defensive rigidity and indifference to non-Catholics that had characterized the reign of his predecessors. And he could take pleasure in the knowledge that it would once again be a Church of which Pope Leo and Uncle Zaverio could be proud.

On the eve of the council, in September 1962, John had learned that he had stomach cancer. He knew he had little time left, and his determination to work for world peace intensified. Central as the council was to his concerns, he did not let preparations for it or its activities to monopolize his time. He was determined to alleviate Cold War tensions, to assert that communists were also a part of humanity, to demonstrate that Moscow, too, hoped for peace. Whereas Pius XII was willing to excommunicate Italians who voted for Communist Party candidates, John angered Church conservatives by refusing to excommunicate Fidel Castro. In September 1961, he sent a message to a conference of nonaligned nations meeting in Belgrade to endorse its disarmament proposals. When Soviet leader Nikita Khrushchev remarked favorably on the pope's message, John perceived an opportunity to improve relations between the Vatican and the Kremlin. Working through the Italian Communist leader Palmiro Togliatti, John and Khrushchev reached out to each other cautiously. On John's eightieth birthday in November, Khrushchev sent greetings. John responded warmly, sending not only thanks for the greeting but also his best wishes to the Russian people.

Leaders in both Washington and Moscow recognized that the Vatican approach to communism and the Cold War had changed radically. American Cold Warriors were clearly unhappy about a pope who seemed dangerously soft on communism, but found John's credibility with Khrushchev useful in the midst of the Cuban missile crisis of October 1962. As Khrushchev and the American president, John F. Kennedy, struggled to escape the abyss of nuclear war, the crisis caused by the Soviet surreptitious introduction of intermediate-range ballistic missiles into Cuba, Kennedy asked for the pope's help, asked John to call for negotiations. John did so, and the text of his speech was carried on the front page of *Pravda*, mouthpiece of the Soviet government. Conceivably the speech gave Khrushchev additional cover for his retreat, and publication of the pope's message was perceived in Washington as a signal of Khrushchev's intent to retreat. Both Khrushchev and Kennedy appear to have been grateful for the pope's role. Kennedy sent a message of thanks, and Khrushchev subsequently acquiesced to the pope's request for the release of seventy-year-old Ukrainian metropolitan Josef Slipyi, who had been in a Soviet labor camp since 1948. In return, John promised not to use the release for anti-Soviet propaganda.

The pope and the Soviet leader exchanged Christmas greetings in December 1962—at Khrushchev's initiative. John typed the response himself, to be certain the Curia did not edit out the warmth he wished to convey. On the morning after Christmas he awoke, knelt before the crucifix in his bedroom, and consecrated his last days to the conversion of Russia to Catholicism. Khrushchev doubtless would have been horrified. The connection between the two men deepened a few months later when John received Khrushchev's daughter and her husband, a prominent Soviet journalist, in a private audience. The record of that meeting was suppressed by the Curia, contrary to John's instructions. It's worth noting that John used the contact with Khrushchev to urge the Kremlin to take action against Russian anti-Semitism, perhaps hoping to have better luck with the Soviets than he was having with the Roman Curia on this issue.

Conservative churchmen in Italy were terribly troubled by John's relationship with Khrushchev and his tolerance of communists. Every word or act of his implying that communists could be decent men and women, could be trusted and accepted as collaborators in the struggle for world peace and prosperity, undermined decades of efforts by the Church to place communism beyond the pale of human decency. The pope's attitude toward communism might well affect the Italian elections set for April 1963. Indeed, in Washington, Dean Rusk, Kennedy's secretary of state, echoing Cardinal Siri, condemned John as the pope who made it possible for five hundred thousand Italian women to vote for communist candidates.

John was not focused on the Italian elections, however, but rather on world peace. He was working on his second great encyclical, *Pacem in Terris*, published April 11, 1963, just two months before his death. Nowhere in the document was there an explicit criticism of communism. Near the end of it he referred to a "false philosophy," unquestionably Marxism, but insisted that some good had been done in its name. Half of the encyclical was a powerful demand for the protection of human rights, probably the strongest statement of its kind any world leader had ever put forward. The rest was a rejection of Realpolitik, imperialism, and the arms race.

His focus on human rights was weighted toward social and economic rights. Man had an inalienable right to food, clothing, shelter, medical care, and social services. He was entitled to respect as well as to freedom of speech and freedom of religion. He had the right to emigrate and immigrate freely. As he had in *Mater et Magistra*, John stressed the importance of fair wages for workers. They should not be subjected to arbitrary treatment. He insisted that justice and equity might require the state to give more attention to the weaker members of society—a suggestion of what Americans would call "affirmative action." He even called attention to the just demands of women for rights and duties as human rights: Women could not be treated as instruments, presumably for procreation only. And he expressed satisfaction that racial discrimination, although not eliminated, could no longer be referred to with approval.

The state, the pope argued, must not deprive individual citizens of their freedom of action. Civil authority, he insisted, exists for the attainment of the common good. He declared that "any government which refused to recognize human rights or acted in violation of them, would not only fail in its duty; its decrees would be wholly lacking in binding force." Quoting Leo, he reminded his readers that true freedom safeguards the dignity of the human person.

And then he turned specifically to issues of world affairs. He was appalled by the idea that men who accepted the responsibility of public office were thus "compelled to lay aside their own humanity" in the service of the state, in the national interest. He would not countenance inhumane actions in the name of national security. Some day he hoped the Universal Declaration of Human Rights, set forth by the United Nations in 1948, would protect the rights of everyone, but it was clear that he had no illusions about the UN's ability to do so in his lifetime.

John's concern for poorer nations was underlined by repetition of the appeal he had made in *Mater et Magistra* for wealthy nations to provide needed aid. He asked that assistance be given with respect for the national characteristics and civil institutions of the recipient peoples and insisted that advanced nations were not entitled to dominate others—perhaps a gentle hint to his friends in Washington. No country, he declared, had the right to oppress another or to interfere "without warrant" in its internal affairs.

His strongest appeal was for an end to the arms race. He again demonstrated his understanding of the "security dilemma" and was searching for a way out of it. Peace, he contended, rested on mutual trust, not a balance of arms, but he had no fresh insight into how to achieve that trust, nowhere to be found in Moscow or Washington. He called for a ban on nuclear weapons and expressed his opposition to the testing of such weapons—an issue with greater resonance. Kennedy and Khrushchev were already working toward a treaty to ban at least atmospheric testing. For John, who had served in one world war and observed the horror of a second, the idea of war in the atomic age was inconceivable. He demanded negotiations, diplomacy, as the necessary alternative to the use of force to adjust differences. But most striking in his approach was his unwillingness to condemn one side, the Soviet side—to hold the Soviets responsible for the world's ills. For the first time in the era of the Cold War, the Church's appeal was neutral and truly universal, however dissatisfied it may have left anticommunists the world over.

Two months later, good Pope John was dead. He would have been pleased to know that Montini was chosen to succeed him, despite the hostility of the Curia. Perhaps no candidate was more likely to fight to realize John's vision for the modern Church. Paul VI, as he was known, was prepared to go even further in some areas, even to liberalize the Church's position on contraception, but he was unquestionably committed to the broad modernization for which John had hoped. Unfortunately, after his death in 1978, the Curia struck back and found a pope for whom anticommunism was central and who did not share the dreams of John and Paul, whose names he chose for himself. Not all was lost—only the hope for a Church in tune with the realities of the modern world.

Angelo Roncalli, Pope John XXIII, was not a great intellectual. He will not be read by later generations as I read Augustine and Aquinas in my undergraduate days—and might read Hans Küng, John Courtney Murray, or Pierre Teilhard de Chardin today. But he was an intelligent as well as a good and decent man—the kind of man everyone would want in a pastor: loving, forgiving, eager to find good in everyone. He recognized his vices early—eating and ambition—and struggled unsuccessfully against both, but he did contain his lust.

Roncalli served his people—all people—well, wherever he was, whatever his assignment. His eyes and ears were open to their needs and dreams. He saw a Church that was failing workers, failing the people of the Third World, failing to do its part for world peace. As pope he attempted to redress these failings in his encyclicals and through the reforms he set in motion when he called the Vatican Council.

As a Jew, I cannot help but be struck by his efforts on behalf of Jews fleeing the Holocaust and Jews oppressed by anti-Semitism in Soviet-bloc nations. I am grateful for his efforts to eliminate anti-Semitism from Catholic teaching and ritual—and regret the deliberate speed with which the Church has chosen to move on the issue in recent years.

He was a great, wonderful man, worthy of the love the world bestowed on him. Skeptics need only read his two magnificent encyclicals, *Mater et Magistra* and *Pacem in Terris*.

Top: Andrei Sakharov, used by permission of AP Photos; bottom: Mikhail Gorbachev and Ronald Reagan, used by permission of AP Photos/Doug Mills

CHAPTER 12

Mikhail Gorbachev, Andrei Sakharov, and Human Rights in Europe

Like most of us—and like virtually all of the men of whom I write in this book—Andrei Sakharov was not without flaws as a husband and father. Still, he appears more saintly than most. His commitment to the struggle for human rights and democracy in the Soviet Union and for world peace, along with his willingness to sacrifice the extraordinary privilege he had earned as the principal developer of his country's hydrogen bomb, assures him of a place among the heroes for our time. Sakharov alone, however, could not have ended the Cold War or lifted the heavy yoke of the Communist Party from the necks of his people. The vision, the insistence on respect for "universal human values," may have been Sakharov's, but the man who had the power to end the Soviet-American confrontation and to provide his people with the opportunity to be free was, of course, Mikhail Gorbachev. The relationship between Sakharov's vision and Gorbachev's willingness to use his power to realize it is not unlike that between Eleanor and Franklin Roosevelt.

Gorbachev was born in 1931 to a peasant family in south Russia. Both his grandfathers had run afoul of the Soviet system and one, falsely accused of being a Trotskyite in 1937, had suffered torture and imprisonment. (His wife's grandfather had actually been executed on similar false charges.) Gorbachev easily found Khrushchev's 1956 denunciation of Stalin's crimes credible. Similarly, as a child following his father in the fields, he was aware of the pain caused by the forced collectivization of agriculture. There was little in his early experiences to foster unquestioning faith in the practices of the regime. After the war, in which his village endured a German and Ukrainian occupation, he worked the land with his father and, trapped in the village, began to equate their life with serfdom.

Gorbachev was also very lucky through most of his life—so lucky that he might have imagined that his creator had great plans for him. As a teenager, he won an award for helping to turn out a record harvest. He was endowed with a first-rate mind and excelled in school. His success in his studies won him a scholarship and admission to Moscow State University. His peasant origins and award for manual labor seem to have worked in his favor; the suspect dossiers of his grandfathers appear to have been overlooked. His loyalty to the system was never questioned, and in 1952 he was admitted to the Communist Party. In 1955 he graduated at the top of his class.

Although committed to socialism, convinced throughout his adult life of the superiority of socialist democracy to capitalist democracy, by the time he graduated from Moscow State, Gorbachev had seen enough and learned enough to know that Soviet-style socialism was deeply flawed and in need of reform. He understood that change, of necessity, would have to come from the top. He was confident of his ability, ambitious, and determined to rise to a position that would allow him to have an impact. Shrewdly, he concluded that trying to work his way up the Moscow bureaucracy would bring nothing but frustration. He chose instead to return to his home region of Stavropol, where he hoped to have more freedom of action and more influence. He calculated correctly that if he performed well, he was more likely to be noticed and to rise rapidly in a profoundly hierarchical organization.

Gorbachev spent twenty-three years as a party official in Stavropol. In 1969, a year before he became first secretary there, he met Yuri Andropov, chairman of the KGB, who was vacationing at a spa in the area. Thereafter they met often. Archie Brown, a leading student of Gorbachev's career, contends that Andropov was greatly impressed by the young man's intelligence and charm. Andropov was to play the major role in Gorbachev's rise to power. The head of the KGB, ruthless in his suppression of dissent, was also determined to reform the system—at minimum to make it less corrupt. He perceived in Gorbachev a potentially valuable ally, just as Gorbachev understood that as a protégé of Andropov, his prospects in the party would be enhanced greatly.

In the late 1960s, before he met Andropov, Gorbachev and his wife traveled outside the Soviet Union as tourists. In 1966, they visited France. In 1967, they vacationed in Italy. In 1969, a year after Brezhnev sent Warsaw Pact troops to crush the Prague Spring, the Gorbachevs went to Czechoslovakia and surveyed the scene for themselves. In France and Italy, they were struck by how much better ordinary people lived than they did in the Soviet Union. Gorbachev was struck by the freedom people enjoyed to complain about their government and to criticize their leaders. In Czechoslovakia, he was quickly disabused of any credence he might have put in Brezhnev's rationalizations for intervention in 1968: It was not required by any foreign threat nor did it have the support of Czech workers. These observations may well have informed his conversations with Andropov.

In 1978, Gorbachev was called to Moscow to serve on the party Secretariat with responsibility for overseeing Soviet agriculture. In 1980, at the age of forty-nine, he was elevated to full membership in the Politburo, its youngest member. These were heights he might not have reached without Andropov's patronage—and certainly not as fast. At last, in 1982, a senescent and barely functional Brezhnev died, and Andropov succeeded him as General Secretary. As Andropov moved to consolidate his power, Gorbachev emerged as the leader of his faction within the Politburo—the man in whose political skills and values Andropov had the most confidence.

Gorbachev worked at the side of the General Secretary in Andropov's efforts to reform the party and modernize the Soviet system. But Andropov's health did not allow him enough time to accomplish much, and it seems unlikely that he would have attempted the radical changes the rapidly deteriorating Soviet condition required. Aware that his death was approaching, he tried to arrange to have Gorbachev succeed him, but the party elders were not interested in anointing a young man likely to challenge their perquisites. They chose Konstantin Chernenko, a man almost as doddering as Brezhnev had been in his last years. Gorbachev was content to wait—he had no choice.

His travels outside the Soviet Union contributed mightily to Gorbachev's answer to Lenin's question "What is to be done?" In 1983, in Canada, he met with Alexander Yakovlev, then Soviet ambassador, with whom he developed a close relationship. Yakovlev, a war hero who studied briefly at Columbia University, had strong views on what needed to be done at home—views that had not been well received by Brezhnev and his supporters. An embassy in the West was a pleasant enough exile. In Canada, Gorbachev was enormously impressed by the efficiency of Canadian agriculture, and Yakovlev reinforced his growing conviction that the West did not pose a threat to the Soviet Union. He arranged for Yakovlev's return to Moscow.

In 1984, Gorbachev went to London, had serious conversations with Margaret Thatcher, and spoke to Parliament about foreign policy. Thatcher was impressed by both his intelligence and his views. She perceived him as a man with whom the West could work to reduce tensions, perhaps even end the Cold War. He came away with an understanding that it was essential to assure the West of its security if the arms race was to be ended without risk to the security of the Soviet Union.

Chernenko died early in March 1985, and Gorbachev was selected quickly to replace him. He had made no secret of his views on the necessity for reform, but awareness of the desperateness of the Soviet condition facilitated his election. Had his colleagues perceived the range of changes he contemplated, however, the outcome might have been different. Gorbachev had come to believe that for socialism to succeed it required contested elections, rule of law, public accountability, and a free press. Almost certainly he did not appreciate the impact such reforms would have on the party and the country. He was also determined to end the Cold War in order to focus on the nation's internal problems. He had to curb the military—at least its budgetary demands—to find the funds he needed for his domestic program.

Meanwhile, off in Gorky, Andrei Sakharov chafed in exile. The great physicist, human rights activist, and winner of the Nobel Peace Prize in 1975 had pushed the Soviet leadership once too often. He had been forced out of Moscow and denied anything more than minimal contact with friends and colleagues other than his wife, Elena Bonner, another thorn in the side of the Communist Party. In poor health, he nonetheless resorted to hunger strikes to impose his will on the regime—which retaliated by force-feeding him. But he realized he had little power and he despaired.

His early years had not presaged the life he led in the 1970s and 1980s. Unlike Gorbachev, he was born into an educated family and a comfortable existence in Moscow. His grandfather had been a founding member of the Kadet party, constitutional democrats who, on the eve of the First World War, showed promise of leading Russia away from autocracy. His father was a physics teacher who wrote textbooks and explanations of physics for laymen and seems to have been apolitical.

Homeschooled until he was twelve, Sakharov, like Gorbachev, demonstrated a powerful intellect. At seventeen, he was admitted to the physics program at Moscow State, from which he graduated, in the midst of the Second World War, in 1942. His questionable health cost him admission to the air force academy, but after digging trenches for a while he was sent east of the Urals to work in a munitions factory. It was there that he found his first wife in 1943.

His first great worldly success came at the factory, where he developed a quality-control test for armor-piercing shells and received an award, much as Gorbachev was to receive one for his agricultural achievement. Before the war ended, he was admitted as a graduate student to the Institute of Physics at the prestigious Academy of Sciences. He defended his dissertation in 1947 and was appointed to a junior research position in theoretical physics. The atomic age had guaranteed great status for theoretical physicists, and in 1948 he was assigned to a group tasked with finding a way to develop thermonuclear weapons, or H-bombs. He appears to have accepted the assignment without reservation—as a patriotic duty.

By all accounts, Sakharov loved his work and was minimally troubled by the distance it put between him and his family. For all his inherent decency, he seemed insensitive to his wife's intense unhappiness and neglectful of his parental obligations. He was not much troubled by leaving his family in Moscow while he went off to the heavily guarded secret workplace, nor did he dwell on his wife's discontent when she was allowed to join him in that isolated warren. His choice companions were the men who were his intellectual peers, the colleagues with whom he discussed the realities of the Soviet system—the terror, the Gulag, and the rampant anti-Semitism—as they worked together to enhance the power of the state.

Sakharov's subsequent fame and status in the Soviet Union derived from his role in developing the new weapon, tested successfully in 1953. Thereafter he was known as the father of the H-bomb. He was elected that year to the Soviet Academy of Sciences, at thirty-two the youngest ever so honored. His accolades included Hero of Socialist Labor, the Stalin Prize, and the Order of Lenin. And with the medals came extraordinary privileges—among them access to housing such as the average Soviet citizen could not imagine, to the special shops where the elite could find goods available nowhere else in the country, to foreign publications, and a telephone that enabled him to speak directly to his nation's leaders. And he did not even have to join the party to enjoy his perquisites. He could easily have imagined that he had the power to change the world—or at very least the minds of Soviet leaders.

Sakharov had both a sense of his own great power and of great responsibility to use it well on behalf of his countrymen, perhaps even the entire world. Always elitist, in the tradition of the Russian intelligentsia, encouraged by his early successes, he expected Soviet leaders to follow his advice. His frustration when they failed to do so fueled his discontent and drove him gradually into opposition.

He had understood in his quest for thermonuclear weapons—and especially in the successful test of one—the incredible devastation the bomb would cause if used. He had thought less about the effects of radioactive fallout from the tests alone. In the late 1950s he read the warnings of Robert Oppenheimer, Linus Pauling, and Albert Schweitzer, who wrote of the long-term contamination of areas reached by the fallout and of the deaths that might be caused over time by exposure. He quickly came to share their view that the testing of nuclear devices had to be stopped.

One day Sakharov picked up the telephone that connected him to the Kremlin, explained the danger of radioactive fallout to General Secretary Nikita Khrushchev, a man he admired greatly, and advised him that the Soviet Union should cease testing nuclear weapons. Dissatisfied with Khrushchev's response, he sent the Soviet leader a memo spelling out his views. In July 1961, Khrushchev called together the scientists responsible for testing and informed them of his intent to break his public promise not to test again unless the Americans did first. William Taubman, Khrushchev's biographer, concluded that Khrushchev thought the best way to restrain the United States was to scare it, as he had tried to intimidate Kennedy at their meeting in April of that year.

Sakharov's arguments angered Khrushchev, who took the occasion of a dinner following the meeting with scientists to attack him. Sakharov had overstepped the bounds: He was a scientist who dared to give political advice to the leader of the Soviet state. "Sakharov," he yelled, "don't try to tell us what to do or how to behave. . . . I'd be a jellyfish and not chairman of the Council of Ministers if I listened to people like Sakharov." The Soviets went ahead with the planned test.

Both men came away from the dinner angry. For many months, Khrushchev had other more pressing matters to distract him—the Cuban missile crisis, for example. Sakharov, on the other hand, lost whatever faith he might have had in the wisdom of his leaders and was ready to challenge them on all fronts. In 1962, perceiving the punishment to exceed the crime, he intervened in an unsuccessful attempt to prevent the execution of a counterfeiter. The next major confrontation came in 1964, when a protégé of T. D. Lysenko, the internationally ridiculed Stalinist scientist, was nominated for full membership in the Academy of Sciences. Leading the opposition, Sakharov argued that the nomination was an unacceptable intrusion of political considerations in science. Khrushchev was outraged and announced he would teach Sakharov a lesson, but he was forced out of office before he could act.

Richard Lourie, Sakharov's biographer, reports that by the mid-1960s Sakharov, while continuing his scientific work, did not hesitate to challenge the regime on political issues. Reading samizdat, clandestine writings circulated by critics of the Soviet system, he became aware of a wide range of government transgressions, such as forcible psychiatric hospitalization of dissidents. He forwarded his concerns to the chairman of the Supreme Soviet but received no reply. He participated in quiet demonstrations in support of political prisoners and signed petitions in defense of dissidents. The government responded harshly, removing him from his post as head of theoretical physics at the Academy of Sciences and cutting his salary sharply.

Sakharov may have been surprised by the punishment, but he was undeterred. He was convinced that scientific progress required freedom of thought. He insisted that free exchange of ideas was essential to the realization of the Soviet utopia he had imagined as a young man. In 1968, listening to BBC and VOA broadcasts about the Prague Spring, he was entranced with the possibilities. He wrote an impassioned essay denouncing the Maoist approach to communism and insisting on human rights, the rights of every individual in any society—inviolable rights. "Socialism with a human face" was enormously appealing to him, and he called for comparable reforms at home. Wary of Western capitalism, he nonetheless dismissed the idea of irreconcilable differences between the West and the Soviet Union. He wanted a convergence of the two systems. He also argued against anti-ballistic missile systems which he considered easily overwhelmed and thus useless.

Sakarov's essay was circulated in samizdat in May and June without any significant impact. The Kremlin, focused on events in Czechoslovakia, seemed unperturbed by the musings of an irritating physicist. But on July 22, the essay was published in the *New York Times* and gained international attention. Suddenly Sakharov became a hero in the West, embarrassing the Soviet leadership as it moved to crush the reformist movement in Prague. Retribution came quickly: Sakharov was removed from all secret projects—and lost the special telephone that had given him access to his country's leaders. His life as an insider in the Soviet system was over. Published in book form, Sakharov's *Reflections on Progress, Coexistence, and Intellectual Freedom* sold more than eighteen million copies outside the Soviet Union in 1969.

Yuri Andropov, then head of the KGB, profiled Sakharov for the Central Committee. Sakharov's views were wrong, of course, but he was a good man, "honest, compassionate, and conscientious." He was a man of principle, "courageous in defending his principles." But he was naïve and forces hostile to the regime were using him, perhaps taking advantage of guilt he might feel for contributing to the development of the H-bomb. There was a danger that he would slide into open dissidence, followed by other scientists. Andropov urged his superiors to have someone from the Central Committee talk to Sakharov. His advice was not followed.

The year 1969 was probably as traumatic a year as Sakharov ever faced. In addition to his expulsion from the Eden of the Soviet elite, his wife died. Their relationship had long been troubled, and Sakharov knew he had not done well by her. Unlike several of the other men of whom I write, the problem was never infidelity. By all accounts, Sakharov's only mistresses were his work and the causes to which he became dedicated. Having failed to meet his wife's needs, knowing how she suffered at the end of her life, he was too decent a man not to feel guilt. His biographer, Richard Lourie, suggests that the combination of loss of work and wife "unhinged" him.

Powerful friends were able to find him work at the Institute of Physics as a senior scientist, and he found emotional refuge among the dissident intelligentsia. In 1970, one of them, the physicist Valery Chalidze, persuaded him to join in the founding of the Human Rights Committee. Chalidze also appears to have played a key role in involving him in attending the trials of dissidents—and in his initial contacts with Elena Bonner.

None of these activities escaped the notice of the KGB. Quite likely the apartments of both men were bugged. Andropov seemed very well informed about their conversations and suspected hostile Western forces of instigating their activity. Sakharov's role was particularly troubling because of his international prominence, and Andropov hoped in vain to convince him that he was harming his country. Andropov feared that Sakharov's relationship with Bonner was inimical to the interests of the Soviet state—that Bonner was an irreformable troublemaker. Stalin would have known how to deal with her, but the KGB of Andropov and Brezhnev was relatively tame. Gradually Andropov's conviction that Sakharov could be turned evaporated. Bonner and Sakharov were married in January 1972, and Andropov's apprehension proved justified.

Over the next few years, Sakharov became a symbol of the dissident struggle in the Soviet Union and an inspiration to the international human rights movement. In December 1972, a British newspaper published an interview in which he denounced the treatment of political prisoners. The appalling practice of confining them in psychiatric wards and subjecting them to treatments for psychotics outraged him. Unsurprisingly, the KGB was displeased by his contact with foreign journalists; it orchestrated criticism of him but was not ready to isolate him. In July 1973, a Sakharov interview with a Swedish journalist was broadcast in Sweden. Sakharov spoke of the moral imperative to speak out against injustice, even if there seemed little hope of success. He was critical of Soviet society for its apathy and of the regime's central planning for its failure to improve the economy. A few weeks later he was called in for a warning by the deputy prosecutor and told to stop speaking to foreigners. He responded by holding a press conference five days later.

Andropov and the Politburo were angry: Sakharov was darkening the benign image of the Soviet Union cultivated by advocates of détente at home and abroad. They were reluctant to give the Western press further ammunition by treating Sakharov harshly; however, the press conference exhausted Andropov's patience. Sakharov criticized détente, suggesting that it was dangerous in the absence of steps toward the democratization of the Soviet Union. He even supported the notorious Jackson-Vanik amendment to the Trade Act of 1974, about to be passed by the American Congress, denying the Soviets most-favored-nation trade privileges unless they allowed free emigration. Andropov recommended that Sakharov be stripped of all of his awards and sent into exile in a city closed to foreigners, but the Politburo held back. Instead, the government arranged for forty Academicians to sign a letter in *Pravda* attacking Sakharov for allowing himself to be used by hostile propagandists and planted suggestions that he might be guilty of treason—or even Jewish.

In fact, in late 1973 the Politburo was much more concerned about the publication in Paris of Alexander Solzhenitsyn's *Gulag Archipelago*, with its revelations about the regime's crimes against its own people. In February, Solzhenitsyn was arrested and deported to Germany, sparking an enormous uproar in the West. Andropov recommended waiting until the furor subsided before resuming the assault on Sakharov.

Sakharov and other Soviet dissidents called for publication of *Gulag Archipelago* in the Soviet Union and urged formation of an international tribunal to investigate the gulags. Pissing in the wind, they demanded publication of the relevant documents from the archives of the KGB and its predecessors. Not surprisingly, Sakharov was elevated to public enemy number one. The only question was how to dispose of him. He was too well known internationally to be killed and knew too many state secrets to be deported. Internal exile, favored by Andropov, seemed the most effective course, but the Brezhnev Politburo decided against it. Sakharov was arguing against détente on the grounds that the West should be pressing Moscow to respect the human rights of the Soviet people. Leaving him free to fulminate harmlessly was the best evidence the government could offer that it tolerated opposition and was generous toward its critics. And in August 1975, to achieve legitimatization of its gains in World War II, the Soviet leadership continued its playacting by signing the Helsinki Accords, accepting the provision guaranteeing human rights and fundamental freedoms.

In October, however, word reached Moscow that Sakharov would be awarded the Nobel Prize for Peace, a decision the Politburo could only view as hostile. He would not be allowed to leave the country to accept the award, but Bonner went and read his address. In the same month, the first of several "Sakharov hearings," conferences on human rights in the Soviet Union, was held in Copenhagen. Subsequent sessions were held in Rome in 1977 and in Washington in 1979. There was no doubt that Sakharov was a major irritant to the Soviet leadership, but it held off taking any major action against him that would arouse world opinion and jeopardize the benefits of détente. The KGB continued to harass him, to do what it could to make his life miserable, but was careful not to cross the threshold—even after he struck an agent in 1976, the same year he and his comrades formed the Moscow Helsinki Watch Group.

Sakharov was heartened by the election of Jimmy Carter in November 1976. Carter had campaigned against Kissingerian Realpolitik and promised to make human rights the centerpiece of his administration's foreign policy. Sakharov opened a correspondence with Carter, again infuriating Soviet leaders, but it was not until Sakharov denounced the Red Army's invasion of Afghanistan in 1979 that the Politburo's tolerance of his transgressions was exhausted. In January 1980, he was sent off to internal exile in Gorky. And there he sat, fighting the regime with the only weapon he had left, the threat of dying through hunger strikes—until Gorbachev moved into the Kremlin.

Gorbachev's primary concern, much like that of Andropov, was to revitalize the Soviet economy. Like his mentor, he was receptive to new ideas; yet both men expected the party to spearhead the reforms. Not surprisingly, the bureaucracy and the party apparatus proved resistant to change. It did not take long for Gorbachev to conclude that the system would require significant political reform if he was to make any progress toward liberalizing the economy, a goal he had settled on after travel abroad, intensive reading, and discussions with the Soviet intelligentsia. His promise of *perestroika*, never easily defined, initially appeared to be a call for economic restructuring, but quickly came to encompass the political system and major shifts in foreign policy as well.

Gorbachev also spoke early of *glasnost*, a familiar term in Soviet discourse, meaning little more than openness, but when demanded by Sakharov and other Soviet intellectuals it implied freedom of speech as well as the more transparent government Gorbachev seemed to be promising. Archie Brown sees the concept evolving during the Gorbachev years, as dissidents tested the limits and interpreted it to mean freedom of speech and of the press and a government that kept its people fully informed. The initial failure of the regime to be open and honest about the Chernobyl nuclear disaster in April 1986 embarrassed Gorbachev and strengthened the position of those demanding greater public access to information.

Throughout 1985 and 1986 Gorbachev struggled to carry out his reforms with increasing opposition from those in the party who realized his success likely would diminish their power and privileges. By June 1986, most of the rest of the leadership was fighting him, eager to undermine his programs and get rid of him if they could. To bolster his status at home and abroad, in December he decided to free Sakharov from exile, to invite him back to Moscow. Gorbachev was sympathetic to much that Sakharov had argued, but the decision to call him personally and end his exile was a brilliant public relations maneuver. It signaled a major departure from the Brezhnev era and alerted Soviet citizens and world leaders to the possibility that Gorbachev genuinely meant to transform the Soviet Union into a social democracy. The promise of socialism with a human face that had been repressed in Prague in 1968 and was reappearing in the Eurocommunism of the West had reached Moscow at long last. Spring came early that year.

One day in December, a telephone was installed in Sakharov's apartment in Gorky, and the next day, Gorbachev called to tell him he was free. Characteristically, Sakharov urged him to free *all* prisoners of conscience—and to withdraw Soviet troops from Afghanistan. Gorbachev was not quite ready to take on either assignment, but two hundred dissidents were freed over the next year. Equally indicative of Gorbachev's vision for the country was the fact that there were no subsequent arrests for anti-Soviet activities, signaling abandonment of the totalitarian state's favorite means of silencing its critics.

Soon after he returned to Moscow, Sakharov resumed work at the Academy of Sciences, and by the end of 1987 he was publishing his views in the Soviet press. A year passed, however, before he met with Gorbachev, who evidenced no pressing need for his advice. Nonetheless, Sakharov was pleased with the direction in which Gorbachev seemed to be leading the country.

The Soviet leader was pushing and manipulating the party apparatus toward accepting the need for democratization, for "free labor and free thought in a free country." He denounced Stalin's crimes publicly. A few months after the two men met, Gorbachev fought off an effort by party conservatives to derail his reforms—an effort highlighted by publication and widespread distribution of the notorious Nina Andreyeva letter of March 1988. Andreyeva was an obscure academic whose neo-Stalinist views were supported by several, perhaps most, members of the Central Committee and, in an attempt to retake the helm, they published her complaints while Gorbachev was out of the country—provoking fear among reformers that a new era of repression was about to begin. But upon his return, Gorbachev called for and persuaded the Politburo to print a comprehensive rebuttal in *Pravda*. Gradually he pushed aside most of Andreyeva's supporters in the Politburo. The reform intellectuals came back out of the woodwork.

In his foreign policy statements, Gorbachev also sounded some of the themes that Sakharov had voiced earlier. Much of the "new thinking" put forth by the party intellectuals who advised Gorbachev had appeared a decade or more earlier in some of Sakharov's writings, especially variations on the concept of universal values. When the Soviet leader warned of the dangers of a nuclear holocaust, he echoed the arguments with which Sakharov had enraged Khrushchev, but his emphasis on nations having "freedom to choose," which led to the disintegration of the Soviet empire in Eastern Europe, was reminiscent of Woodrow Wilson's 1918 call for self-determination.

Gorbachev had easily concluded that the only way to achieve his goals was to arrogate more power to himself. Sakharov noted the concentration of power and was worried by it. He suspected, however, that Gorbachev alone could and likely would move the country toward democratic socialism. But Gorbachev's course changes, his frequent tacking to counter the winds of opposition, irritated Sakharov. He was never fully persuaded that Gorbachev's concessions to the conservatives were necessary, that the constraints the party secretary perceived actually existed. Tension arose between the two men. Gorbachev was no less irritated by Sakharov's criticism. He saw himself as the pragmatic politician who maneuvered through the shoals to reach his objective and was dismissive of Sakharov as an impractical idealist. Long after Sakharov's death, Gorbachev was loath to credit him with any influence on his thinking.

In March 1989, Gorbachev succeeded in staging the first free election in Soviet history. It was not, however, a multiparty election. The Central Committee of the Communist Party, allotted one hundred seats in the First Congress of People's Deputies, was presented with a slate of one hundred candidates, all of whom received the 50 percent vote necessary to be presented to the electorate. The Academy of Sciences put forward twenty-three names for the twenty seats it had been allotted, enraging its members by excluding Sakharov. The membership balked, rejecting fifteen candidates and forcing a second round—at which Sakharov and other pro-reform candidates were elected.

The Congress, televised live, met in May, and was dominated by party members, many unsympathetic to Gorbachev aims. Gorbachev, presiding, honored Sakharov by inviting him to be the session's first speaker. The political posture of most representatives, almost 90 percent of whom were Communist Party members, was revealed immediately when those jeering him greatly outnumbered those applauding. Despite his support for Gorbachev, Sakharov insisted that the Soviet leader's election as head of state should be debated. Disregarded, he left the hall in protest. After he returned, a question was raised by another delegate about the composition of a commission to draft a new constitution: Why were all members communists? Cleverly, Gorbachev added Sakharov to the commission, an "honor" Sakharov accepted on condition he be allowed to dissent from its recommendations.

A few weeks later, Sakharov asked to meet Gorbachev privately. Gorbachev agreed, but the conversation went badly. Sakharov thrust, demanding acceleration of the reforms, warning that public support was eroding. Gorbachev parried: There would be no great leaps forward—and the people would understand. It was not a relationship made in heaven, and it continued to deteriorate, especially after Sakharov drew close to Boris Yeltsin as part of a group of deputies determined to force the pace of change. Polls indicated that Sakharov was rated "best deputy" by the public, with Yeltsin second and Gorbachev a distant seventeenth. On the last day of the Congress, Sakharov rose to challenge the constitutional provision preserving the leadership of the Communist Party and to demand that all senior officials, including the president, be freely elected by the deputies. Infuriated by what he perceived as Sakharov's dangerous radicalism, Gorbachev cut power to his microphone.

Despite Sakharov's growing impatience with Gorbachev, he was obviously living and working in a Soviet Union that was a far better place than he had ever known. In his eagerness to see a westernized social democracy emerge in his homeland, he seemed unable to appreciate the enormous progress toward that goal that Gorbachev had made possible. In June, he and his wife left Moscow to spend the summer with their children in Massachusetts, conceivably never reflecting on the fact that this freedom to travel had been won by Gorbachev.

The great events of 1989—the destruction of the Berlin wall, the disappearance of the Soviet empire, the end of the Cold War—these were Gorbachev's extraordinary achievements. Deservedly, he was awarded the Nobel Peace Prize and won the praise and gratitude of much of the Western world. At home, the perception of the Soviet leader was radically different. Conservative communists and Russian nationalists condemned him for undermining Lenin's vision, for losing much of what Stalin had gained, and what millions of Soviet citizens had fought and died for. They were outraged by separatist movements within the Soviet Union and by Gorbachev's temporizing responses. Ordinary people asked what they had gained in return:

What had perestroika and glasnost done for them? They thought little about freedoms granted while the quality of their lives seemed to decline. And among intellectuals and noncommunist political activists, those who had benefited most from Gorbachev's efforts, there was anger at what they perceived as his inconsistency, his cowardice—his failure to create the pluralist social democracy of which they dreamed.

Sakharov was, of course, one of the disaffected. He had returned to Moscow in August and resumed his efforts to promote democracy, working on the constitution, speaking everywhere, attending meetings, providing aid and comfort as best he could to the victims of Soviet society. As in the past, the KGB missed none of his activities, and its leaders expressed frustration at their inability to deal with him effectively. They insisted he was dangerous, a man determined to wrest power from the Communist Party. Perhaps fortunately for Sakharov, Gorbachev, too, was determined to break the party's monopoly on power, to shift power from the party to the state. He was almost ready to act—but not yet.

When the Second Congress convened on December 12, 1989, Sakharov, true to form, argued for elimination of Article 6 of the constitution, wherein the leadership role of the party was inscribed. He appeared with thousands of telegrams and letters supporting his position. At several points during his address, he was shouted down by the party faithful. Once again he angered Gorbachev, who accused him of trying to manipulate the people and denied him extra time to present his case. Calling for a voice vote, Gorbachev declared Sakharov's move to have been defeated.

It's not difficult to understand Gorbachev's fury. Sakharov was demanding action toward a goal Gorbachev was maneuvering cautiously to reach. On the one hand, he feared Sakharov was undermining his efforts to drag the Central Committee along, making his task more difficult. On the other, there was an egotistical, even petty displeasure over the presumably powerless Sakharov being viewed by the public, indeed by the world, as the great force for freedom and democracy in the Soviet Union—which only he, Gorbachev, could produce.

A few days later, on December 14, Sakharov died. In February, Gorbachev won the Central Committee's approval for elimination of Article 6. In March, the deputies dutifully voted to eliminate the leading role of the Communist Party.

In the months that followed, Gorbachev struggled to hold the Soviet Union together, move the state toward democratic socialism, and retain power. He failed on all counts. Yeltsin, who had become his principal nemesis on the left, soared in popularity, especially in Russia. Party conservatives obstructed liberalization in every way they could, and ultimately attempted a coup in August 1991. Yeltsin was the key player in defeating the coup attempt and easily outmaneuvered Gorbachev in the days that followed to obtain supreme power for himself—and Gorbachev was left with nothing.

Gorbachev was never the visionary that Sakharov had been, but in his effort to reform and strengthen the Soviet state, he reached some of the same conclusions: that Soviet troops had to be withdrawn from Afghanistan, that the Cold War had to end, that there were universal human values that capitalists and socialists shared, that the Communist Party's monopoly of power had to be broken. Sakharov might provide a powerful voice sounding these views, but he could do little if anything to move the Soviet government to act on them. Gorbachev was no angel, and the course and speed he chose may have been problematic at times, but he was the essential catalyst. He opened the door to social democracy in the Soviet Union and enhanced the prospects for world peace enormously. He was surely one of the great statesmen of the twentieth century, deserving of a place alongside Franklin Roosevelt and Winston Churchill. He cannot be held responsible for the disappointments that followed, compliments of Boris Yeltsin and Vladimir Putin.

Liu Binyan, courtesy of Zhu Hong

CHAPTER 13

Liu Binyan: The Quest for Truth and Justice in China

Having spent most of my adult life studying Chinese-American relations, it seemed essential for me to include a Chinese among those whose vision I was sketching—but I had trouble coming up with a name. Surely with a billion, more or less, to choose from, I could find one that met my standards. And then, reminiscing one night about my days as a fellow at the Woodrow Wilson Center with Mary Bullock, former director of the Center's Asia Program, we remembered another fellow we had both come to know and admire: Liu Binyan.

Liu was a Chinese journalist, famous for his exposés of corruption and other abuses of power by Communist Party officials. Needless to say, his work was controversial—welcomed by victims and factional leaders within the party who derived advantage from his work, despised by the perpetrators and the factional leaders closest to them. When I met Liu in 1991, he was living in involuntary exile in the United States, fortunate to have escaped the repercussions that followed the Tiananmen massacres of 1989, but depressed by living in America, where he could contribute little to his country.

Liu's story fits well with the traditional Chinese narrative of the place of the intellectual and writer. Historically, it was usually the intellectual who spoke truth to power, often at great personal risk. It was a role justified by Confucianism, which called upon educated men to advise emperors to replace officials and correct policies deemed detrimental to the people. A half century ago, when I studied modern Chinese history, I learned about Kang Youwei, one of a group of Confucian intellectuals who, in 1898, persuaded a young emperor to carry out reforms that might lead to the modernization of China—over the objections of the Dowager Empress, Cixi, and conservative officials enjoying the perquisites of the existing system. Cixi prevailed in the contest, the emperor died where she kept him imprisoned for a decade, some of the reformers were executed, and Kang was fortunate to escape with his life to exile in Japan. Liang Qichao, one of Kang's students and perhaps China's foremost nationalist intellectual in the early years of the twentieth century, was also forced into exile at the same time.

The tradition with which Liu Binyan doubtless would feel more comfortable was that of the May Fourth Movement and especially the role played by the great writer Lu Xun. After the student demonstrations that began in Beijing on May 4, 1919, in protest against provisions of the Treaty of Versailles that left Chinese territory under Japanese control, leading Chinese intellectuals launched an assault on traditional society. Led by men such as Peking University's president, Cai Yuanpei; its prominent young Deweyite philosopher, Hu Shi; and the radical historian Chen Duxiu, they condemned Confucianism and called attention to political, social, and cultural evils, the many appalling aspects of Chinese life. In their quest for a cure they stressed the need for the modernization of China along Western lines, calling upon their followers to embrace "Science and Democracy."

Throughout the 1920s and 1930s, a number of scholars and writers came forward as China's first modern public intellectuals, men with a powerful sense of responsibility to address political and social issues before the nation. They did so in the face of intensifying government censorship—and the threat of arrest and even assassination. They persisted out of patriotism and a profound concern for intellectual and professional autonomy. Lu Xun was considered China's outstanding writer of this era, famous for his essays and short stories attacking and ridiculing corrupt officials and the passivity of the Chinese people, conditioned by their culture to accept mistreatment. As the government of Chiang Kai-shek became more repressive, Lu joined the Left and supported the Chinese Communist Party (CCP), which Chen Duxiu had helped found in 1921. He had always had great sympathy for the oppressed, and in the last years of his life he became committed to the ideals of the revolution.

Lu Xun was adamantly opposed to accepting outside direction of what he wrote. Good writing, he insisted, could never be dictated. He and his followers, some party members, some not, would not tolerate interference from party bureaucrats. Leo Ou-fan Lee insists that Lu Xun's political commitment derived from a "humanistic moral ethos," that there was no place in his mind for modifications of what he wrote based on the needs of the party at any given time—for what Lee calls "operational pragmatism." In 1936, when the party's cultural organization in Shanghai dismantled the League of Left-Wing Writers, of which Lu Xun was a founder, and informed its members that the party's new "United Front" policy, calling for cooperation with Chiang's regime, required adjustments in their writings, Lu Xun went into open rebellion. He would not be controlled by the party. His whole being, his identity, was dependent upon his sense of personal integrity, his critical spirit, and his intellectual honesty. At the time of his death in 1937, he was disillusioned with the Communist Party and its path to revolution. After his death, although the party deified him—and claimed that he had been a devoted follower of Mao Zedong—most of his prominent followers were purged from the party for continuing to insist on their intellectual independence. Mao and the party saw writers in utilitarian terms: They existed to serve the party, to follow its line no matter how tangled it became. Mao made this clear in his notorious speeches on art and literature delivered in Yan'an in 1942.

Liu Binyan was born in 1925, roughly of the generation that followed that of the May Fourth Movement. His father, a poor railroad worker, seems to have been the major influence on him, wanting him to grow up to be a great man and to work for social justice. He fulfilled his father's vision on both counts. The elder Liu had served in Russia during World War I, learned Russian before he could read or write Chinese, and served as an interpreter on the Central Manchuria Railway. He had returned from the Soviet Union in 1921 persuaded that it was a country without class divisions and without injustice, and when he returned to China he often spoke to his son of the utopia he had left behind. Binyan accepted his father's paeans to socialism, although he admitted to being puzzled by the Soviet invasion of tiny Finland in 1939.

The family had insufficient funds to send Binyan to high school, but he read voraciously at home in Harbin. He was befriended by a young leftist writer who introduced him to Marxist literary theory, and he joined a study group affiliated with the CCP. In 1940, he moved to Beijing to stay with a married sister, who helped him return to school.

In Harbin, in Beijing, and in Tianjin, where Liu studied when his sister could no longer provide assistance, awareness of the Japanese occupation was oppressive. Like many a patriotic young Chinese, he joined an underground anti-Japanese group and in 1944 was admitted to membership in the CCP, doing what he could to undermine the rule of the invaders. During the civil war between the CCP and Guomindang that followed soon after the Japanese surrender, Liu and his colleagues were involved in land reform efforts. He was firmly committed to land redistribution, to taking land away from wealthy landlords and giving it to poor peasants, but he was troubled by the actual practices, which too often involved vicious beatings and lynchings. He also discovered he was a good teacher; he could hold audiences for long periods and persuade the people of the justness of the communist cause.

After the establishment of the People's Republic in 1949, Liu was assigned to be an investigative reporter for the *China Youth News*, the country's leading newspaper for young people. He loved the work, although he was not happy about the rigid discipline the CCP attempted to impose—its insistence that all publications be filled with only good news about happy peasants and workers. He was puzzled by its apparent mistrust of educated young people. To circumvent restrictions, in the early 1950s he developed a form of literary journalism, thinly veiled criticism of the party bureaucracy— examples of its corruption and its efforts to control the press. His stories soon became national sensations. He was widely read and widely admired, but he found himself suspected of committing anti-party acts, of being a counter-revolutionary. He survived an attempt to incriminate him with forged letters in which he was alleged to have attacked Zhou Enlai and Hu Yaobang—and saw this as proof of the reliability of the party.

In 1956 and 1957, when Mao seemed open to suggestions for improving the party's work and eventually launched his "Hundred Flowers" campaign inviting criticism, Liu was delighted with Mao and thought Chinese society was becoming more humane. He wrote two particularly striking stories. "At the Bridge Site" was based on an accident that had occurred when a railway bridge was being built across the Yellow River. A bright young engineer, who cared for and inspired his workers and acted as he thought necessary, came into conflict with his superior, an able enough man who did nothing without instructions from Party Central. In a flood emergency, the young man did not wait for orders, took preventive measures, and saved the structure for which he was responsible. His boss waited for instructions and lost the structure for which he was responsible. The result was that the successful young man was demoted for violating party discipline and the older man who failed was rewarded for following the leadership. Liu perceived this sort of outrage to be endemic, only one of countless transgressions by party bureaucrats.

"Inside Story" was an account of how a newspaper was destroyed by tyrannical and ignorant editorial leadership that stifled the initiatives of its reporters. Liu was implying that party leadership and press censorship were detrimental to the country, and that there was a need for press reform to allow the negative aspects of society to be revealed and corrected—much as the May Fourth intellectuals had argued in the 1920s and 1930s.

In 1957, Liu even wrote directly to Mao to call attention to the emergence in China of what Milovan Djilas had called the "new class": a party bureaucracy that considered itself omnipotent, above the law, and beyond reproach. Unbeknownst to Liu, Mao had read his articles and had not liked what he saw. He apparently suspected Liu of trying to replicate the conditions that had led to the 1956 uprising in Hungary. Liu was marked for punishment and with Mao behind the attack, there could be no recourse.

Threatened by criticism from intellectuals, much of which suggested that conditions in China were worse in 1957 than they had been under Chiang Kai-shek, the party struck back. Beginning in June, hundreds of thousands of intellectuals were labeled "rightists," accused of betraying the revolution by attempting to undermine the party. Many were sent to labor camps or sent to the countryside to do manual labor for the rest of their lives. Some were jailed, some were driven to suicide by attacks and harassment, and some were executed. The moment of free speech, of freedom of the press, had passed quickly; it would be a long time before intellectuals would risk their lives again.

As soon as the anti-rightist campaign began, Liu understood that his hopes for greater freedom, for the democratization of China, were endangered. It does not seem to have occurred to him that *he* might be attacked. When a senior official, Hu Yaobang, came to the offices of the *China Youth Daily*, Liu challenged the labeling as rightist of those who, like himself, were opposed to bureaucratism as an obstacle to progress. Shortly afterward, a staff meeting was called and the newspaper's party secretary denounced Liu as a rightist. To Liu's astonishment, his colleagues, one after another, rose to accuse him. He tried to defend himself, but he was forced to attend countless self-criticism sessions in which his tormentors demanded that he confess his "crimes." He was attacked in all the country's major newspapers. His friends and even his wife were forced to denounce him. He became a notorious figure throughout the country, targeted as one of the worst offenders precisely because of his growing influence as a muckraking reporter.

Curiously, Liu came to accept the verdict. Mao had labeled him a rightist—and Mao could not be wrong. Over the years, other Chinese intellectuals labeled rightists in 1957 have told similar stories—of being surprised, but accepting the verdict, because they believed Mao to be infallible. A rare exception was Li Shenzhi, a prominent administrator in the Chinese Academy of Social Sciences—and public critic of the 1989 Tiananmen massacre—who began to question Mao's judgment when Mao labeled him a rightist. Liu Binyan would not confess to trying to overthrow the leadership of the CCP, but he did admit to being guilty of individualism and of harboring other symptoms of bourgeois ideology. He was stripped of his party membership and sent to the countryside for reform through manual labor. His sentence was three to five years, but he spent almost all of the next twenty-one years away from his desk and his family—planting rice, making bricks, tending pigs, and carrying night soil (human excrement) from Beijing to farms in the countryside.

In 1966, the rightist label was finally removed from Liu and he was allowed to return to his office, but the reprieve lasted only a few months. A colleague came upon his diary, in which he had scribbled some notes about the realities of life for the peasantry as opposed to party propaganda—and betrayed him. He was relabeled a rightist and sent back to the countryside. His son was forced to denounce him and his daughter was expelled from her Red Guard unit because of the status of her father. The Great Proletarian Cultural Revolution was under way, and Liu was a major target. Astonishingly, he liked the idea of the Cultural Revolution. He was hopeful that it would actually result in a cleaning out of corrupt CCP bureaucrats and that it might yet bring democracy to China.

Liu's return to the countryside lasted eight years—more brick making and pig tending. For the first time, he contemplated suicide. In 1969 he was allowed seven days at home and then sent to a May Seventh Cadre School, where targets of the Cultural Revolution performed manual labor between endless sessions in which they were attacked verbally for their alleged sins. He was not allowed to return to Beijing until 1975, after Mao had agreed to the rehabilitation of Deng Xiaoping. And then in 1976, after a huge demonstration in Tiananmen Square commemorating the death of Zhou Enlai, the pendulum swung again; he was shipped back to the May Seventh school. In 1977, once more he was excoriated in all the major newspapers. It seems incredible that he did not give up then, a tribute to his profound optimism—or perhaps he simply hoped the next cycle would come quickly, as it did. In January 1979, Liu was "rehabilitated," his rightist label was removed, he was readmitted to the CCP, and he was assigned to write for the *People's Daily*, the county's most important newspaper.

Despite the horrendous experiences of the past twenty-one years, Liu remained committed to the CCP and imagined that it could be purified and lead the country to democracy. Once again, he saw himself playing an important role: He would reveal the corruption and the abuses of power, and Deng and his cohort would provide the necessary cure. He believed that it was for this purpose that he had been rehabilitated and that the rapidly rising Hu Yaobang, who became secretary general of the party in 1980, had spoken for him.

Free to report and write again, Liu's incredible optimism soared. Immediately after he joined the *People's Daily*, he began searching for situations that demanded rectification. Alerted to some apparent problems in the northeastern province of Heilongjiang, he traveled up there to investigate. He was horrified by the scale of corruption that he found in the party apparatus, the excess of one provincial cadre in particular. In September he threw down the gauntlet, publishing an article, "People or Monsters," that exposed the extent of bribery that had enabled one party secretary to amass a fortune at the expense of ordinary people—and he waited to see how the CCP leadership would respond. He gave speeches disparaging Mao, criticizing the party's management of the Cultural Revolution. And nothing happened! He was not punished for criticizing the party. Moreover, he received letters from all over China lauding him as the people's conscience, filling him with stories of abuses by party officials that they had experienced or witnessed. Overnight, he became the most admired writer in the country.

Of course, there were officials in Heilongjiang and, more importantly, in Beijing, who were not pleased by Liu's work. But the years 1979–1980 have been called the golden age of the *People's Daily*, usually attributed to the moral courage of the paper's leadership—and the encouragement and protection of Hu Yaobang. Nonetheless, the offended party leaders were critical of Liu and hostile to the relative freedom of the press Hu allowed, and they worked assiduously to rein in Liu and to undermine Hu. Rumors abounded of plans to silence Liu, to punish him one way or another. In 1981, Deng approved a campaign against "bourgeois liberalism" that had a chilling effect on intellectuals so soon after the Cultural Revolution, especially those like Liu who had suffered from the anti-rightist campaign in 1957. Even some of the latter, presumably desperate to protect themselves, joined in the criticism of Liu.

The tide of press freedom ebbed and flowed for several years. When the struggle against bourgeois liberalism washed away in 1982, a new campaign against "spiritual pollution" was instituted in 1983. In the teeth of that campaign, Hu Yaobang called for more exposure of corruption. To the delight of Liu Binyan, Hu asked that three thousand cases a year be brought to public attention. Liu went to Xi'an and wrote a withering report revealing the abuses of the Xi'an party apparatus. On this occasion, Deng apparently required Hu to declare that Liu had gone too far. Liu suspected Hu's heart had not been in the negative response to his report and went on undeterred.

He had become a folk hero. In December, at the Fourth Congress of the Writers Association, Hu insisted that the officers be elected democratically rather than being dictated by the party. Liu was immediately elected vice president, insisting that the top spot be reserved for Ba Jin, China's most revered writer.

Tempting fate, reveling in his role, sometimes naïvely surprised by the outrage of his targets, Liu continued to challenge the CCP to stand by the ideals of the revolution, to provide social justice for the downtrodden, to stop abusing its power. In March 1985, in a new magazine, he published "A Second Kind of Loyalty," an article too sensational for the *People's Daily*. The new magazine in which it was published was banned immediately afterward, and its publisher and editor went down with it. But the article won Liu still more popular acclaim. His argument was simply that the blind loyalty the party demanded was inferior to the loyalty demonstrated by those who challenged the leadership and held party leaders accountable for their transgressions. Implicitly, he was calling for the legitimization of a loyal opposition.

Deng was apparently displeased by the article. Calls for silencing Liu resumed in the Central Committee, but Liu, despite awareness that he had offended some of the party elders, refused to back off. In September he was forced to participate in a self-criticism session in which he conceded that he might be arrogant and that he might have made some minor errors of fact in his writings, but yielded nothing of consequence. His enemies were not satisfied, but in 1985 they lacked the power to destroy him.

Indeed, in 1986, the situation changed for the better. Wan Li, a senior party official, spoke in praise of Liu's "Another Kind of Loyalty" and invited Liu to his office in a show of support. It was evident that Hu Yaobang still had sufficient support on the Politburo and from Deng to allow considerable space for freedom of expression.

Nonetheless, there was considerable unease among party leaders. Students were getting restless, and pressures for political reform were growing. Changes in the Soviet Union, where Gorbachev had ascended to the leadership of the Communist Party and was calling for glasnost and perestroika, were troublesome. Above all, the party leaders were determined to maintain the CCP's monopoly of power and to retain their own personal power and perquisites. By December 1986, Hu Yaobang was in trouble, and yet another campaign against bourgeois liberalization was under way. In January, Deng pushed Hu aside and in the absence of Hu's protection, Liu Binyan and the other two most prominent reformist intellectuals, Fang Lizhi and Wang Ruowang, were expelled from the party.

Expulsion from the CCP in 1987 proved to be quite different from the experience of 1957. None of the three targeted "bourgeois liberals" was sent to the countryside. Liu found that rather than being ostracized as in 1957, in 1987 his friends stood by him and total strangers wrote and visited to offer their support. China had changed, and its people were no longer willing to play "follow the leader" blindly. Liu's writings had resonated, at least among educated Chinese. Quickly, the campaign against bourgeois liberalization faded away.

But for Liu, the inability to write, to publish was almost unbearable. Sitting home and chatting with friends and admirers was far better than carting bricks or night soil, but for a writer it was not enough. His writing defined him, constituted his identity—and he was miserable. After initial refusals to allow him to accept invitations to travel abroad, the leadership relented in 1988. Liu and his wife flew to the United States, where he gave some lectures and took up a Nieman Fellowship at Harvard.

Liu was a Chinese patriot who rejected the label of dissident and intended to return to Beijing after his fellowship to renew his efforts to bring about a socialist utopia. The huge demonstrations in Tiananmen Square that followed the death of Hu Yaobang proved to him that the Chinese people would no longer tolerate the CCP's abuse of power. He thought of returning immediately, hesitated—and then it was too late. The June 4, 1989, massacres that resulted from Deng's determination to crush, to bloody, the demonstrators who dared to challenge the party left no doubt that he would not be welcomed home.

In the years that followed, Liu asked to be allowed to return to China. There was no chance as long as Deng lived, but after Deng's death and especially after the rise of the new leadership of Hu Jintao and Wen Jiabao, there was a spark of hope. His letters, however, went unanswered. Even when it was evident that he was dying of cancer and wanted desperately to die at home among his friends and relatives, Beijing would not relent. No CCP leader was willing to risk the outpouring of support that Liu's return might elicit. And as the party leaders anticipated, Liu, like most exiles, was soon forgotten. My Chinese students in 2007 did not recognize his name.

China today is a far more prosperous and open society than Liu ever knew, and yet were he alive and able to return, he would be far from satisfied with what he found there. In the 1990s he did not approve of Deng's economic reforms, predicting accurately that without a free press and political freedom, the result would be massive corruption, with party bureaucrats and their friends and relatives being the principal beneficiaries of economic growth.

He would be appalled by the abuse of farmers and workers in a country that claims to be socialist. For all the advances apparent in China today, there is enormous need for—and no room for—men with the moral vision of the May Fourth intellectuals, of Lu Xun, and of Liu Binyan. Those who try to play that role are quickly silenced by a party apparatus that brooks no challenge, living in constant fear of its own people.

Liu Binyan died in New Jersey in December 2005. In his memoir, *A Higher Kind of Loyalty*, translated by his wife, he suggested his own epitaph: "Here lies a Chinese who had done what he should do, and said what he should say." And he never gave up hope that some day, China would evolve into the just society to which he had dedicated his life.

PART V

FREEDOM FROM WANT

Franklin and Eleanor Roosevelt, Library of Congress, Prints & Photographs Division, NYWT&S Collection, LC-USZ62-111583

CHAPTER 14

Franklin D. and Eleanor Roosevelt and the Welfare State

I remember the day Franklin Roosevelt died—and the tremendous sense of loss that spilled down the street where I lived, in Brooklyn. I met Eleanor once, nearly ten years later, in September 1954. It was my senior year at Columbia and I had joined a group of Democrats attempting to block Tammany Hall's candidate, Averell Harriman, from winning the Democratic nomination for governor. Our candidate was Franklin Roosevelt Jr. The convention was a hilarious travesty—Tammany workers using all sorts of tricks to displace Roosevelt supporters in the galleries. Tammany controlled the convention site, as was made evident to me when I was roaming the floor as one of the organizers of the pro-Roosevelt demonstration. Suddenly, Carmine De Sapio, Tammany's leader and, to my mind, the personification of crooked politics, stood, raised his arms, and the police swept us off the floor. As Harriman's victory appeared imminent, I was sent backstage to ask Eleanor to address the convention—our last-ditch effort to play on the Roosevelt name. She refused.

Historians, including me, generally consider Franklin Roosevelt to have been one of America's great presidents. The criterion for greatness is a simple one: the men who sustained democracy in the midst of crisis, who demonstrated that grave threats to the nation could be met without sacrificing the principles, the values for which we stood. Washington, who united his fractious countrymen at the outset; Lincoln, who led us through a terrible civil war—and Roosevelt, who preserved democracy when the Great Depression gave rise to totalitarian movements in the United States as well as abroad.

No one should doubt that Roosevelt was a consummate politician who manipulated his wife as well as his friends and enemies. But he came to the presidency when tens of millions of Americans were out of work, millions of families destitute, and all hoping that a new president would alleviate their misery—that the political system would work. Unlike his predecessor, he committed himself and his administration to accepting responsibility for the people's economic well-being. He didn't know how he would do it, but he would keep trying until he succeeded, even if it meant changing the role of government beyond anything he had ever imagined. He gave the American people hope, put some back to work, provided relief for others, and sustained almost all in their faith in democracy. Some historians have argued that he saved capitalism, albeit capitalism with a human face. And, of course, there was his leadership of the United States and its allies to victory in World War II.

Eleanor is usually portrayed as more idealistic than her husband, as his conscience. Perhaps she was, but there is little if any evidence of this before he became president. There can be no doubt that when they were in the White House, Eleanor was far more outspoken, far more aggressive in pursuit of equality for African Americans. She disagreed with Franklin's decision to order the internment of Japanese Americans during the war. After his death, she yielded to no one in her commitment to the civil rights movement, universal human rights, and opposition to the stain of McCarthyism in American politics.

FDR was a devious man in his public life as well as his private life. We rarely know with certainty what his thoughts were. Our best bet is that he and Eleanor shared values most of the time, that apparent differences were tactical rather than strategic. Late in life, she insisted he had been the major influence on her thinking. He was a political leader with a perceived need to keep his followers in line, compromise on some issues to gain support on others, and avoid giving openings to his enemies. There is evidence that he encouraged her to speak out on issues on which he chose to remain silent. When they disagreed, it was usually because she thought he could do more and he was convinced he didn't have sufficient support to do what she—and perhaps both of them—would have liked to have seen done. Ultimately, only he could get things done; only he could order the policies that would implement their vision.

There is nothing in the early years of either Franklin or Eleanor that foretold the concern for poor or oppressed Americans—and for the victims of injustice abroad—that they demonstrated in their maturity. Both were born into wealthy, privileged families, the aristocracy of New York. She was the niece of Theodore Roosevelt, Franklin a distant cousin. Both accepted their social status and their roles in high society without a second thought. Neither evidenced anything but contempt for minority peoples. Eleanor in particular accepted and gave voice to racist, anti-Semitic, and anti-Catholic sentiments.

Franklin had an idyllic childhood, after which he enjoyed the education that men of his class took for granted: Groton, Harvard, Columbia Law School. He was a mediocre and indifferent student and, after passing the New York bar examination, accepted a nonpaying position as a law clerk with a white-shoe firm in the city. His mother financed and remained an important part of his life, long after he married. Eleanor had a less agreeable childhood. Her mother died when she was eight, and she was sent to live with her maternal grandparents. Her father, whom she adored, was an unstable alcoholic and womanizer. He died when she was ten. College was not an option—her grandmother thought it ruined young women—but she attended an elite private high school in England, where her intellectual awakening seems to have occurred.

Franklin and Eleanor were of the same social circle and not long after her return to the United States, they decided to marry. He was good-looking and lively; she was plain and shy—presumably they complemented each other. They were married in 1905 with Uncle Theodore, president of the United States, giving away the bride. Over the next eleven years, she bore six children and had little time for anything else. She was a typical society matron and he was the quintessential clubman and yachtsman.

Teddy Roosevelt seems to have been the model for Franklin's ambition and may well have been the catalyst for both Franklin and Eleanor's drift into progressive politics. Franklin imagined himself choosing a political career with the ultimate goal of becoming president. If one Roosevelt could, why not another? He definitely did not see a future for himself as a lawyer. In 1910, running as a Democrat (he probably would have accepted the Republican nomination had it been offered), he was elected to the New York state senate, embarrassing his mother and friends by his choice of career.

The move to Albany was unsettling for Eleanor. It was the first time she had ever lived without her grandmother or her mother-in-law overseeing the household. She had little knowledge of politics and the issues of the day—and was not terribly interested. When her husband hesitantly came out in support of women's suffrage, she was appalled. She had always assumed politics was a man's world.

In office, Roosevelt aligned himself with political reformers against Tammany Hall. James MacGregor Burns reports that machine politicians such as Al Smith and Robert Wagner found him insufferable. It was only toward the end of his first term in the senate that he evidenced interest in social reforms: women's issues, environmental issues, and labor issues. Burns contends that the transformation resulted from his admiration for Woodrow Wilson, the governor of New Jersey and Democratic candidate for president in 1912. Roosevelt was active at the Democratic convention and upset both Eleanor and Teddy by supporting Wilson against Teddy in the election campaign. He wanted a post in the Wilson administration.

He won that appointment, partly by charming the secretary of the navy, Josephus Daniels, and largely on the Roosevelt name. He became assistant secretary of the navy, precisely the post from which Teddy had won acclaim by ordering Dewey's Asiatic Fleet into action against the Spanish navy in the Philippines. He was willing to give that up for a seat in the U.S. Senate, but stayed with it after he lost in the Democratic primary in 1914.

When the United States went to war in 1917, Franklin, like Teddy, was eager for a combat assignment, but the president professed to need him in Washington. During the war, Eleanor, having delivered her last child in 1916, became active in relief work, especially the navy's branch of the Red Cross. Increasingly, she was on her own as Franklin's work—and his affair with Lucy Mercer—kept him busy.

Eleanor discovered the affair in 1918 and confronted him with the evidence. A divorce was out of the question—his mother would have cut off her financial support and his political career would have ended. He agreed to pay her price for continuing the marriage: He was never to see Lucy again—a promise on which he reneged many years later. Eleanor and Franklin rebuilt their relationship in the years that followed, but James MacGregor Burns and others have contended that physical intimacy was never resumed.

In 1920, the appeal of the Roosevelt name gained Franklin the vice-presidential nomination on the Democratic ticket. The ticket lost and he was briefly rudderless. It was not the best of times: He had lost the election, lost Lucy, and undermined his marriage.

Eleanor was no happier, trying to remake her life, and resentful of her husband's activities, political as well as private. Several writers have suggested that it was Louis Howe, Franklin's closest political adviser, who befriended Eleanor in 1920, who encouraged her to trust her instincts and become active politically on her own. When they returned to New York in 1921, she joined the board of the League of Women Voters and became engaged with women activists on issues such as national heath insurance, child labor, working conditions for women, birth control, and American membership in the League of Nations.

It was in the summer of 1921 that Franklin came down with polio. Lucky to survive, he was paralyzed from the waist down for the remainder of his life. For several years he convinced himself he would recover through physical therapy and exercised strenuously, but without success. Nonetheless, a year later he was active politically again and able to travel with assistance. The crisis appears to have enabled Eleanor to forgive him for his transgressions—perhaps she imagined divine punishment. He was grateful for her care and her forgiveness. A warm friendship and political collaboration ensued.

Franklin's reemergence as a national figure came in 1924, when Al Smith asked him to head his New York campaign to gain the Democratic nomination for president. Both Franklin and Eleanor seized the opportunity. When Franklin was invited to nominate Smith at the national convention, Eleanor chaired a committee to devise planks for the party platform that would appeal to women voters. Both Roosevelts were enormously successful at the convention. She succeeded in imposing her will over that of the Tammany bosses in the selection of women delegates from New York, and his widely praised nomination speech marked him as a power within the party. Smith, however, did not get the nomination and settled for reelection as governor of New York.

The next few years were relatively quiet. Franklin had discovered and purchased Warm Springs in Georgia and was convinced its waters would improve his condition and his mobility. He spent a great deal of time there. Eleanor built a cottage away from the Hyde Park house over which her mother-in-law presided and lived there, working closely with two of the women activists with whom she had joined forces. She taught a couple of days a week at a private school in Manhattan. They both seem to have enjoyed these years—Eleanor perhaps more than Franklin, who craved more political action.

In 1928, Democratic Party leaders urged him to run for governor of New York. Smith anticipated winning the nomination for president and he and the others thought Roosevelt would enable them to carry New York. Roosevelt was skeptical. He thought that Smith had little chance of defeating Herbert Hoover and that victory for himself was questionable if Smith were beaten badly. But he could not turn down the invitation without risking alienating men whose support he would need in the future. He ran for governor and won by a slim margin—while Hoover overwhelmed Smith.

Eleanor was not overjoyed by the prospect of moving back to Albany and playing the role of governor's wife. She accepted the responsibilities that came with that role but continued to teach in New York City, retaining as much of her private life as was humanly possible. In Albany, she pressed her husband to appoint women to major posts and he proved responsive. However, she did not hide her contempt for Smith or her distaste for several of the Jews—especially Belle Moskowitz—who had served as Smith's top advisers.

As governor, Franklin immediately set his sights on the White House. His policy goals reflected those of his last year in the state senate. He was concerned especially with conservation issues, but he had admired Smith's social program and was determined to continue to focus on labor rights and old-age pensions. He and Eleanor shared a sense that government had a responsibility for the well-being of the people.

In those days, the term of the governor of New York was two years—and 1929 and 1930 proved to be relatively quiet years. When Franklin ran for re-election in 1930, he won easily, becoming an obvious presidential possibility, but 1931 and 1932 were far from tranquil. The impact of the Great Depression was readily apparent, and the governor had to act to alleviate the misery of his constituents. On the one hand, he committed the state government to providing relief and spoke of the state as a laboratory for testing potential national action. On the other, his vision was narrow and conventional: He would provide relief without allowing the state to go into debt. The funds would come from an increase in the state income tax. This was not the kind of experimentation or imagination the times required.

Nonetheless, Roosevelt was one of the men in a position to contest the Democratic nomination for president in 1932, a year in which Hoover's inept handling of the Depression promised a victory for the Democrats. He denied interest, but it's hard to believe that any of the party leaders took his words at face value. Initially, it was Eleanor rather than Franklin who seemed to have a presidential platform. She pushed a liberal agenda that he, hesitant to alienate potential supporters, was not yet ready to endorse. He even repudiated his past support for the League of Nations to appease William Randolph Hearst. His excuse then—as always—was that he had to act in accordance with political realities. But in one important speech, he revealed the approach he would use as president, promising to experiment until the needs of the people were met. He called for more social planning and immediate action. Nominated after a difficult struggle at the convention, he offered Americans a New Deal which, somehow, would include a balanced budget. And, of course, he won the election easily.

Certainly Eleanor wanted him to win, although she had qualms—as did he—about whether he could find a path out of the Depression. She could think of no one more committed to improving the lot of the average man—and she could reasonably expect to have some influence over policy. But most of all, she dreaded moving to the White House. America's first lady could not have a private existence.

In 1933, the inauguration of a new president was still scheduled for March, four months after the election, presumably allowing the winner ample time to ride his horse to Washington. The four-month interregnum served the country poorly, as neither the sitting president nor his successor could lead effectively. Herbert Hoover, despite having been defeated overwhelmingly, used his last months in office to try to persuade Roosevelt to abandon the New Deal. Obviously, he failed, but neither man could have enjoyed the experience.

In desperate times, with banks failing at an incredible rate, as many as one in four Americans unemployed, millions of families fearing starvation, the country waited anxiously for Roosevelt to solve its problems, to see what the New Deal would mean. In his inaugural address, he famously told the American people that "the only thing we have to fear is fear itself," but he himself hadn't a clue as to how he would feed his people, put them back to work, and end the Depression. Although he had assembled a team of brilliant young advisers, his cabinet choices were discouraging. He bypassed powerful Democrats and filled the table with appointees he could dominate. His economic ideas were conventional, as indicated by his expressed determination to balance the budget. He was determined even more, however, to do whatever proved necessary to bring about a broad economic recovery.

What he delivered initially, in the first "hundred days" of his administration, was a flurry of activity in a furious effort to help everyone: businessmen, workers and farmers, men and women. One of the first and most popular acts passed legalized the sale of beer and wine, ostensibly so it could be taxed and raise revenue needed to pay for other programs. Before the end of the year, the constitutional amendment prohibiting the sale, manufacture, or transportation of alcoholic beverages was repealed. Roosevelt's own favorite program was the Civilian Conservation Corps (CCC), created as a means of putting 250,000 unemployed young men to work on reforestation, flood control, and national park projects. The men lived in work camps under military direction and received a small monthly stipend. Eleanor thought it too militaristic but succeeded in having provisions included for young women.

Early in May, Congress passed the Federal Emergency Relief Act, allowing for direct grants to the states and giving Harry Hopkins his first opportunity to fund work projects to reduce unemployment. On the same day, Congress established the Agricultural Adjustment Administration (AAA), intended to drive up commodity prices and restore the purchasing power of farmers—and it provided for the refinancing of farm mortgages to stem the flood of foreclosures. Before the month was over, Congress brought joy to the heart of Senator George Norris (R-NE), longtime advocate of what became the Tennessee Valley Authority (TVA), a public corporation that would build the dams and power plants necessary for the economic—and social—development of the seven-state region.

Subsequent legislation attempted to regulate the banking system and the issuance of stocks and bonds. The Banking Act of 1933 included provision for creation of the Federal Deposit Insurance Corporation (FDIC), and the Federal Securities Act ultimately led to the creation of the Securities and Exchange Commission (SEC). In June, Congress authorized creation of the National Recovery Administration (NRA), which Roosevelt and his advisers hoped would stimulate business activity and reduce unemployment. Considerable additional legislation followed, but the main pieces of the president's initial program were in place.

The results were disappointing. To be sure, the Depression did not continue to worsen and there were some gains in employment. But there were still millions without jobs and millions of hungry families. Some senators, specifically Robert Wagner (D-NY) and Robert LaFollette (R-WI), pressed for a major public works program, but Roosevelt resisted. He was still committed to balancing the budget. Nonetheless, the New Deal programs of the spring of 1933 changed the existing economic system: The government was intervening in the economy to an extent unprecedented in peacetime. Most important, the Roosevelt administration was acting on behalf of all the people, for the general welfare—and not just that sector of American society, the Anglo-Saxon Protestants, who had traditionally assumed the government existed to serve their interests.

Roosevelt's vision of uniting all classes behind his efforts to bring about recovery was not realized. Business elites did not go quietly into the night as New Dealers strove to bring about a more equitable and just society. Bankers and Wall Street brokers bridled over efforts to regulate their industries. In 1934 the Liberty League, led by DuPont and General Motors executives, organized to attack Roosevelt's programs, eventually contending that the president was violating the Constitution and comparing him to Mussolini—or was it Stalin they had in mind? But he was buoyed by the 1934 mid-term election results, which gave the Democrats enormous majorities in both houses of Congress.

Roosevelt began 1935 with the promise of what some historians have called the second New Deal. He was troubled by the hostility of businessmen whom he had wooed with evidence of his conservatism—and who had fared better than most from his early policies. He was also increasingly aware of the appeal of populist demagogues who insisted he was ignoring the needs of the great mass of the people and who were proposing appealing measures to re-distribute wealth. And his new Congress was committed to spending its way out of the crisis rather than balancing the budget. Encouraged by Eleanor, he groped again for policies that would provide the American people with economic security and better living conditions—and he edged away from efforts to appease business interests.

In the spring of 1935, Roosevelt's supporters in Congress created the WPA (originally the Works Progress Administration and later the Work Projects Administration) under Hopkins, which had the authority to spend billions to build highways, bridges, parks—but mostly to put people to work, including, at Eleanor's behest, artists, actors, musicians, and writers. There can be no doubt that the WPA was inefficient, that money was wasted, but in the eight years of its existence, its achievements were monumental. Beyond its legacy of construction projects and art work was the fact that it put millions to work and contributed mightily to a rise in national purchasing power that neither the NRA nor the AAA had achieved.

In July, Senator Wagner won passage of the National Labor Relations Act, upholding the right of workers to join labor unions and to bargain collectively. Roosevelt had no particular fondness for unions, but he had great sympathy for the plight of workers. It's unlikely that he would have initiated this piece of legislation, but he did not withhold his support—and probably could not have, had he wanted to, given the alignment of forces supporting and opposing him. The U.S. Chamber of Commerce had already declared war on the New Deal, and Roosevelt could hardly afford to alienate workers or their champions in Congress.

In August came the iconic Social Security Act, often perceived as the foundation of the welfare state. In part, it reflected the commitment of both Roosevelts to providing government guarantees of individual social and economic rights—and in part it was an effort to draw support away from populist demagogues. The act established a federal-state system of unemployment compensation, a tax for old-age and survivors' pensions, and authorized grants to the states to subsidize welfare payments for the poor and disabled and other forms of relief. It was a relatively conservative bill, since the payroll tax meant workers were contributing to—and thus earning—the pensions to which they would be entitled. Critics have noted that the payroll tax reduced workers' spending power and argued that it delayed recovery, but the fact that the act established the worker's moral and legal right to benefits has proved enormously important over the years. Many of us have grumbled about the deduction from our paychecks, but few would support elimination of the Social Security Administration and the assurance of old-age pensions.

Roosevelt's first term in office did not bring an end to the economic crisis in the United States, but the president succeeded in stemming the tide of misery and in winning the confidence of most Americans that he was deeply committed to their well-being. Denouncing "economic royalists," he campaigned as a liberal crusader in 1936. Even African Americans, for whom he had done little—indeed the AAA had hurt black tenant farmers and sharecroppers in the South—began to move away from the party of Lincoln to support Roosevelt, leader of the party that had long been dominated by Southern racists. It was Eleanor, rather than Franklin, who was perceived as the champion of equal rights for black Americans, who befriended black leaders and invited them to the White House. Franklin may have shared her views on issues of race, but he could not conceive of risking the support of Southern Democrats. Her role in pressing for anti-lynching legislation irritated him.

Striking and insufficiently understood was Eleanor's gradual overcoming of the racism and anti-Semitism that she had continued to exhibit and express in the 1920s and to a lesser extent in the 1930s. She had developed close friendships with assimilated Jews such as Bernard Baruch and Elinor Morgenthau in the 1920s and with black leaders such as Mary McLeod Bethune and Walter White in the 1930s, and doubtless these helped her transcend her prejudices. But she struggled to extend her acceptance to less distinguished Jews and blacks. Initially she could not bring herself to embrace and kiss Bethune as she did when greeting her white women friends, and she was slow to respond to the plight of German Jews under assault in Hitler's Germany. But she understood intellectually that her prejudices were wrong, and she struggled with considerable success to put them behind her.

Huey Long's assassination in September 1935 weakened what might have been a formidable third-party challenge to Roosevelt in the 1936 election. Kansas governor Alf Landon, the Republican candidate, was a good and decent man who had the support of the great majority of newspapers—resulting in a *Literary Digest* prediction of his victory—but he never had a chance. Roosevelt won an overwhelming victory, and the Democrats gained yet more seats in the House and the Senate. Americans still hung on to the belief that this man who seemed committed to their well-being was their best hope for a complete recovery from the Depression.

In his second term, Roosevelt felt himself thwarted by a Supreme Court that struck down major portions of the New Deal program and by a conservative coalition of Republicans and Southern Democrats in Congress. He decided to attack both and miscalculated in each attempt. His notorious "court-packing" effort, a plan to increase the size of the Supreme Court from nine judges to a maximum of fifteen, adding a judge whenever one over seventy chose not to retire, alienated even many friends and supporters, given his transparent deviousness. But soon after, two of the judges most hostile to the New Deal retired, and Roosevelt was able to appoint men whose values were closer to his own. A near-collapse of the economy in August 1937 made him more determined to purge Democrats in the House and Senate who were obstructing his program. Although he rid the party of one conservative New York congressman, he failed in his efforts to defeat senators Walter George (GA) and Millard Tydings (MD) in the 1938 primaries. Neither man became more compliant in the years that followed.

The economic crisis that began with a business recession in August resulted once again in massive unemployment, demonstrating that the New Deal reforms had not solved the problems that led to the Great Depression. Roosevelt had learned that attempting to balance the budget was not an adequate response, and he poured federal funds into relief efforts, including expansion of the numbers of men and women employed by the WPA. But nine million remained in the ranks of the unemployed in the summer of 1938. Ultimately, it was probably expenditures on the military, preparations for the defense of the nation in an increasingly threatening world situation, that put Americans back to work. Unemployment remained a concern even after the United States went to war in 1941, disappearing only in 1943.

Eleanor proved to be an unusual first lady. As Teddy Roosevelt's niece, she was well aware of and grudgingly accepted the social responsibilities that came with the position. But she would not surrender her life to the role of White House hostess. She wanted to be an adviser to the president. She was determined to press her own agenda, her own causes. Franklin rejected the idea that she serve as an administrative assistant, but she found ample outlets for expressing her views publicly, as well as to her husband. She became a de facto journalist, beginning with a monthly column for the *Women's Home Companion* and later as a syndicated columnist for United Features; held press conferences (for women reporters only); and gave dozens of speeches every year. She built a network of women activists who worked with her to lobby Congress and the president. She pushed through her own program of government-subsidized subsistence homesteads, contributing her own money and raising more among friends.

Although she tried not to embarrass the president, her views, openly stated, were often more reformist than his actions. She attempted to win over middle- and upper-class voters by warning against the social upheavals that occurred in Europe, insisting that reform would deflate comparable pressures in the United States. Franklin's "politics as the art of the possible" often disgusted her, especially on race issues, but on a range of foreign policy affairs as well. In 1940, a Gallup Poll found her more popular than her husband.

In his first term in the White House, Roosevelt had not had the luxury of focusing much attention on foreign policy issues. Most analysts agree that his "torpedoing" of the London Economic Conference of 1933 was at best inept, even if arguments can be made in favor of resisting European pressures for currency stabilization. He had disappointed those Americans who expected him to follow Henry Stimson's lead in attempting to coerce Japan into ending its aggression against China. In response to pressures from William Randolph Hearst, he had dropped his earlier support for American membership in the League of Nations. Cautiously, perhaps goaded by Eleanor, he urged ratification of the World Court protocol in January 1935, but he was stung by defeat in the Senate. In 1935 and again in 1936, however grudgingly, he accepted Congress's neutrality laws, designed to keep America out of war by surrendering neutral rights. If there was ever an "isolationist" era in American history, it probably coincided with Roosevelt's first administration.

Italy had attacked Ethiopia in 1935, Italy and Germany supported the rebellious Spanish generals in their overthrow of their democratic government, and Japan renewed its aggression against China on a massive scale in 1937. None of these actions appeared to pose a direct threat to the security or economic interests of the United States and there was little inclination to act, either in Congress or the White House, however sympathetic many were toward the victims. But Roosevelt was troubled and groping for a way to respond to the violence, to keep it away from America's shores. Eleanor, who was a member of the board of the American Friends Service Committee (AFSC)—to which she contributed the earnings from her writings—thought aggression might be stopped by economic sanctions. She wanted him to do more to oppose Mussolini in Ethiopia and to support the Spanish government against fascist rebels.

In October 1937, Roosevelt was scheduled to speak in Chicago. Before he headed west, he consulted with Clark Eichelberger, a prominent advocate of collective security to stop aggression. As a result of their conversation, Roosevelt added a few lines to his speech advocating an international quarantine of aggressors. The public response was overwhelmingly favorable, but he had no plan for action nor was there much likelihood of congressional support if he'd had one.

A few months later, in broad daylight, Japanese planes attacked the USS *Panay* on patrol in the Yangtze River in China. The *Panay*'s American markings were clear, but the Japanese pilots sank the gunboat anyway and strafed crew members who survived the initial attack. Although Japanese officials in Tokyo claimed the incident was an accident and issued the necessary apologies and assurances, it was evident that the Japanese military in China did not welcome an American presence. The reaction in the United States was muted. Some on the Hill, fearful of being dragged into the Sino-Japanese conflict, rather than expressing outrage, asked what a U.S. warship was doing in a war zone.

Most analysts, in and out of government, recognized the intensifying threat to American interests in Asia and in Europe, where Hitler's Germany was clearly determined to revenge its defeat in the First World War. German forces reoccupied the Rhineland in March 1936, signed the Anti-Comintern Pact with Italy and Japan later that same year, annexed Austria in March 1938, and prepared to invade Czechoslovakia in September. Roosevelt easily won congressional support for a major naval building program in May 1938, which provided work for thousands of Americans as well as preparing the United States to confront dangers that might arise in the Atlantic or Pacific. At the same time he encouraged advocates of collective security and of support for China to educate the public and to lobby Congress for legislation that would enable the president to punish aggressors and aid their victims. Eleanor, too, had moved away from the pacifism of the AFSC toward rearmament and collective security.

It took the outbreak of war in Europe in September 1939 to enable Roosevelt to win repeal of the neutrality legislation of the mid-1930s. The American people were overwhelmingly favorable to China in Asia, but rather less so to Great Britain in Europe. Many Americans of European ethnicity and some anti-imperialists had their reservations about the British cause, however repugnant they may have found Nazi Germany. Roosevelt, however, perceived the war in Europe to pose the greater threat to the security of the United States and was eager to aid the British cause and to avoid conflict with Japan. The critical point, however, is that by 1939, foreign policy concerns trumped Roosevelt's domestic concerns. One of the great attractions of focusing on the president's role in foreign affairs and as commander-in-chief in military affairs is that the Constitution allows a president frustrated by congressional obstruction in domestic affairs far more leeway to exercise the powers of his office abroad than at home. And Roosevelt was certainly frustrated by the obstructionism of the conservative coalition that dominated Congress.

Throughout 1940 and 1941, the struggle to prepare the United States for war and to find means to provide aid to friends abroad without provoking war consumed the president. It had made his decision to run for a third term easier; he never doubted that he was the best man to lead the country in such a time of crisis. Promising to keep the country out of war, he narrowly overcame the two-term tradition, winning reelection in 1940 and again in 1944, serving as president until his death. In the summer of 1940, he abandoned pretense to neutrality by sending military supplies to Great Britain and most dramatically by the destroyers-for-bases deal, in which he gave the British warships to help their fight against German submarines in exchange for bases on territory belonging to the British empire.

In January 1941, Roosevelt, with remarkable simplicity, summed up what his policies at home and abroad promised—his glorious four freedoms: freedom from want, freedom from fear, freedom of religion, and freedom of speech. It was his answer to totalitarian dictators, and now he had the support of Congress and the American people as his administration colluded with Winston Churchill's government and extended aid under the Lend-Lease Act, permitting the cash-strapped British to acquire arms and other supplies. In August Roosevelt and Churchill met at sea and proclaimed the Atlantic Charter, including the four freedoms, along with a promise of self-determination among the principles for which those fighting aggression professed to stand.

The previous June, Germany, in violation of the nonaggression pact signed in 1939, invaded the Soviet Union. Few American or British leaders had illusions about the nature of Josef Stalin's brutal dictatorship, but Soviet resistance to Hitler's armies relieved much of the pressure on Great Britain and increased whatever chance there was of the United States avoiding a major combat role in the war. In November, the United States began extending lend-lease aid to the Soviets.

As early as September 1941, however, the U.S. Navy was engaged in an undeclared war with Germany. German submarines attacked an American destroyer assisting in the protection of convoys headed for Great Britain, and Roosevelt ordered the navy to shoot on sight any German or Italian vessels in the waters he claimed essential to the defense of the United States—roughly the western half of the North Atlantic.

On December 7, 1941, came the brilliant Japanese attack on the American fleet at Pearl Harbor. Roosevelt had tried to avoid provoking a Japanese attack while providing aid to China and increasing economic sanctions against Tokyo. He saw the outcome of the war in Europe as a more immediate concern and wanted to concentrate as much as possible on supporting the anti-Axis struggle there. However, he could not risk the utter collapse of the weak Chinese war effort for fear a Chinese surrender would free Japan to attack the Soviet Union as German troops stormed Leningrad and Moscow. But the Japanese would no longer tolerate American assistance to China, and their military machine was endangered by the cutoff of American fuel supplies. Preparing to seize control of the oil fields of the Dutch East Indies, they chose to cripple the American fleet to give them time to consolidate their hold over the Western Pacific.

Despite the Japanese attack, Roosevelt and his military advisers persisted in their Europe First strategy, facilitated by Hitler's decision to declare war on the United States. The Japanese military swept across American, British, Dutch, and French possessions in the Western Pacific with remarkable ease in the early months of 1942. Its reach into the Central Pacific and goal of taking the Hawaiian Islands was thwarted in June 1942 when a Japanese fleet was defeated by U.S. naval forces in the Battle of Midway. The American holding action in the Pacific became an offensive in August, when U.S. Marines landed on Guadalcanal. Three months later, General Dwight Eisenhower landed U.S. troops in North Africa. In May 1943, Axis forces in North Africa surrendered. A few months later, the Soviets blunted a German offensive and began to push the Wehrmacht out of their territory, while Anglo-American forces invaded first Sicily and then Italy. The war was far from being over. Millions more would die first. But the Axis powers were being driven back on all fronts.

Eleanor had not anticipated Franklin's decision to run for a third term. She understood the toll four more years in the White House would take on her husband—and on her—but she accepted his belief that the country needed him, though she was not easily reconciled to his role as Dr. Win-the-War. Although she had long since concluded that pacifism was no answer to the likes of Hitler and the Japanese militarists, she had never thrilled as he did to the sight of warships. The war that seemed to exhilarate him horrified her. In general she stood aside. On occasion, however, she fought him.

His willingness to acquiesce in the internment of Japanese Americans in 1942 precipitated their angriest disagreement. She knew he was condoning an egregious violation of the rights of American citizens. He was indifferent.

A man who accepted as a moral responsibility the protection of his people's welfare was acting immorally—and she could not budge him. His discrimination against Japanese Americans was reminiscent of his unwillingness to take a stand against the lynching of African Americans. His was a democrat's acceptance of the racism of the majority of Americans—a failure to protect minorities. And he had rejected her belated, post-Kristallnacht, efforts to gain admission to the United States for Jews fleeing Hitler. He was unwilling to fight against the powerful anti-immigrant and anti-Semitic currents running through the country.

Mostly, Eleanor was frustrated during the war years by the inadequate attention the administration was giving to social welfare programs and civil rights. She occupied herself in part by working with Fiorello La Guardia in the Office of Civil Defense, but in her writings, in her speeches, and in conversations with her husband she pushed hard for support for New Deal measures, irritating the president and his advisers. In 1944, resigned to Franklin's determination to run for a fourth term they both knew he might not survive, she urged him to choose Henry Wallace as his running mate. She saw Wallace as the man most committed to continuing and expanding the programs of the New Deal. The president ignored her, choosing Harry Truman instead.

On April 12, 1945, Franklin Roosevelt died in Warm Springs of a cerebral hemorrhage. Eleanor was not with him at the time, but Lucy Mercer was. On his deathbed, he had betrayed Eleanor once more—and she learned that he and Lucy had been meeting again for some time, with the connivance of her own daughter. But his life and her marriage were over, and soon the war ended as well.

Eleanor Roosevelt outlived her husband by more than seventeen years. She was not sorry to leave the White House in 1945 but had reservations about turning it over to Truman, whose commitment to liberal reforms she doubted. She could not push the new president as easily as she had pushed her husband, and she expected a decline in whatever influence she had had on national policy. But the career she had carved for herself as a political writer and speaker remained and she was free to pursue her own agenda, as blatantly as she pleased. And she emerged as an important power broker among liberal Democrats.

The causes with which Eleanor was identified were civil rights and civil liberties. She understood that racism handicapped the United States in its appeal to people of color throughout the world. As the Cold War evolved, she recognized the advantage segregation in America gave the Soviets in the competition for friends in Africa and Asia. Her activism on behalf of black

Americans in the 1930s had earned her the enmity of white supremacists throughout the country, and her views became more vehement, more radical after the war. She no longer counseled patience to her black friends. She was no longer merely advocating equal opportunity, calling for fair employment legislation. By the 1950s she was demanding an end to segregation and supporting demonstrations to that end. As a young woman, she would have found racial integration unthinkable. By the 1930s she had surrounded herself with black friends, and in the 1950s she was demanding integration for the whole nation.

Eleanor had consistently favored civil liberties, specifically the right to dissent. In the context of the Cold War, she recognized the threat to those liberties, specifically to people on the Left. She fought McCarthyism and, despite her own anticommunism, defended the right of American communists to express their views. Her unwillingness to support John F. Kennedy in 1956 and her continued reluctance in 1960 was based in large part on his evasiveness on the issue of McCarthyism.

Perhaps surprisingly, it was in world affairs that she made her mark in the postwar years. In December 1945, Truman asked her to serve as a member of the American delegation to the General Assembly of the United Nations. She remained a member of the delegation until Dwight Eisenhower succeeded Truman in 1953.

At the United Nations Eleanor was assigned to work on humanitarian, educational, and cultural issues, and she suspected she was being kept away from the vital political issues of the day—men's work. Ultimately, however, her efforts proved to be of enormous importance and a source of great satisfaction to her. She was chosen to make the American case against forced repatriation of refugees and carried the day. Appointed to the Human Rights Commission, she played a major role, perhaps *the* major role, in the drafting and the 1948 adoption of the Universal Declaration of Human Rights.

Her dealings with the Soviets on both refugee and human rights issues were unhappy and disappointing to her. She had hoped, as had her husband, that the United States and the Soviet Union could cooperate in the postwar world, but she found it impossible to have private and frank discussions with Moscow's representatives and had good reason to despair of the relationship. The experience left her skeptical of her old friend Henry Wallace's campaign to soften the American approach to Stalin and his minions in his 1948 presidential campaign.

Eleanor's work with the Universal Declaration of Human Rights was most indicative of what she and her husband had fought for in the 1930s. The goal was an international treaty that would guarantee the political, civil, economic, social, and cultural rights of the individual—an extension of Franklin Roosevelt's four freedoms and a worldwide governmental commitment to the economic and social well-being of all. Shrewdly, she did not seek to obtain the treaty at the outset. First she would gain international acceptance of a statement of principles, a guideline for measuring violations of human rights in the future. Then she would seek a treaty that bound all signatories to govern by those principles. She gained her universal declaration, but however disappointed, she was probably not surprised that the support necessary for the treaty could not be mustered in her lifetime. The principles for which Eleanor Roosevelt fought were eventually split into two conventions, one for political and civil rights and the other for economic, social, and political rights, and accepted at last by the United Nations in 1966. She would have been appalled and embarrassed to watch her own country stall until 1992 before ratifying the convention on political and civil rights—and it has yet to ratify the other.

Eleanor Roosevelt died in 1962. The major moral and political role she played as the president's wife and widow was not assumed by Bess Truman or Mamie Eisenhower, both of whom stayed at home and out of the spotlight. Jackie Kennedy certainly matched her in media attention, but she was America's equivalent of Princess Diana, physically attractive, beautifully dressed, and a political naïf—everything Eleanor Roosevelt was not. Ladybird Johnson and Pat Nixon suffered through their husband's presidency, making the necessary appearances and enjoying them not at all. Betty Ford gained America's sympathy as she recovered from substance abuse. Rosalynn Carter, the "steel magnolia," never won the affection of even her husband's supporters.

Perhaps the most influential first lady of the twentieth century was Nancy Reagan, but she worked behind the scenes, guided in part by her astrologer, and offered neither political nor moral leadership. Barbara Bush did not appear to play any role during her husband's presidency, but is sometimes blamed for the transgressions of the son, who became the first president of the twenty-first century. Of course it was Hillary Rodham Clinton who "channeled" Eleanor Roosevelt and aspired to have the active political role that Eleanor had. And Hillary Clinton's nontraditional role as first lady, much like Eleanor's, aroused considerable hostility—although I must confess I voted for her husband in 1992 after reading an article Gary Wills wrote about her for the *New York Review of Books*. Senator Clinton, Secretary of State Clinton—who may yet someday be President Clinton—has Eleanor Roosevelt to thank for changing our expectations about a woman's place in American politics.

If Eleanor seems destined for sainthood, Franklin is not likely to join her—and probably wouldn't want to. Nonetheless, he did provide much of the moral leadership his country needed between 1933 and 1945. The moral vision was shared—and Eleanor appears to have been readier to implement it—but only the president had the political power needed to convert it to national policy. He fell short, especially on racial issues, of what she—and I—think was necessary and right, but in both domestic and foreign affairs, he made most Americans proud of their government and confident they could count on it should they need it. And he left his country with unsurpassed standing in the hearts of millions liberated by American forces in World War II.

Mohammad Yunus, used by permission of AP Photos/Fabian Bimmer

CHAPTER 15

Muhammad Yunus, Microfinance, and an End to Poverty

Once upon a time, in the 1960s, American president Lyndon Johnson declared war on poverty in the United States. That "war" was quickly overshadowed by the war he chose to wage in Vietnam. To the everlasting shame of the inhabitants of the wealthiest country in the world, poverty persists in America and thousands of children go hungry every day, a situation that exists because other Americans lack sufficient concern or the political will to help the poor, because American politicians choose to serve the rich and powerful. In the last quarter of the twentieth century and in the early years of the twenty-first, the maldistribution of wealth in the United States worsened indecently. Worldwide, poverty may well be the most neglected human rights issue.

Also in the 1960s, Muhammad Yunus, a young Bengali economics teacher and successful businessman, won a Fulbright Scholarship to study at Vanderbilt University in Tennessee, where he obtained his PhD. In 1971, while he was in the United States working on his degree, war erupted in his homeland. Long-standing grievances among the people of East Pakistan against the dominance of West Pakistan in their bifurcated country led leaders in the East to fight for an independent country they would call Bangladesh. During the war, despite the demands of a doctoral program, Yunus spent much of his time in Washington, lobbying on behalf of Bangladeshi independence. Although he had married an American woman and taught briefly at Middle Tennessee State University, he chose to return to Bangladesh in 1972 to help in the reconstruction of his country after its successful but devastating war.

He and his wife moved from a country of extraordinary wealth back to one of the poorest lands in the world, where poverty was endemic. He anticipated that his Vanderbilt PhD would gain him a senior appointment at the University of Dhaka, his nation's preeminent university, from which he had been awarded a master's degree. Dhaka disappointed and probably offended him, offering only a junior-level position, which he rejected. Instead, he accepted a prestigious post on the government's Planning Commission, where he was quickly frustrated. He had a fine title and an attractive office, but he was given little to do and felt he was accomplishing nothing. He decided to return to teaching. Failing to win an acceptable appointment to Dhaka, he agreed to head the Economics Department at the less highly esteemed University of Chittagong, where he had studied as an undergraduate.

Yunus enjoyed teaching and the university gave him leeway to develop new projects, allowing him to utilize his enormous energy. Unfortunately, Chittagong, unlike the capital, cosmopolitan Dhaka, offered little to occupy an educated American woman. Yunus's wife, a student of Russian literature, read a great deal, but grew increasingly dissatisfied with her life. National capitals such as Dhaka usually are filled with interesting people and entertaining diversions. The port city of Chittagong was not. Yunus spent most of his free time in the field, in nearby villages, groping for ways to alleviate the incredible poverty he encountered. His ideas about providing villagers with credit began to take shape in 1976. His wife might have become engaged in some of his activities, but in that same year, she became pregnant. She left Bangladesh in July 1977, a few months after their daughter was born. Five years there proved to be more than enough. Yunus would not go with her and rarely saw his daughter in the years that followed. As with many men and women who devoted themselves to worthy causes, Yunus saw his family life suffer—although a second marriage, to an English-educated Bengali physicist, seems to have prospered.

In 1974, Bangladesh was afflicted with one of its periodic famines, and many died. Yunus, wandering through the villages near his university, was not only horrified by the miserable conditions he saw everywhere but also determined to do something about it. He was contemptuous of the efforts of most of the foreign aid projects, convinced that too little of the aid reached the poor—that contributions from abroad enriched local bureaucrats and enabled aid workers to live well. They were not Peace Corps volunteers. The development theory he had studied in the United States and was teaching in Bangladesh seemed useless in the context of the misery he observed. Why were these people starving? What did they need to provide for themselves? What could he do to help them?

The simplest answer was that the desperately poor peasants needed money, in most instances tiny sums to make life possible, even bearable. Yunus asked them how much they would need and for what purpose. He came up with a list of forty-two villagers, all of whose lives could be turned around for a *total* of $27 (on occasion he remembered $21) in Bangladeshi *takas*. Saving them from exploitation by professional moneylenders, he advanced the loan himself, asking to be repaid as soon as possible. And it occurred to him that if so small a sum could be so useful, so transformative, minimal loans to the poor for productive purposes might prove to be a valuable instrument in the struggle against poverty.

An academic's salary allowed Yunus a comfortable life in Bangladesh, but there were obviously limits to how many people he could assist on his own income. He went to the local bankers to discuss his idea. They were not unsympathetic but saw no way to help. The people to whom he wanted to lend money had no collateral—no property, no paychecks, nothing the banks could take away from them if they failed to repay their loans. Bankers were not in the business of offering unsecured loans. And they perceived the transaction costs of small loans to be prohibitive. Thus was created the opening in all poor societies into which the moneylender stepped with his or her exorbitant interest rates, usually in excess of 150 percent in Bangladesh.

Yunus decided to gamble. In December 1976, he arranged for a local bank to lend the money to him. Then he went back to the villages and gave money to those who approached him with what he deemed worthy projects, productive projects that would allow the recipient to generate some small income, to become an entrepreneur—albeit on a very small scale. One might buy a cow, sell the milk, clear a profit sufficient to buy a second cow. Another might buy unhusked rice, husk it, make a small profit from selling the clean rice, and buy a larger quantity the next time. The gains were tiny, but enough to allow repayment of the loans with interest—and for families to eat. His scheme was working and his vision of its possibilities grew—more people, more villages—perhaps some day the whole country. Perhaps he could lift all of Bangladesh out of abject poverty. And tomorrow the world,

Implementing his vision was not going to be easy. In 1977, when he began lending, he was able to work with only sixty-five borrowers. Yunus, academic economist, decided he needed more flexible financing and decided to become a banker. Thanks to friends in high places (some of whom arranged for him to serve on the Bangladesh delegation to the UN General Assembly from October to December 1977), he was able to overcome the usual bureaucratic resistance to any new idea and, as project director, opened a small branch office of the Bangladesh Agricultural Bank in April 1978. By September, he had issued loans to 398 people, more than six times the number he had been able to fund between January 1977 and March 1978.

Over the course of the two years in which he had been extending loans to destitute peasants, he developed by trial and error, often upon the recommendation of the villagers he sought to help, a system that had worked extraordinarily well, with repayment levels rarely seen in the world of conventional banking—usually 95–98 percent. He required a would-be borrower to form a group of four nonfamily members, an idea that originated with the villagers. Two members of the group would receive loans. If they did well, the other members of the group would then also receive loans. The borrowers were encouraged to help each other. He handed out the cash publicly and returned every two weeks for an installment repayment, also arranged publicly. Social pressure played an important part in ensuring that his money would be returned. Once the loan was repaid, the borrower was allowed to apply for another loan to expand his or her operations.

Over time Yunus determined that women were better risks—more likely to use the money for productive purposes and to repay the loan. Equally important was his observation that when peasant women became petty entrepreneurs, their entire family benefited—not always the case with male borrowers. As a result, more than 90 percent of the bank's loans eventually went to women. The bank charged 20 percent interest and required repayment within one year. He also required borrowers to join a center formed by bringing together seven or eight groups and to attend weekly meetings there.

Yunus did not want his efforts to be seen as charity. He considered his program to be a "socially conscious capitalist enterprise." His vision called for the creation of millions of petty entrepreneurs who would become self-sustaining through businesses of their own conception. Some would provide services. Others might be shopkeepers or craftsmen. In his study of what became the Grameen ("rural" in Bengali) Bank, David Bornstein calls Yunus's plan "bubble-up" economics, whereby the poorest of the poor gained some control over their lives and came to enjoy modestly better living conditions.

At a seminar for development specialists in 1978, Yunus tried to win support for his ideas, but found his audience skeptical. The professionals attributed his success to the fact that he was working with villages near the university, in a small area in which his personality and reputation radiated. They doubted it could be replicated across the district, in villages where he would not be a presence. He rose to the challenge eagerly. His political contacts enabled him to get funds from the national Bangladesh Bank, albeit only a fourth of the amount he requested. At some point in the next year or two he also won a small grant from the Ford Foundation. By early 1980, he had set up fifteen project offices in the district with forty-nine staff members, led by his own best students. Over the next several years, he was able to demonstrate that his program could be expanded without his direct personal involvement. Tens of thousands of poor Bangladeshis were taking out small loans and dragging themselves out of the direst poverty.

A coup at the national level in 1983 resulted in a Yunus friend becoming finance minister. Yunus persuaded him to set up the Grameen Bank as an independent institution—although the government initially retained a 60 percent share. The Ford Foundation sent a pair of Chicago bankers, who helped Yunus improve his accounting procedures. They were so favorably impressed with his project that they established a comparable program in the United States. By the end of the year, the Grameen Bank was operating in five districts, employing over eight hundred staff members and lending to nearly a hundred thousand families.

The mid-1980s were momentous for the bank and for Yunus personally. 1984 was the first year in which women borrowers exceeded men, despite some resistance from male staff. The Ford Foundation gave the bank substantial grants for staff training and as a guarantee against default. It was also the year in which eligibility for loans required memorization of and commitment to the "Sixteen Decisions," a social contract drafted by center chiefs eager to overcome the social and cultural context of poverty. The decisions included family planning, elimination of the dowry, nutritional advice, a promise to educate children and keep them clean, calls for physical exercise, safe drinking water, home repair, and pit latrines. The bank set up workshops at which the members could discuss the decisions and be instructed in their implementation. And before the year ended, Yunus won the Magsaysay Award for community leadership—a prize likened to an Asian Nobel. Recognition of his success with microcredit was spreading beyond South Asia.

In 1986, as Malaysia began a pilot project modeled after his program, Yunus returned to the United States to testify before a congressional committee about his success with generating entrepreneurship among destitute villagers. The American media was entranced, however briefly, with his ideas. There was considerable editorial support for microcredit. He was invited to Arkansas, where Governor Bill Clinton and his wife expressed interest in incorporating Yunus's program into their efforts to improve conditions in that benighted state. In 1987, Congress and the Reagan administration included $125 million for loans to microenterprises in the annual U.S. Agency for International Development (USAID) legislation. Yunus, by this time almost certainly the Bangladeshi with the greatest international fame, was granted his country's highest honor, the Independence Day Award, for his contribution to rural development.

As the operations of the Grameen Bank mushroomed across Bangladesh, Yunus expanded his vision to encompass other kinds of programs. His field staff perceived a need for better housing for the bank's clients and proposed that Grameen offer mortgages. Drier and warmer homes would presumably reduce the spread of disease—the principal cause of failure to repay loans and the greatest obstacle to upward mobility. Mortgages were offered to members with perfect repayment records over the duration of two loans. Each recipient was required to purchase four reinforced concrete pillars and a concrete latrine and to build according to a design provided by the bank. The resulting homes were palatial in comparison to the mud shacks in which the borrowers had long lived. A roomier house also provided additional space for a family's microenterprise.

One of the criticisms of the bank was its focus on tiny projects that provided only a slow and limited rise out of poverty. Although Yunus continued to focus primarily on improving the lot of the destitute, he had not been unwilling to try larger enterprises by lending to centers or combinations of groups. These experiments had proved unsuccessful, largely because the villagers lacked managerial experience. In 1986, however, he decided to accept an offer to take over a failed fish farming project from the government. To overcome the initial inadequacies of the villagers, the bank's staff would provide management until the ponds became profitable and its clients had demonstrated their ability to take charge. It took seven years for the project to break even.

Less successful was Yunus's decision to take over a deep tube well program that the government offered at a fraction of what it had already invested. Most potential donors thought poorly of the idea and shied away. On the basis of Yunus's track record, the United Nations Development Program gambled to provide him with the necessary funding. He might well have succeeded, but the government changed policy and began providing clean water at half the market price, undercutting the Grameen program. Years later, dangerous levels of arsenic were discovered in some of the aquifers the Grameen wells were tapping.

The bank had other troubles, perhaps more fundamental. As it expanded and its employees multiplied into the thousands, many, perhaps most of them, did not seek employment with Grameen because they shared Yunus's vision. Decent jobs were scarce in Bangladesh and young people could not be choosy. Some were exhilarated by the work, by the ability to lift poor people out of their misery. Others were unhappy with the working conditions. Educated youth, generally of urban origin, disliked being posted in remote rural areas—and some were contemptuous of the people they were there to help. One bank branch failed and an investigation discovered various abuses of clients and staff corruption. Bank managers were occasionally abusive toward their staff, especially toward the few women Yunus was able to recruit. The larger the bank grew, the less supervision Yunus could provide. Grameen was not immune from the kinds of problems that afflict organizations that expand rapidly.

In 1991, Yunus was shocked to discover that his employees had registered a union. He reacted as most capitalist CEOs would: He fought it. The courts determined that many signatures on the petition for unionization were forgeries and cancelled the registration. Given Yunus's contacts with Bangladesh's leaders and the considerable political power available to a man to whom millions of Bangladeshis looked as a benefactor, it is not inconceivable that the court tilted in his favor. Using another time-honored union-breaking tactic, he designated his bank workers as managers, making them ineligible to join a union.

Another—perennial—problem the bank faced was the opposition of wealthy landowners. The Grameen Bank was a threat to rural elites. To the extent that their wealth and power derived from moneylending, Yunus's lower interest rates undermined them. A more secure peasantry, confident of obtaining credit for microenterprises, was likely to force up wages. The landowners fought back by attempting to intimidate villagers and by contending that the bank was a violation of the tenets of Islam. One year village elders persuaded many husbands of borrowers to stop payment on loans, slashing the repayment rate. Occasionally Islamicists demonstrated against the bank, and Yunus could never be certain of prevailing against them. He was careful not to open branches in the vicinity of mosques, even though the Mosque of the Internet (provenance unknown) designated Yunus as the epitome of what a Muslim banker should be and suggested that Grameen was the only true Islamic bank.

In 1998, the usually astute, politically sensitive Yunus slipped. He accepted $150,000 from the Monsanto Corporation, the world's largest agrochemical company, to launch the Grameen Monsanto Center for Environment-Friendly Technologies. Monsanto was notorious for its development of genetically altered crops and had become the bête noire of some environmental and development groups across the globe—and they were outraged by the alliance. Yunus, who treasured his international reputation as "a kind of bankers' Mother Teresa," was shaken by the barrage of criticism. Hardly more than a month after the joint venture was announced, he pulled out.

His international standing and domestic popularity led several Bangladeshi governments to offer Yunus major official appointments, but he was not interested. He perceived that his political influence was greater if he remained aloof from partisan politics, free to criticize all parties that failed to meet the needs of the people as he thought necessary. He was shrewd enough to understand that the bank's operations might be jeopardized if he were seen to harbor political ambitions. Yunus wanted a Nobel Prize—not the presidency of Bangladesh.

The awards and the glory accumulated, although the Nobel, for which he was an oft-mentioned candidate, remained out of reach. In 1990, CBS did a segment on the bank for 60 *Minutes*. Yunus was able to place an op-ed in the *New York Times*, presenting his argument for "Credit as a Human Right." Newspapers across the United States picked up the story again. In 1994, the first year the Grameen Bank actually showed a profit, Yunus won the World Food Prize. In 1995, Hillary Clinton visited the bank and invited Yunus to the White House. Peter Jennings interviewed him on American national television, and ABC named him its Man of the Week. Once more, there was widespread media attention in the United States to the idea of microcredit.

In 1996 Yunus was awarded the Simón Bolívar Prize. In 2000, the bank shared the Gandhi Peace Prize with Nelson Mandela. A Village Phone program the bank established to enable women to provide wireless pay phone service in rural areas of Bangladesh was awarded a €100,000 Petersberg Prize in 2004—sponsored by Deutsche Telekom AG and Microsoft. A few months later, the *Economist* gave Yunus its annual award for social and economic innovation, noting that the Grameen Bank now had thirteen hundred branches serving more than 3.5 million people in forty-six thousand villages in Bangladesh. His microcredit model was being replicated in fifty countries around the world, including the United States—where several dozen nonprofit organizations had begun Grameen-type operations. A November 2004 UN report on implementation of the first United Nations Decade for the Eradication of Poverty (1997–2006) focused on the role of microcredit. The authors found that worldwide, 67 million poor and low-income people had access to microcredit in 2003—and noted that the programs had proved especially beneficial to women.

In December 2006, Yunus was at last awarded the long-coveted Nobel Peace Prize, to be shared with his beloved Grameen Bank. Once again, the world's media called attention to his extraordinary accomplishments—and once again his vision of microcredit, and variations on it, won widespread praise. The people of Bangladesh appear to have responded with great delight to having one of their own acclaimed an international hero. But when Yunus decided to come forward as the potential savior of his country, the white knight who would rescue the land from the two major political parties notorious for their corruption—and from the army, which had seized power in a coup in late 2006—the response was surprisingly cool.

The political elite of Bangladesh was not prepared to welcome him, the media was critical, and the major political parties evidenced no interest in making room for Citizen's Power (Nagarik Shakti), the party Yunus formally announced in February 2007. Rumors spread that the army was exploiting his name as a means of keeping power after the coup. Three months later, in May 2007, Citizen's Power was gone and Yunus had abandoned his political aspirations. But the Grameen Bank and its imitators across the globe still flourish, even in the for-profit sector—and nothing can diminish Yunus's contribution in that arena.

Almost certainly the most important feature of Yunus's model is the fact that it can be replicated—or, as Alex Counts puts it, it can be "franchised." Yunus's genius was to create an antipoverty program that could reach millions of people all over the world—even in the United States. In Bangladesh, the Grameen Bank has helped millions rise above the poverty line, and it is likely that its clones elsewhere will enable millions more to improve their lives substantially—to have better food, clothing, shelter, some medical care, and opportunities for education. Of course, Yunus is not satisfied. Although he is unquestionably a gradualist, convinced that social change would come slowly—not through revolution—he has had to concede that his system is too slow. He estimates that it took ten to fifteen years of borrowing from the bank for the average destitute villager to climb out of poverty. He wants to reduce that to seven to ten years. We can only wish him success.

Conclusion

Little has happened in the early years of the twenty-first century to mitigate concern for human rights, for the future of humanity. Moral vision has been lacking among the world's leaders. Brutal, oppressive regimes persist in Africa, Asia, and Eastern Europe. Some governments in Central America and the Middle East are only marginally better. Nonstate actors, most notably al-Qaeda, have emerged as a major source of misery, their atrocities facilitated by the relative ease of movement of people and goods we call globalization. The United States, once widely perceived as providing moral leadership, is now reviled for betraying its values by condoning torture and other deplorable practices in its "war against terrorism." It is some small consolation that Americans who abhor their government's conduct remain free to criticize it—and Americans were able to vote to replace the men and women who had sullied their nation's reputation. Elsewhere dissidents are beaten, imprisoned, and murdered. Nonviolent resistance continues to have its advocates, such as Suu Kyi and the Dalai Lama, but it shows little promise of success for the people of Burma or Tibet.

Women, in much of the world, seem likely to fare better in the twenty-first than they did in the twentieth century. Female presidents and prime ministers are no longer rare, certainly not in Europe, South America, or South Asia. Bangladeshi, Indonesian, Pakistani, and Turkish Muslims have voted for women to lead them. Huda Sha'rawi and Doria Shafik would have been astonished and delighted, perhaps hopeful that such enlightenment would someday soon reach Egypt and other parts of the Arab world. Women hold positions of power and influence in Africa, East Asia, and North America as well. In many countries, they serve in the armed forces. In Saudi Arabia, however, they are not even allowed to drive cars. Men in most of the world remain unwilling to concede women full equality, whether it be equal pay for equal work—or control over their own bodies. There have been advances: Thanks to Margaret Sanger and her followers everywhere, access to contraception is widespread and legal abortions are available in many countries, but women are still forced into brothels, especially in Europe and Southeast Asia. "Honor killings" abound. Rape as an act of war has been condemned by the international community, but it is rampant in Africa. As I write, the Taliban is still on the loose in Afghanistan, maiming and murdering young women for daring to go to school. Nonetheless, however grudgingly, in most of the world the patriarchy is being forced to give ground. The prospects for my granddaughters are far brighter than they were for women when I was an undergraduate a half century ago.

Racism, unfortunately, remains endemic throughout the world, the election of an African American president in the United States notwithstanding. It seems to satisfy some human need for an "other" to look down upon. There are still millions of Americans who would not vote for a black politician and are hostile to immigrants of color. Europeans, long contemptuous of racial attitudes in the United States, have demonstrated their own intolerance, increasingly virulent as migrants flock to Europe from Africa in larger and larger numbers. Russians and Chinese demonstrate hostility toward Africans who study in their countries. Japanese continue to despise those of Korean ancestry who live among them. Sudanese Arabs commit genocide against black Sudanese as guiltlessly as Nazis murdered Jews and Slavs. Black Africans still have not come close to economic equality in Nelson Mandela's South Africa, despite more than a decade of presidents chosen from the African National Congress, to the despair of men and women who share the values of Bram Fischer, Donald Woods, and Helen Suzman. There will doubtless be breakthroughs across the globe, the triumphs of men such as Barack Obama, for whom Martin Luther King Jr. opened the door. But of all human sins, racism seems least likely to disappear.

The broader struggle for human rights, of necessity, will go on forever. One of the grimmer aspects of the human condition appears to be a predisposition to mistreat one's opponents, minority groups, perhaps anyone who appears different. Abusive behavior by police is not an activity limited to dictatorships; nor, we have learned to our horror, is torture. Murders stemming from religious intolerance are reported almost daily. Catholics and Protestants have achieved a truce in Northern Ireland, but Christians are being killed by Hindus in India and by Muslims in Indonesia, Nigeria, and

Pakistan. Hindus in India riot against Muslims as well. Shiite and Sunni Muslims slaughter each other in Iraq and Pakistan. No subsequent pope has matched John XXIII's efforts to bridge religious divides, and Benedict XVI seems determined to undo what John achieved.

Sexual identity also has long been a human rights issue. Gay men, lesbians, and transgender men and women have been targets of abuse in many, perhaps most societies. Reports of beatings, torture, and murder abound, even in the United States.

Sadly, many regimes across the globe tolerate no political opposition; permit no freedom of speech; and imprison, torture, and kill those who dare to challenge them. Russians have little conception of how much they have lost since the days of Gorbachev and Sakharov. Investigative reporting is a highly dangerous profession in many countries. Liu Binyan was perhaps fortunate to die in bed.

Who besides Suu Kyi and the Dalai Lama, both of whom have proven ineffective against the overwhelming power of the state, will lead the fight for human rights in the twenty-first century? Václav Havel keeps trying, with eloquent speeches and writings, to little avail. The answer seems to be NGOs. Amnesty International has long led the fight to free prisoners of conscience across the globe. Human Rights Watch, an outgrowth of the organization created to oversee Soviet adherence to the Helsinki agreements on human rights, to which Jack Greenberg contributed mightily, has exposed violations all over the world, energetically defending victims. Both organizations have received Nobel Peace prizes, Human Rights Watch sharing one with other groups, including Physicians for Human Rights, that worked to eliminate land mines. And billionaire investor George Soros founded the Open Society Institute, which works assiduously to promote democracy and human rights, including economic, legal, and social reforms—an organization of which Eleanor Roosevelt would have been proud.

Another Nobel Prize–winning NGO is Doctors without Borders, whose work is predicated on the assumption that adequate medical care is a basic human right. Doctors who work with it can be found in poverty-stricken areas of Africa, Asia, and the Americas—and risking their lives in war zones. Physicians for Peace, a newer and smaller group, attempts to do much of the same work, sending volunteers into war-torn regions and occupied territories where the occupier appears indifferent to the health of the occupied.

For many years, the American Friends Service Committee (AFSC), a Quaker organization, has been in the forefront of efforts to reduce human misery everywhere, working to avoid military confrontations and to end them or mitigate the conditions they cause once they occur. In addition to peace activism, the AFSC has contributed greatly to social reforms wherever it operates. Peace Now, an Israeli-based group with an active American affiliate, focuses narrowly—and in vain—on improving Palestinian-Israeli relations, largely by opposing Israel's occupation of Arab lands and its mistreatment of Palestinians.

Another organization with a limited but enormously important role is Reporters without Borders, winner of the 2005 Sakharov Prize for Freedom of Thought awarded by the European Parliament. Press freedom, including Internet communications, is central to all efforts to protect human rights. Regimes that violate human rights must be exposed, and toward that end the investigative reporter is essential. Understanding the role of the reporter, oppressive governments increasingly act against them with beatings, imprisonment, and murder. Murders of journalists and their aides have soared in the early years of the twenty-first century, as have nonlethal physical attacks and imprisonments. Several high-profile journalists have been murdered in Russia alone. The Chinese government is notorious for its efforts to suppress Internet reporting. Reporters without Borders publicizes violations of press freedom, fights censorship, defends imprisoned journalists, and attempts to provide safety for those working in war zones.

Finally, the quest for freedom from want appears to be another lost cause. Muhammad Yunus's efforts, despite widespread duplication, have barely made a dent in the needs of the world's poor. Hunger is rampant across the globe, even in parts of the United States, where inequality of income has reached obscene levels. The United Nations' vision of cutting global poverty in half by 2015 seems certain to fall way short. In its wealthiest "unipolar" days, circa 2000, the United States contributed less than 1 percent of its GDP to foreign aid. The percentage subsequently dropped in the early years of the twenty-first century. The United States now contributes the least amount in percentage terms of any major donor nation. The prospects for the future are grim. Who will step forward, like Franklin Roosevelt, to provide a New Deal for the world?

The men and women whose biographical sketches appear in this volume all behaved heroically, in the best humanist tradition. They all tried to live up to the time-honored injunction to leave the world a better place than they found it. Some were obviously more successful than others, and some were awarded the recognition they deserved in their lifetime. Others went to the grave unsung. Their greatest achievements may very well have been the way in which they forced much of the world to recognize the evils they fought and the extent to which they allow us to hope that we have taken some small steps toward easing human suffering. The question that remains is: Who among us will be the heroes of the next century?

Suggestions for Further Reading

Chapter 1: Mahatma Gandhi

Dalton, Dennis. *Mahatma Gandhi: Nonviolent Power in Action*. New York: Columbia University Press, 1993.

DeLuca, Anthony R. *Gandhi, Mao, Mandela, and Gorbachev: Studies in Personality, Power, and Politics*. Westport, CT: Praeger, 2000.

Erikson, Erik H. *Gandhi's Truth: On the Origins of Militant Nonviolence*. New York: Norton, 1969.

Gandhi, Mohandas K. *Autobiography: The Story of My Experiments with Truth*. New York: Dover, 1983. First published 1948.

Nanda, B. R. *Gandhi and His Critics*. New Delhi: Oxford University Press, 1985.

Orwell, George. "Reflections on Gandhi." In *A Collection of Essays by George Orwell*. Garden City, NY: Doubleday, 1954.

Wolpert, Stanley. *Gandhi's Passion: The Life and Legacy of Mahatma Gandhi*. New York: Oxford University Press, 2001.

Chapter 2: Václav Havel

Ash, Timothy Garton. *The Uses of Adversity: Essays on the Fate of Central Europe*. Cambridge, UK: Granta Books, 1989.

Havel, Václav. *Disturbing the Peace: A Conversation with Karel Hvizdala*. New York: Vintage Books, 1991.

———. "A Farewell to Politics." *New York Review of Books*, October 24, 2002.

———. *Open Letters: Selected Writings, 1965–1990*. New York: Alfred A. Knopf, 1991.

Kriseova, Eda. *Václav Havel: The Authorized Biography*. New York: St. Martin's Press, 1993.

Chapter 3: Aung San Suu Kyi

Aung San Suu Kyi. *Freedom from Fear and Other Writings*. Edited by Michael Aris. London: Penguin, 1995.

———. *Letters from Burma*. London: Penguin, 1997.

———. *The Voice of Hope: Aung San Suu Kyi Conversations with Alan Clements*. New York: Seven Stories Press, 1997.

Ling, Bettina. *Aung San Suu Kyi: Standing Up for Democracy in Burma*. New York: Feminist Press at CUNY, 1999.

Selth, Andrew. *Burma's Armed Forces: Power without Glory*. Norwalk, CT: Eastbridge, 2002.

Steinberg, David I. *The State of Myanmar*. Washington, DC: Georgetown University Press, 2001.

Chapter 4: Margaret Sanger

Chesler, Ellen. *Woman of Valor: Margaret Sanger and the Birth Control Movement in America*. New York: Simon & Schuster, 1992.

Kennedy, David M. *Birth Control in America: The Career of Margaret Sanger*. New Haven: Yale University Press, 1970.

Sanger, Margaret. *Margaret Sanger: An Autobiography*. New York: Norton, 1938.

Chapter 5: Muslim Feminists

Badran, Margot. *Feminists, Islam, and Nation*. Princeton: Princeton University Press, 1995.

Karam, Azza M. *Women, Islamisms, and the State: Contemporary Feminisms in Egypt*. New York: St. Martins, 1998.

Manji, Irshad. *The Trouble with Islam Today*. New York: St. Martins, 2005.

Nelson, Cynthia. *Doria Shafik, Egyptian Feminist: A Woman Apart*. Gainesville: University Press of Florida, 1996.

Chapter 6: Jack Greenberg

Greenberg, Jack. *Crusaders in the Courts*. New York: Basic Books, 1994.

Kaufman, Jonathan. *Broken Alliance: The Turbulent Times between Blacks and Jews in America*. New York: Scribner, 1988.

Tushnet, Mark V. *Making Civil Rights Law*. New York: Oxford University Press, 1994.

Williams, Juan. *Thurgood Marshall: American Revolutionary*. New York: Times Books, 1998.

Chapter 7: Martin Luther King Jr.

Appiah, K. Anthony. "The House of the Prophet." Review of *Martin Luther King, Jr.*, by Marshall Frady. *New York Review of Books*, April 11, 2002.

Carson, Clayborne, ed. *Autobiography of Martin Luther King, Jr.* New York: Warner Books, 1998.

Frady, Michael. "A Man in Full: A Biographer's Encounter with the Radical Legacy of Martin Luther King, Jr." *Los Angeles Times Book Review*, March 31, 2002.

Garrow, David J. *Bearing the Cross: Martin Luther King, Jr., and the Southern Christian Leadership Conference*. New York: Morrow, 1986.

Lemann, Nicholas. "The Long March." *New Yorker*, February 10, 2003.

Lewis, David Levering. "The Mission: Martin Luther King's Final Chapter." *New Yorker*, January 23 and 30, 2006.

Thelen, David. "Symposium on Martin Luther King, Jr.'s Plagarism." *Journal of American History* 78:11–123.

Chapter 8: Donald Woods, Bram Fischer, and Helen Suzman

Clingman, Stephen. *Bram Fischer: Afrikaner Revolutionary*. Amherst: University of Massachusetts Press, 1998.

"Donald Woods" obituary. *Daily Telegraph* (London), August 20, 2001; and see the film *Cry Freedom* (1988).

Lelyveld, Joseph. "Minority of One in South Africa's Parliament." *New York Times Magazine*, March 20, 1966.

Suzman, Helen. *In No Uncertain Terms: A South African Memoir*. New York: Knopf, 1993.

Swarns, Rachel L. "Donald Woods, 67, Editor and Apartheid Foe." *New York Times*, August 20, 2001.

Woods, Donald. *Asking for Trouble: Autobiography of a Banned Journalist*. Boston: Beacon, 1982.

Chapter 9: Nelson Mandela

DeLuca, Anthony R. *Gandhi, Mao, Mandela, and Gorbachev*. Westport, CT: Praeger, 2000.

Mandela, Nelson. *Long Walk to Freedom*. Boston: Little, Brown, 1994.

Sampson, Anthony. *Mandela: The Authorized Biography*. New York: Knopf, 1999.

Chapter 10: Holocaust Rescuers

Block, Gay, and Malka Drucker. *Rescuers: Portraits of Moral Courage in the Holocaust*. New York: Holmes & Meier, 1992.

Crowe, David M. *Oskar Schindler*. Cambridge, MA: Westview Press, 2004.

Gilbert, Martin. *The Righteous*. New York: Henry Holt, 2003.

Levine, Hillel. *In Search of Sugihara*. New York: Free Press, 1996.

Milton, Sybil. "The Righteous Who Helped Jews." In *Genocide: Critical Issues of the Holocaust*, edited by Alex Grobman and Daniel Landes, 282–87. Los Angeles: Simon Wiesenthal Center, 1983.

Paldiel, Mordecai. *The Righteous among the Nations: Rescuers of Jews during the Holocaust*. New York: HarperCollins, 2007.

Todorov, Tzvetan, ed. *The Fragility of Goodness: Why Bulgaria's Jews Survived the Holocaust*. Princeton: Princeton University Press, 2001.

Chapter 11: Pope John XXIII

Alberigo, Guiseppe, and Joseph Comonchak, eds. *History of Vatican II*. Maryknoll, NY: Orbis, 1995.

Cousins, Norman. *The Improbable Triumverate: John F. Kennedy, Pope John, Nikita Khrushchev*. New York: Norton, 1972.

Elliott, Lawrence. *I Will Be Called John: A Biography of Pope John XXIII*. New York: Dutton, 1973.

Hebblethwaite, Peter. *John XXIII: Pope of the Century*. London: Continuum, 2000.

Kaiser, Robert Blair. *Pope, Council, and World: The Story of Vatican II*. New York: Macmillan, 1963.

Pope John XXIII. *Journal of a Soul*. Garden City, NY: Image Books, 1980.

Chapter 12: Mikhail Gorbachev and Andrei Sakharov

Bailey, George. *Galileo's Children: Science, Sakharov, and the Power of the State*. New York: Arcade, 1990.

Brown, Archie. *The Gorbachev Factor*. Oxford, UK: Oxford University Press, 1997.

Chernyaev, Anatoly S. *My Six Years with Gorbachev*. University Park: Pennsylvania State University Press, 2000.

Doder, Dusko, and Louise Branson, *Gorbachev: Heretic in the Kremlin*. New York: Viking, 1990.

Gorbachev, Mikhail. *Memoirs*. New York: Doubleday, 1995.

———. *On My Country and the World*. New York: Columbia University Press, 2000.

Kelley, Donald R. *The Solzhenitsyn-Sakharov Dialogue: Politics, Society, and the Future*. Westport, CT: Greenwood Press, 1982.

Lourie, Richard. *Sakharov: A Biography*. Hanover, NH: Brandeis University Press, 2002.

Sakharov, Andrei D. "How I Came to Dissent." In *The First Anthology: Thirty Years of the* New York Review of Books, edited by Robert B. Silvers et al., 141–57. New York: New York Review of Books, 1993).

Chapter 13: Liu Binyan

Goldman, Merle. *China's Intellectuals: Advise and Dissent*. Cambridge, MA: Harvard University Press, 1981.

———. *Sowing the Seeds of Democracy in China: Political Reform in the Deng Xiaoping Era*. Cambridge, MA: Harvard University Press, 1994.

Lee, Leo Ou-fan, ed. *Lu Xun and His Legacy*. Berkeley: University of California Press, 1985.

Liu Binyan. *A Higher Kind of Loyalty: A Memoir by China's Foremost Journalist*. New York: Pantheon Books, 1990.

Chapter 14: Franklin D. and Eleanor Roosevelt

Black, Allida M. *Casting Her Own Shadow: Eleanor Roosevelt and the Shaping of Postwar Liberalism*. New York: Columbia University Press, 1996.

———, ed. *Courage in a Dangerous World: The Political Writings of Eleanor Roosevelt*. New York: Columbia University Press, 1999.

Burns, James MacGregor, and Susan Dunn. *The Three Roosevelts: Patrician Leaders Who Transformed America*. New York: Grove Press, 2001.

Cook, Blanche Wiesen. *Eleanor Roosevelt: The Defining Years, 1933–1938*. New York: Penguin, 1999.

Glendon, Mary Ann. *A World Made New: Eleanor Roosevelt and the Universal Declaration of Human Rights*. New York: Random House, 2001.

Leuchtenberg, William E. *Franklin D. Roosevelt and the New Deal, 1932–1940*. New York: Harper & Row, 1963.

Roosevelt, Eleanor. *The Autobiography of Eleanor Roosevelt*. New York: Harper, 1961.

Chapter 15: Muhammad Yunus

Bornstein, David. *The Price of a Dream: The Story and the Idea That Is Helping the Poor to Change*. New York: Simon & Schuster, 1996.

Bruck, Connie. "Millions for Millions." *New Yorker*, October 30, 2006.

Counts, Alex. *Give Us Credit: How Mohammad Yunus's Micro-Lending Revolution Is Empowering Women from Bangladesh to Chicago*. New York: Random House, 1996.

Johnson, Jo. "Give the Man Credit." *Financial Times*, December 9/10, 2006.

Yunus, Muhammad. *Banker to the Poor: Micro-Lending and the Battle against World Poverty*. New York: Public Affairs, 1999.

Index

About the Author

Warren I. Cohen is Distinguished University Professor Emeritus of History at the University of Maryland, Baltimore County (UMBC); University Distinguished Professor Emeritus at Michigan State University; and Senior Scholar with the Asia Program at the Woodrow Wilson International Center for Scholars in Washington, D.C. He is a historian of America's foreign relations, especially relations with East Asia. He has published eighteen books, the best known of which is *America's Response to China* (fourth edition, 2000). His most recent book is *America's Failing Empire* (2005). His Reischauer Memorial Lectures at Harvard were published as *The Asian American Century* (2002). He was general editor of *The Cambridge History of American Foreign Relations* (1993), to which he contributed the fourth volume, *America in the Age of Soviet Power*. In addition to his scholarly publications, he has written for the *Atlantic Monthly, Baltimore Sun, Christian Science Monitor, Foreign Affairs, International Herald Tribune, Los Angeles Times, Nation, National Interest, New York Times, Times Literary Supplement,* and *Washington Post*. He is an occasional commentator on National Public Radio, the Voice of America, and the BBC. In past years he has served as president of the Society for Historians of American Foreign Relations; chairman of the U.S. Department of State Advisory Committee on Historical Diplomatic Documentation; and consultant on Chinese affairs to the Senate Foreign Relations Committee, the CIA, the Department of State, two governors of Michigan, and three directors of the Michigan Department of Commerce. During the thirty years he taught at Michigan State University, he was also director of the Asian Studies Center at the university and director of the Michigan China Council. In 2004 he received the Laura and Norman Graebner Prize of the Society for Historians of American Foreign Relations, granted biennially to a senior scholar for excellence in teaching, scholarship, and service. In 2005, he received an award for research and scholarship from the University of Maryland Board of Trustees.